I0814011

A Graphic Guide to Making the Perfect Cocktail

The text in this book previously appeared in *The Complete Cocktail Guide* (2003)
This edition published in 2025 by OH
An imprint of HEADLINE PUBLISHING GROUP LIMITED

1

Cataloguing in Publication Data is available from the British Library

Hardback ISBN 978-1-03542-443-6

Printed and bound in China

Headline's policy is to use papers that are natural, renewable and recyclable products and made from wood grown in well-managed forests and other controlled sources. The logging and manufacturing processes are expected to conform to the environmental regulations of the country of origin.

HEADLINE PUBLISHING GROUP LIMITED
An Hachette UK Company
Carmelite House
50 Victoria Embankment
London
EC4Y 0DZ

The authorised representative in the EEA is Hachette Ireland, 8 Castlecourt Centre, Castleknock Road, Castleknock, Dublin 15, D15 YF6A, Ireland

www.headline.co.uk
www.hachette.co.uk

PUBLISHER'S NOTE: In this book, one measure is equal to one jigger. For more information on jiggers, please see p.28.

LESSONS

IN MIXOLOGY

A Graphic Guide to Making the Perfect Cocktail

JORDAN SPENCE

CONTENTS

INTRODUCTION 6

A-Z OF COCKTAILS 7

THE WELL-STOCKED BAR 10

Whisky 12
Rum 13
Gin 14
Vodka 16
Brandy 17
Tequila 19
Liqueurs 21
Champagne 22
Mixers & Garnishes 23
Fruit 24
Shakers 25
Glasses 26
Other Equipment 28
Bartending Techniques 29

RECIPES

Classic Cocktails 32
Vodka Cocktails 54
Gin Cocktails 78
Brandy Cocktails 104
Rum Cocktails 126
Whisky Cocktails 150
Tequila Cocktails 174
Champagne Cocktails 198
Liqueur Cocktails 220
Shots 240

INDEX 252

INTRODUCTION

Cocktails stepped out of the speakeasy and into the mainstream around the 1950s, and since then they've shown no signs of slowing down. Having found a new popularity among younger generations, cocktails are now available almost everywhere. No longer confined to glitzy bars and exclusive socialite parties, they've now infiltrated your local pub, bar, pizza restaurant, and even food trucks.

In the digital world, social media is awash with cocktails, whether it's a good-looking Hollywood star mixing the perfect martini or an up-and-coming influencer creating something new and experimental, it seems everyone has caught cocktail fever.

When made properly, cocktails are a drink experience unlike any other, satisfying several senses at once: sight, smell, taste. Perfectly balanced, layered and complex, and served in iconic glasses, they can make you feel classier than any other drink can.

The enjoyment of a cocktail may be in the drinking, but the process of making it is everything. To a serious mixologist, creating the perfect cocktail is as scientific as splitting the atom and as artistic as painting the Sistine Chapel. The discussions about how to make the perfect Martini, for example, have been raging since its creation, and its numerous reinventions have sparked both delight and outrage.

This book breaks each cocktail, from an Acapulco to a Zombie, into easily digested, graphic components, simplifying the process as much as possible while keeping the same delicious end result. Keep this book next to your spirit bottles, shaker and glasses, so you're always ready to mix up your 5pm aperitif or your dinner party showstopper.

Just remember to take it easy: you may feel fantastic drinking your cocktail of choice, but you may not feel as fantastic the following morning. Cheers!

A-Z OF COCKTAILS

A

Acapulco 176
Adam and Eve 106
After Eight 222
Afternoon Delight 128
Alabama Slammer 242
Alaska 80
Algonquin 152
All Night 177
Amaretto Comfort 223
American Beauty 107
Angel Wing Shooter 244
Angel's Kiss 243
Angelic 153
Apollo 13 129
April Shower 108
Aristocrat 224
Astoria 81
Aviation 2 56

B

B-52 245
B & B 109
Bad girl 227
Bahia 130
Ballantine's 154
Banshee 225
Barracuda 131
Bastile 200
Bee Stinger 226
Bee's Kiss 132
Bella Donna 133
Bellini 34
Between the Sheets 110
Bikini 57
Black and Tan 228
Black Jack Shooter 246
Black Magic 58
Black Russian 59
Black Velvet 201
Blackjack 229
Blood and Sand 155
Bloody Mary 35
Blue Hawaiian 134
Blue Monday 82
Bombardier 83
Brandy Alexander 36
Brandy Cocktail 111
Brandy Daisy 112
Brandy Kiss 113
Brighton Rock 230
Broadway 84
Brooklyn 156
Bullshot 60

C

Cadillac Lady 85
Caipirinha 37
Canadian Sherbet 157
Cape Codder 61
Casablanca 135
Casanova 202
Champagne Cobbler 203

A-Z OF COCKTAILS

Champagne Cocktail 204
Champagne Cooler 205
Chapala 178
Chapel Hill 158
Chastity Belt 247
Cherry Picker 114
Chicago 115
Clam Digger 179
Cocoloco 136
Colonel Fizz 159
Cool Cucumber 206
Cool Gold 180
Corpse Reviver 116
Cosmopolitan 38
Cuba Libre 137

D

Daiquiri 39
Death by Chocolate 231
Death in the Afternoon 207
Deep Throat Shooter 248
Dirty Martini 86
Dizzy Dame 117
Dizzy Gillespie 138

E

Eggnog 118
El Diablo 181
El Presidente 139
Eldorado 182

F

Floridita 140
Fluffy Duck 87
French 75 88
French Kiss 62
French Martini 63
French Sherbet 208
Frenchie 119
Frisco 160
Frostbite 183
Fuzzy Navel 232

G

Gimlet 40
Godfather 161
Grasshopper 233
Gumdrop 162

H

Harry's Cocktail 89
Harvey Wallbanger 64
Honeymoon Paradise 209
Hurricane 141

I

Imperial 90
Iron Lady 234

J

Jack Rose 120
Jacuzzi 91
James Bond 210
Jasmine 92
Joe Collins 65
Jungle Juice 142
Juniper Royale 93

K

Kaiser 94
Kentucky Sunset 163
Kir Royale 211

L

La Bomba 184
La Dolce Vita 212
Laser Beam 185
Last Emperor 164
Leap Year 95
Liberty Bell 165
Lieutenant 121
Long Island Iced Tea 42
Love for Sale 66
Lychee Martini 67

M

Madonna 143
Mai Tai 43
Manhattan 41
Margarita 44
Martini 45
Matador 186
Metropolis 68
Mexican Mule 187
Mexicana 188
Mikado 122
Milk Punch 166
Mimosa 213
Mint Julep 46
Mojito 144
Moulin Rouge 96
Mudslide 69

N

Naked Lady 145
Negroni 47
Nicky Finn 123

O

Old Vermouth 97
Old Fashioned 48

P

Painkiller 146
Piña Colada 147
Pink Cadillac 235
Pisco Sour 49
Poinsettia 214
Poison Arrow 70
Pussy Foot 148

R

Raja 124
Raspberry Sip 215
Red Death 236
Red Desert 189
Red Snapper 98
Ritz Fizz 216
Rob Roy 167
Rosalita 190
Rusty Nail 168

S

Salty Dog 71
Sazerac 169
Screaming Multiple Orgasm 237
Screwdriver 72
Sea Breeze 73
Sea Horse 74
Sex on the Beach 249
Shamrock 170
Shooting Star 238
Short Fuse 191
Sidecar 50
Silk Stocking 192
Singapore Sling 51
Slippery Nipple 250
Soixante-Neuf 217
South of the Border 193
Swan Song 239
Sweet Surrender 218
Swinger 99

T

Tequila Sunrise 194
Tijuana Taxi 195
Tom Collins 52
Tom Fizz 100
Tomahawk 196
Traffic Light 251
Tulip 125
Typhoon 219

U

Union Jack 101

V

Vampiro 197
Vesper 75
VIP 171

W

Whiskey Sour 53
Whisky Mac 172
White Russian 76
White Velvet 102
Whizz Doodle 173
Woo Woo 77
Woodstock 103

Z

Zombie 149

THE WELL-STOCKED BAR

Every professional or home bar requires a basic collection of spirits before interesting mixed drinks and cocktails can be made. Always buy the best quality brands to be assured of the purest taste, but, as with most things, good quality can be found at reasonable prices.

ICE

Ice cools the spirit as it is poured into a glass. All ice must be fresh. Only filtered, or even bottled, water should be used to make ice. There are four types of ice used in cocktails: crushed, shaved, cracked or cubed. Ice can be used in a blender, a shaker, a mixing glass or directly in a glass, but cubes should not be served in a cocktail glass. Use cubes in a shaker and crushed ice in a blender. Cracked and shaved ice are more watery than cubes and dilute the spirit more quickly than cubes. Don't put ice from a blender into the glass.

BAR NECESSITIES

Spirits

Bourbon

Brandy

Gin

Pimm's No. 1 Cup

Rum, light and dark

Tequila, white (silver) and gold

Vodka

Whisky

Liqueurs

Amaretto

Baileys Irish Cream

Cointreau

Crème de menthe (white and green)

Crème de cacao (white and brown)

Curaçao, blue

Grand Marnier

Wines

Champagne (or sparkling wine)

Vermouths, dry and sweet

Wine, red and white

Extras

Coconut cream

Cream, double

Egg-white powder*

Tabasco sauce

Worcestershire sauce

Pepper

Salt

Sugar, caster

* Use instead of fresh egg white if preferred

Syrups

Gomme syrup

Grenadine

Bitters

Angostura

Spoiling yourself
At home your cocktail menu can be as adventurous or conservative as you like

WHISKY

How do you like your whisky? Scotch, American, Canadian or Irish? With a few pretenders in between, there is an incredible choice of types, blended or malts. Each method of distillation is just different enough to ensure that the taste experience is always varied.

Scotch whisky is brewed in the northern, eastern, western and central Highlands regions of Scotland, in Speyside (a premier malt whisky region on its own) and on the islands off the mainland, including Islay, Mull, Jura and the Orkneys. The Lowlands and Campbeltown also produce whisky. In the U.S., it centres on the Southern states of Kentucky and Tennessee.

Deer friend
The Glenfiddich stag is one of the best-known Scotch whisky labels

Whisky is made from grain, water and yeast. The difference in taste and colour comes from the distillation methods employed by the producer. Some of the variations are: pot still or patent still; types of yeast; the kinds of wood used for ageing, and the size of the barrel; how long the spirit is in the barrel; the source of the pure water; and the type of cereal grains used (barley, corn, wheat, rye or oats). Flavour and its amber colour are added during the maturation process when the liquid is placed in wood (usually oak) vats or casks.

Scotch must be aged a minimum of three years. In the U.S., federal law states that bourbon must be aged for at least two years.

What do you look for in a whisky? Purity. Colour ranges from light amber to honey and a deeper chestnut brown. Malts are paler versions, whereas bourbons are darker, almost reddish. Kentucky bourbons and Tennessee whiskies are generally sweeter than Scotch; Irish whiskeys are like a light Scotch; and Canadian types, produced in Ottawa and Montreal, are easy-drinking, probably because the majority of the grain is corn. Japan is also a big producer of whisky, and it's becoming increasingly available worldwide.

RUM

Rum is a great mixer, the taste behind great cocktails filled with fresh fruit juices. Without rum we would have no Daiquiri, Piña Colada or Rum Punch, and the world would be an even sadder place than it is.

Rum is, along with tourism, a major industry in the Caribbean. This time-honoured nectar is made from sugarcane, and it has been a favourite drink of sailors for centuries. Islands in the Caribbean are dotted with vast plantations growing sugarcane to meet the demands of distilleries. Rum is produced from molasses and is the byproduct of manufacturing raw sugar from sugarcane. The molasses is turned into alcohol by the process of fermentation. The alcohol is then distilled and becomes clear and colourless.

The spirit is aged in small oak barrels, whether the resulting rum is white or dark. Wood is porous and lets the rum spirit breathe, and with each breath, oxidation takes place. Light rum is matured in pale ash-wood barrels for one year only and then it is transferred to steel vats where it is left to age longer. Dark rum types are in the barrel for three years and longer (some for up to 20 years), after which, distillers believe, they start to lose flavour.

RUM TYPES

White
Also known as silver or light, it is clear and light, and has a dry flavour.

Gold
Also oro or ambré, it is sweeter, with the colour gained from the oak cask or sometimes from the addition of caramel colouring.

Dark
Also black, this type has been aged in a charred barrel.

Premium Aged/Añejo/ Rhum Vieux
Valued by connoisseurs, these are the pick-of-the-crop mature rums.

Flavoured and Spiced
These types are served with fruit juice or a mixer.

Overproof
The white types are used for blending.

Single Marks
These are rare, unblended rums produced by individual distilleries and are sought after. You don't often see them on top shelves.

Most rums are blended from a selection of aged rums and from different styles of rum. How much caramel and flavouring, and which spices are to be added, are up to the blender. Once the mix has been ordained, it is diluted with water to the required bottling strength.

Rum is made all over the world. But it should not be confused with cachaça. This is a spirit distilled in Brazil, made from molasses, sugarcane juice, or a combination of both. Cachaça is probably best known as the spirit underlying the delicious Caipirinha (see p. 37).

Ready for a caning
Molasses and raw sugar come from the cane, and from molasses comes rum

GIN

Gin, known as "Mother's Ruin" in England, has been produced since the 1600s, when the Dutch first produced this full-flavoured spirit. Then it was a distilled grain spirit flavoured with juniper berries, which were thought to have beneficial effects on problems with the kidney and the bladder.

Early gins, such as Old Tom, were more like sweet cordial-type spirits. But, in Britain, over many decades it lost its sweetness to become London Dry in style. Gin was introduced to Britain when British soldiers returned from the series of wars on the European mainland.

In the seventeenth and eighteenth centuries gin was so popular that the government was forced to take control of its production by legislation – the streets and public houses were full of too many gin-soaked people. In 1736 the distilleries were taxed and they, in turn, raised the price for drinkers; 20 years later the distillation of corn was outlawed, and a series of riots ensued. It took until 1760 for the laws to be repealed. Gin was not a respectable drink at that time, and it took decades for it to gain respectability in high society. It's a different matter these days.

The best gin is recognized as that made from a grain spirit – preferably corn – and contains very few impurities. Any gin made with a molasses spirit will taste slightly sweeter. Most gin is made in a continuous still to produce the 96 per cent alcohol by volume ratio required. Once this is achieved, the spirit is redistilled. The second distillation involves the spirit being distilled along with natural botanicals to produce a subtle premium gin.

When you pour a measure of gin, you get a whiff of the aroma instantly. Gin has a neutral-grain base and it is the addition of botanicals that gives gin its character. Each of the contemporary brands is blended to produce an individual taste.

If you have a refined palate, you might taste some of the following herbs in the gin: aniseed, angelica, coriander seeds, juniper berries, ginger, almonds, orange rind, cardamom, cinnamon or liquorice root. For example, extra-dry gins usually contain more angelica or liquorice, whereas gins with a dominant citrus flavour have more orange or lemon peel. The gin is then reduced to bottling strength, 75 proof in America and 35 per cent alcohol by volume (ABV) in Europe.

Many of the best-known classic cocktails are made with gin: the original Martini, Gibson, Pink Gin, Singapore Sling and White Lady.

Basically, there are four types of gin: dry gin (unsweetened), London dry gin (unsweetened), Old Tom gin (slightly sweetened), and Plymouth gin (slightly sweetened). Although you may have to search off-licences for Old Tom gin, the other types are generally available.

VODKA

According to Pablo Picasso in 1950, "The three most astonishing things in the past half-century have been the blues, cubism and Polish vodka." He may well have been right. Vodka, Polish or otherwise, is the perfect base spirit for a cocktail because it is colourless, tasteless and odourless.

Pass someone an orange drink and they'd never know that underneath this colourful exterior might lie the world's "most drunk" spirit. Nearly everybody in the world of drinking age has had a sip of vodka and many of today's drinkers are brand loyal, preferring the flavour and style of one vodka over any other.

Vodka first came into America's consciousness after World War II when Heublein began to distribute Smirnoff vodka. Its advertising played up vodka's very tastelessness and, before you knew it, the classic Martini kissed gin goodbye and became a vodka-based cocktail. We have Ian Fleming's charismatic character, James Bond, to thank for that. Yet, the Bloody Mary (with or without the celery) was born using vodka, just like the ubiquitous Harvey Wallbanger and the Screwdriver.

The name "vodka" derives from the Russian word for water, *voda*. There is a long history associated with this spirit, allegedly born in Russia. Or was it? Scandinavians and Poles claim vodka was made as early as, or even earlier than, the era claimed by the Russians – the fourteenth century.

Note
Vodka should be served chilled, between 2 and 6°C (35–43°F), never higher than 10°C (50°F). Because the aroma of vodka is not perceptible when chilled, distillers put the greatest emphasis on taste

As a general rule, spirit production uses starchy materials (potatoes and grains such as rye, wheat, barley, millet or corn) and sugary materials (molasses, sugar beets, fruit). However, vodka made in America is pure grain neutral spirit distilled from fermented corn, rye or wheat, which is distilled in a continuous still. Charcoal filtration results in a clear and clean-tasting product. In Europe rye grain is traditionally the main ingredient.

New vodkas, aimed at the connoisseur in the same way as armagnac, cognac and whisky, are distilled up to three times, and then a trace of a separately distilled, lower-strength spirit may be added for character. These types are best taken from a shot glass.

Flavoured vodkas have become increasingly popular in recent years. Blackcurrant, cherry, pineapple, lemon, orange, peach and pepper are just some of the flavours on offer. Flavouring spirit can be a very simple process and distillers are secretive about the processes they use. In Poland, flavourings such as fruit and herbs are generally prepared in two ways, using either the classic maceration or the circulation method. With the classic method, ingredients are macerated in spirit which varies in strength (usually 40–60 per cent ABV), according to the type and ripeness of the ingredients.

After the first four weeks, the spirit is drained (and reserved), with another batch of spirit added for a further three-week maceration. These two liquids are blended, together with a residual liquid pressed from the macerated ingredients. Prior to bottling, all three "spirits" are then adjusted to ensure a standard alcoholic strength.

The circulation method uses ingredients such as bison grass spread across a sieve inside a stainless steel vat. The alcohol circulating in the tank passes through the sieve twice every eight hours, usually over a period of four to seven days, according to the ripeness and type of ingredients.

Vodka producers have jumped on the health bandwagon, creating new versions of an ancient ginseng vodka produced by Lancut Distillery, which has mastered the secrets of its production and has obtained access to genuine red ginseng. Red ginseng spirit is increasingly available outside of Asia, often produced in the time-honoured Korean way.

BRANDY

The category "brandy" encompasses perhaps the widest selection in the spirit world. The choice of flavours, textures, aromas and appearances is unique in the world of distilled spirits. At the top of the range, there is probably no more exclusive a drink than cognac.

There is French brandy, including armagnac and cognac, and brandies made in other parts of France. There is Spanish brandy (Brandy de Jérez); Italian types, including grappa; South African, Mexican and American; and pisco from South America. Then there are eaux-de-vie and liqueur brandies. Statistics reveal that two-thirds of the brandy for the American market comes from California, centre of the nation's wine industry.

So, what are you buying when you ask for a drink? "Brandy" is a generic term for a spirit distilled from the fermented juice of fruit. The name itself, brandy, is from the Dutch word *brandewijn* – literally "burnt wine" – and from the perspective of history, the creation of brandy was due almost entirely to Dutch traders who travelled the coastal ports of France and Spain in search of wine for their sailors.

The Dutch demand eventually forced the French to change the way they shipped wine to Holland, where it was used as a raw material in *wijnbranders* ("wineburners"). Distilled spirit was cheaper than wine to ship (it was less bulk), so the French began to use the technique and equipment, introduced by the Dutch for distillation, particularly in the Charente region.

In the modern world, brandy is made from the grapes that have been distilled in either a small copper-pot still (called an alembic), or a continuous still, then transferred to age in oak barrels. After this period of maturation they are allowed to age further in glass jars.

South American brandy is called pisco and hails from Peru and Chile. Made from Muscat grapes, distilled and then aged in oak or in clay jars, pisco is the base spirit of a famous Pisco Sour cocktail.

What should brandy taste like?
You should be able to taste several layers, with sweet, woody and fruity flavours on the tongue. If it burns your throat, try another type. A brandy should make your throat feel warm, but it should not feel harsh and raw

Cognac

Grapes from vineyards of the Charente-Maritime area in France are used to make cognac. Ugni Blanc, Folle Blanche and Colombard grapes are distilled and matured in oak casks from the Limousin or Troncais forests.

All cognac is a blend of cognacs from different houses and vintages, as is most whisky. Any details on a bottle's label refer to the number of years the youngest cognac in the blend has been in the cask. Three Star/V.S. is the youngest at three years; V.S.O.P., V.O. (Very Old), Very Special (or Superior) Old Pale has a four-and-a-half-year-old as the youngest; and XO, Extra, Napoleon, Vieille Réserve has, as its youngest, a six-year-old. The actual ageing is generally longer. When it is aged between 40 and 60 years old, it is considered excellent quality.

Armagnac is the second French region that comes to mind when brandy is mentioned. It is a relatively small player on the scene, and rivalry between the two regions is great, each claiming the benefits of its style of brandy. Armagnaçais producers claim single distillation gives their brandy the edge whereas the Cognaçais dismiss talk of vintages for distilled wines.

Centuries prior to cognac's production, grapes were being distilled by Spaniards in Andalucia, who had learnt distillation from the Moors who occupied Spain for over seven centuries. Generally, these are robust, perhaps sweeter (they are aged in former sherry casks) and simple brandies. Now, no country exports more brandy than Mexico.

TEQUILA

To write of tequila is to write about the true spirit of Mexico, and to recall those nights when the moon shone brightly as you licked the salt, sipped the tequila shot and bit the lemon. The moon shone brighter after that. Oh, by the way, it's the spirit base of a Margarita. But you probably knew that.

Tequila is an unusual distilled spirit produced from the fermented juice of the swollen stem of the blue agave, a flowering succulent plant found all over Mexico. Tequila is a specific mezcal and is not to be confused with the drink with the worm in it. This is mezcal made from a different variety of the agave.

By law, tequila can be produced only in Mexico (in the same way that cognac can come only from Cognac) and is produced in designated regions, mostly in Jalisco, but also in designated villages within four states: Guanajuato, Nayarit, and Tamaulipas.

Types of Tequila

There are two basic types of tequila: 100 per cent agave and tequila mixed with other sugars (mixto). Read the label. If it does not say 100 per cent agave, it is mixto.

Tequila and cocktails go together like sex and the city. Well-known tequila cocktails include Margarita, Tequila Sunrise and Tequila Mockingbird. Each of these exotic names reminds the drinker of holidays in the sun, of lazy days and haunting evenings.

Seasoned drinkers claim it's harder to get a hangover from drinking a 100 per cent agave than with a mixto. Purity excels! At the bar, if

TEQUILA TYPES

Blanco or plata (white or silver)

Clear in colour and bottled immediately after distillation. Can be left for no longer than 60 days in stainless steel tanks before bottling. It may be 100 per cent agave or mixto.

Reposado (rested)

Aged for not less than two months in wooden vats or oak barrels. Can be 100 per cent agave or mixto.

Anejo (aged)

Produced from 100 per cent agave and must be left for a year or more in wooden barrels. Either 100 per cent agave or mixto. The very best are seldom left in the barrel for more than four years.

Joven abocado (often called gold)

Unaged tequila with the characteristics of an aged tequila, but the golden colour is produced by an additive such as caramel. A mixto variety, it can taste more mellow than the usual mixto.

you're set for an evening of tequila, it is preferable to ask for a blanco, a pure agave tequila, regardless of what you mix it with. At least the spirit remains untouched by added chemicals.

Before the Spanish conquest in 1521, Mexico was home to ancient American cultures that regarded the agave as a "gift of the gods" because it was useful in a variety of ways. (Aztecs painted many of their writings on agave fibre.) According to Bob Emmons in his fascinating account, *The Book of Tequila*, the alcoholic properties of the plant were discovered before the rise of the Aztecs. The discovery of the liquid known as *pulque* supplied a means of relaxation. The Aztecs also consumed it as a narcotic during the rather less palatable rites of human sacrifice.

In 1792 Ferdinand IV lifted the ban on spirit production in Mexico and in 1795 he granted a licence to one Jose Maria Guadalupe Cuervo, a Spaniard who set up a distillery in Tequila, Mexico, using cultivated, as opposed to wild, agave to produce the spirit. Now there are over 65 distilleries producing tequila for consumption at home and abroad. And, by the way, the U.S. consumes more tequila than the rest of the world.

What should tequila taste like? Connoisseurs speak of fine tequilas in much the same way as experts in cognac and fine wine drinkers describe their favourite drinks. For instance, of a Tequila Herradura blanco, one expert waxed lyrical with, "Dry complexity to the nose with floral overtones, good herbaceousness and smooth alcohol."

That's before you suck the lemon.

LIQUEURS

It's all sweetness or creaminess in the liqueur business. Coffee, banana, chocolate, strawberry and raspberry flavours abound in delicious mixtures that swirl into the glass in an appealing way. And the colours can be as vivid as an artist's palette or as muted as a warm summer's evening.

Let's get this straight. A liqueur is not a cordial; we're talking true distilled liqueur. The word "liqueur" comes from the Latin *liquefacere*, to melt or dissolve. Centuries ago, liqueurs were distilled from recipes by monks and apothecaries whose main task was to cure ailments.

Dutchman Lucas Bols is responsible for the start of the modern liqueur industry in the sixteenth century. Knowing that caraway was good for the digestion, he created kummel. Benedictine has been made since 1510, and Chartreuse had been made for the brothers at an abbey in France long before it became available in 1848.

Spirits including brandy, cognac, whisky and rum are used as the base for liqueurs. Fruits, plants, fruit skins and/or roots are steeped in alcohol in a still, heated, and the vapours are condensed to produce the spirit. Maceration is used only for fruit with pulp – raspberries, blackcurrants and aromatic plants, such as tea. The picked fruit is put into vats with alcohol and an infusion occurs.

A crème, such as crème de menthe, is a sweet and thick liqueur with 28 per cent sugar content. A cream, such as Baileys Irish Cream, is a combination of alcohol and dairy cream.

If you are serving a liqueur straight, do so at room temperature and in a small liqueur glass. It should be sipped and savoured, not gulped down, like a shot, in a single swallow. Liqueurs are usually served after a meal, without ice, to get the full flavour without it being diluted.

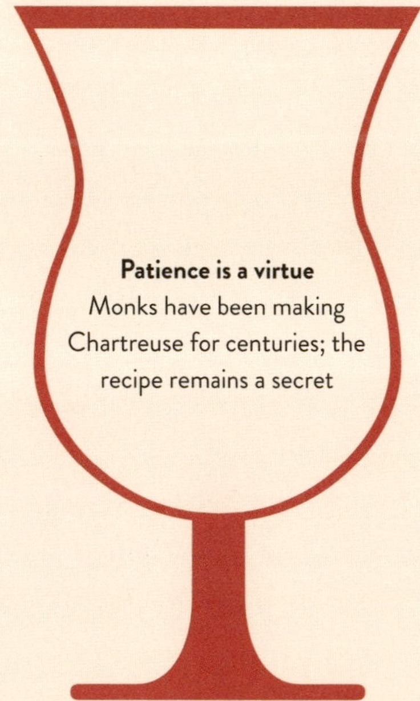

CHAMPAGNE

Ask any champagne producer when is the best time to drink champagne and he will tell you "any time of the day or night". There is a magic about sipping champagne before lunch to which it never quite aspires in the late afternoon or evening. Champagne is also possibly the best apéritif.

The famous British wartime leader Winston Churchill, a great champagne drinker (mainly Pol Roger), called for it as he settled into his seat for a Clipper flight to America, much to the consternation of a colleague.

Many people who have been swilling champagne for a lifetime don't know it is made predominantly from the juice of red grapes. The proportion of juice from white grapes is usually around one-third. Another interesting fact is that a bottle of the best champagne may contain the juice from 15 different vineyards; some superb champagnes have juice from more than 30 vineyards.

Champagne is produced in an appellation controllée region in France. Only wine from this region can be labelled "champagne". Wine labelled "Méthode Champenoise" is made by a similar method, outside the Champagne region.

CHAMPAGNE STYLES

Brut A tiny amount of sweetening is added.

Demi-sec Sweet champagne.

Extra Sec Dry champagne.

Non-vintage Any champagne made using grapes from different years. A non-vintage champagne (NV) is not necessarily of lesser quality.

Rosé Made with some of the still red wine of the Champagne region with white wine.

Sec Medium-sweet champagne.

Vintage A "vintage year" is declared by the authorities when weather conditions have been superb. A bottle of vintage champagne is one for which all the grapes were harvested in the same year.

MIXERS AND GARNISHES

Not every ingredient in a cocktail contains alcohol. Indeed there is probably no more refreshing a drink than a St. Clement's, made with fresh orange juice and bitter lemon. And without grapefruit and cranberry juice, a Sea Breeze becomes a straight vodka.

Mixers

- Ginger ale (punches)
- Lemon-lime soda
- Soda water
- Spring water, still and sparkling
- Tonic water

Juices

- Cranberry
- Grapefruit, white and pink
- Orange
- Pineapple
- Tomato

Garnishes

Garnishes provide the finishing touch to a cocktail. To choose the right garnish, think about the dominant flavour and colour of the cocktail and choose a fruit or leaf that will go with it. Add a piece of fruit that's in proportion to the glass. Don't add a garish touch.

Strawberries are versatile as a garnish added to the drink, particularly in a champagne cocktail, or placed on the rim. Cut out the green stem, make a slit in the bottom of the strawberry and place it over the rim.

BAR CRAFT

Citrus fruit spiral

Press a zester firmly into the rind of a lemon/lime/orange, starting from the top. Carefully cut around the fruit, making a long spiral as you go. Add it to the cocktail.

Twist

Cut a 1- to 2-inch (2.5–5-cm) wide piece of rind from a lemon or orange. Place it on a cutting board, pith down. With a sharp knife, trim a thin strip, about 2 inches (5 cm) long, from the wider piece. Hold it over the glass and twist the ends so that the juice from the rind falls into the drink.

FRUIT

Blackberries (nonalcoholic drinks)
Mint, fresh
Celery sticks (optional for Bloody Mary)
Green olives (for a Martini)
Cherries, maraschino (cocktail cherries)
Pineapples
Raspberries
Cucumber peel (for punches, Pimm's)
Strawberries (for champagne and punches)
Oranges
Lemons
Limes

SHAKERS

The shaker is the most important tool for making great cocktails. As a rule, any recipe with a spirit, a juice and cream is shaken. The shaker used in most bars differs from the types you would find in a normal drinks shop; the professionals' Boston shake is a two-piece unit: one metal, the other clear glass.

Pour the ingredients into the glass section, and add the ice. Place the metal part over the glass, sealing the two sections. Turn the shaker upside down. Shake the drink and let it settle before separating the sections. To serve, pour the cocktail through a bar strainer into a glass.

The shaker most widely available consists of a base, a small lid with a fitted strainer, and a solid cap. When shaking, always hold the lid down firmly. If it becomes stuck, ease the lid up with two thumbs to loosen the vacuum. There's nothing worse than a lid coming loose and having the precious cocktail go everywhere but into the glass.

Cocktail shakers have also become collector's items and can sell at auction for considerable sums. One of the most popular antique shakers is the Penguin, dated circa 1936. It has a hinged beak that lifts to reveal a spout for pouring.

A search of the U.S. Patent Office files disclosed that applications for "an apparatus to mix drinks" were filed in the 1870s. By the late nineteenth century novelty cocktail shakers were all the rage. They included a lighthouse, buoy, skyscraper, golf bag and even a teapot!

Early shakers were made of silver, and as technology progressed, more were made of chrome-plated stainless steel. Today, most shakers are made of plated metal and are relatively inexpensive.

Mr Bond would approve
A Martini with a shaker, not a stirrer

GLASSES

Clear glasses are ideal for cocktails. Since the beginning of the cocktail craze, each type of drink has had a shape specifically for it. For example, a Martini is served in a Martini cocktail glass. Common sense dictates a liqueur should be sipped from a small glass because it is so sweet.

Main Glass Types and Sizes

Most glasses come in regular sizes as an industry standard, but there are some different shaped and sized glasses, particularly double cocktail glasses. This list should provide a useful guide and give an indication of the amount of drink required for a party. Smaller glasses mean less drink is consumed... unless the guests are very thirsty.

Glass Cleaning

Clean the glass with a lint-free towel before pouring a drink. Do not wash with soapy liquids because these can leave a residue on the glass.

GLASS TYPE	CAPACITY	CHARACTERISTICS
Cocktail	4 oz. (12 cl)	Popular for any cocktail served without ice
Flute	6–8 oz. (18–24 cl)	For champagne and champagne cocktails
Highball	10 oz. (30 cl)	Ideal for long drinks filled with ice cubes
Liqueur	2–3 oz. (6–9 cl)	A tiny glass for sipping after-dinner cocktails or a straight liqueur
Old Fashioned	5–6 oz. (15–18 cl)	A short glass with a heavy base
Saucer	5–7 oz. (15–21 cl)	By legend the shape was modelled on the bust of Empress Josephine, but champagne goes flatter more quickly than in a flute
Shot	2–3 oz. (6–9 cl)	Small glass to hold a measure of spirit that will be thrown down the throat
Wine	4–9 oz. (12–27 cl)	For a drink not suited to a cocktail glass but too small for a highball

OTHER EQUIPMENT

A basic cocktail tool kit consists of a few small but important items, listed below. Most can be found in a household goods shop or in the kitchen or bar accessories department of major stores. As with all things, the cheapest is unlikely to be the best, but functional is more important than flashy.

- Bar knife must be very sharp, to slice fruit
- Barspoon mixes and stirs cocktail ingredients in a mixing glass or a shaker
- Blender blends spirits, juice, fruit and crushed ice, especially for frozen cocktails
- Champagne stopper keeps the champagne bubbly once opened
- Chopping board provides a hard, flat surface on which to chop mint, dice garnishes, slice fruit
- Cocktail sticks spear bits of fruit and cherries as garnish
- Corkscrew opens wine bottles; the best is a "waiter's friend"
- Dash pourer adds drops and dashes of other spirits and liqueurs
- Ice bucket saves regular trips to the freezer
- Ice crusher takes cubes and crushes them
- Ice scoop for adding ice to a shaker or blender
- Ice tongs for picking up ice cubes, which hasten the melting process
- Jigger obtains the correct spirit and liqueur measures for a cocktail. In the U.S., one measure is 1 oz., and jiggers for single and double measures are also calibrated to measure common proportions: the quarter, third, half and three-quarters. In the U.K. the law defines one measure as either 25ml or 35ml, with jiggers calibrated for single and double measures. Premises may sell in multiples of 25ml or 35ml but not both
- Juicer for making fruit lemon and lime juices
- Mixing glass to mix two or more ingredients
- Muddler pestle that mashes or pulps mint or fruit berries
- Shaker for shaking cocktails
- Stirrers and straws. Long cocktails should be drunk through a straw
- Tea towel wipes up spills
- Zester peels lemon, orange and lime rinds to make garnishes

BARTENDING TECHNIQUES

Cocktails came back into fashion in the late 1980s and 1990s, as the bar – as opposed to the club or pub – returned to prominence. For a while the job of bartender ranked as one of the most glamorous. But, for all the show, the art of making cocktails should not be taken lightly.

Shaking

It might look simple when the guy behind the bar starts with his act, but for a beginner who has yet to hold a shaker... Firstly, it's very cold, wet and slippery on the outside and that makes it hard to handle. Grip it firmly in both hands, with one hand under the base and the other firmly holding the top while, simultaneously, you splay the fingers around the sides.

Now here's the fun bit. Move only the wrists, not the arms and shoulders. Flick it with finesse, hard, not half-heartedly. The aim is to combine the ingredients inside and chill them as they are swished back and forth over the ice. After about 20 attempts, a personal style will develop. Good bartenders have a personal rhythm to their shake and this is what novices should aspire to.

Using a Mixing Glass

Cocktails with ingredients that need mixing, and are served chilled, are mixed in a mixing glass, then poured through a bar strainer into an Old Fashioned glass or a cocktail glass. Place the ice cubes into the mixing glass and stir the ice around with a barspoon so that it chills the glass. Add the spirits and stir, then strain into a glass. Use a tall glass with a solid base – or a large medicine beaker – if a proper mixing glass isn't available.

Muddling

Muddling is an action that requires a bit of strength in the wrist. And it requires a muddler. Some barspoons have a section on the end that can act as a muddler, but usually they are made of fine wood or marble (as in a pestle and mortar).

Many younger bartenders use muddling to great effect in their new cocktails. The item is placed in the bottom of a shaker/Old Fashioned glass/mixing glass/highball and mashed to release its colour, juice and flavour. A Mint Julep is made with mint muddled in the bottom of a glass. It is imperative to use a glass with a heavy base.

Layering/Floating

Layered drinks look superb. They're impressive, and everyone wonders how it is done. In fact, it's easy. Each spirit in a recipe weighs more or less than the others. Start with the heaviest, then add the second heaviest, and work up to the top until the lightest is floated as a finishing touch.

Usually, layered drinks are made in small glasses such as a shot or liqueur glass. A steady hand is needed, although a barspoon or a small teaspoon may be used to float each liquid over the one already in the glass.

If there are five ingredients in a recipe, begin with the first ingredient in the recipe, because it ought to be the heaviest. To pour, place the spoon on the edge of the first layer in the glass, with the back of the barspoon facing you. Pour the next spirit slowly over the spoon, and watch as it creates a second layer. Repeat the action until each ingredient in the recipe has been used.

Blending

Blended cocktails have a smooth, fruity texture and are a delicious summer drink. It's an unwritten rule that cocktails whose ingredients contain cream, fruit and crushed ice should be blended. With blended drinks, it is possible to make two or three drinks at a time, which is especially useful if there are a few people around for a pool party.

Wash any pieces of fruit before adding them to the blender. Follow instructions for dicing, too. If there isn't enough liquid in the blender when the fruit has been put in, add a teaspoon of water to aid the blades. For a really smooth result, pour the blended mixture through a strainer, and mash the mixture thoroughly, forcing the liquid through into the glass below.

Make this type of drink immediately and serve in a suitable glass, such as a wine goblet, a colada glass or even a margarita glass. Here's a tip: add the ice at the last minute and blend again to chill the drink.

Chilling a Glass

Professional bartenders always chill cocktail glasses and champagne flutes before pouring in any liquid. The opaque glass effect makes a drink look mysterious and as it fades, the drinker is left watching the cocktail itself emerge. Alternatively, place a few glasses in the freezer compartment for about half an hour before guests arrive. If that is impractical, the same effect can be achieved by putting crushed ice in the glass while the cocktail is being shaken or mixed. Remove the ice before pouring in the drink.

Crusting a Rim

For many drinkers, licking the rim of a Margarita, before sipping the drink, is the most pleasurable part of the whole experience. Many classic cocktails were born with a crusting and have remained that way ever since. Crusting a glass is a very simple task.

Rub a wedge of lime around the rim of a glass. Then turn the glass upside down and, holding it by the stem, twirl the rim around a saucer filled with fine salt. Make sure the salt sticks to the rim. If a more crusty effect is required, use slightly crushed sea salt. And, for a very special effect, salt only one half of the glass.

If the recipe requires a sugared rim, the method is exactly the same. Different and colourful effects can also be achieved by using chocolate or cocoa powder or a food colouring in sugar to give an exotic alternative.

CLASSICS

BELLINI

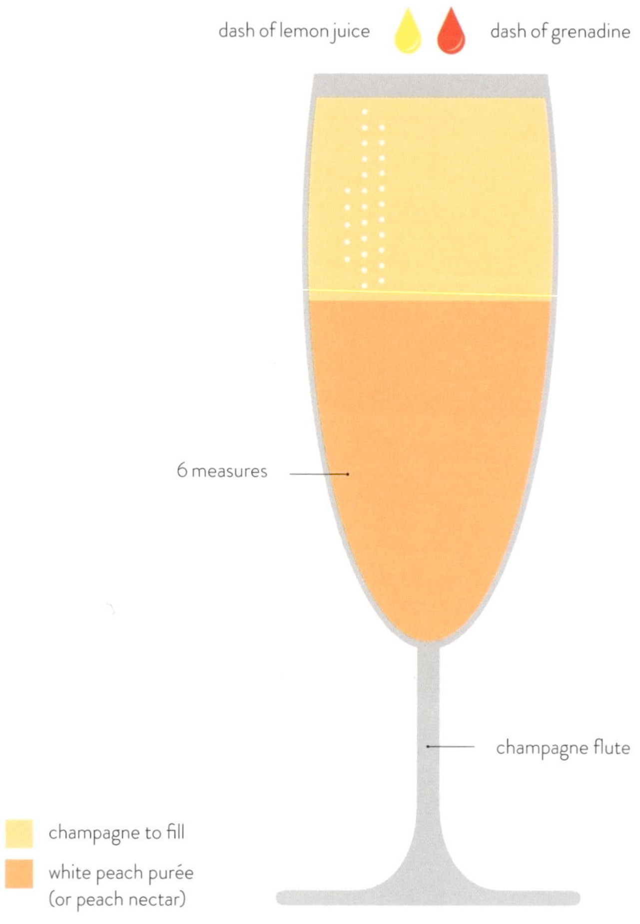

Instructions

1 Mix the peach purée, grenadine, and lemon juice together in a champagne flute. **2** Top up with champagne and serve.

BLOODY MARY

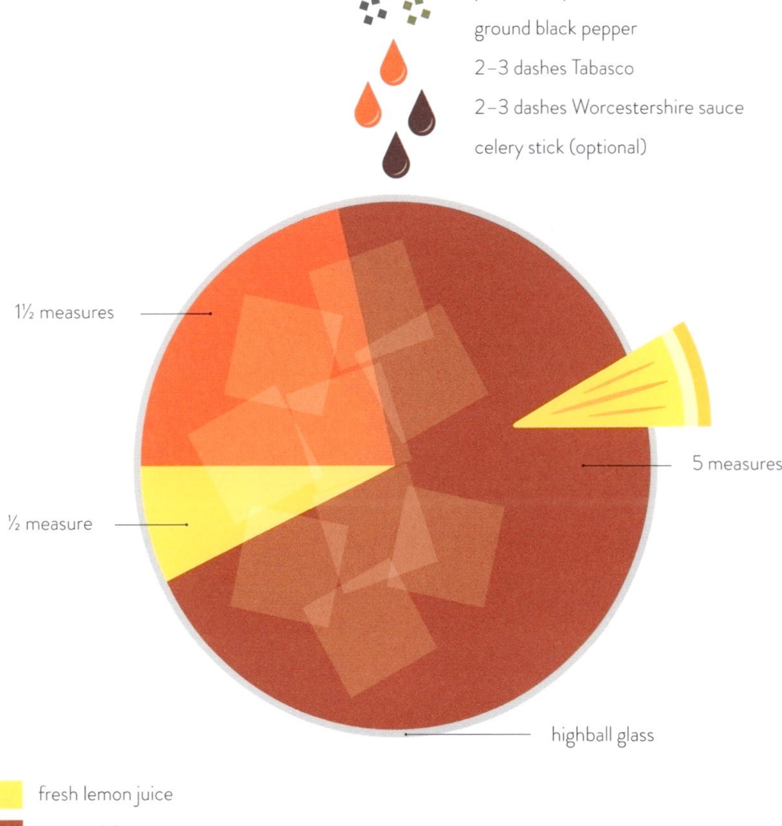

fresh lemon juice

tomato juice

vodka

Instructions

1 Fill a highball with ice, then pour in the tomato and lemon juices. 2 Add the vodka. 3 Add the spices. Stir. 4 Add black pepper. 5 Garnish with a lemon wedge, a stirrer and a celery stick if requested.

BRANDY ALEXANDER

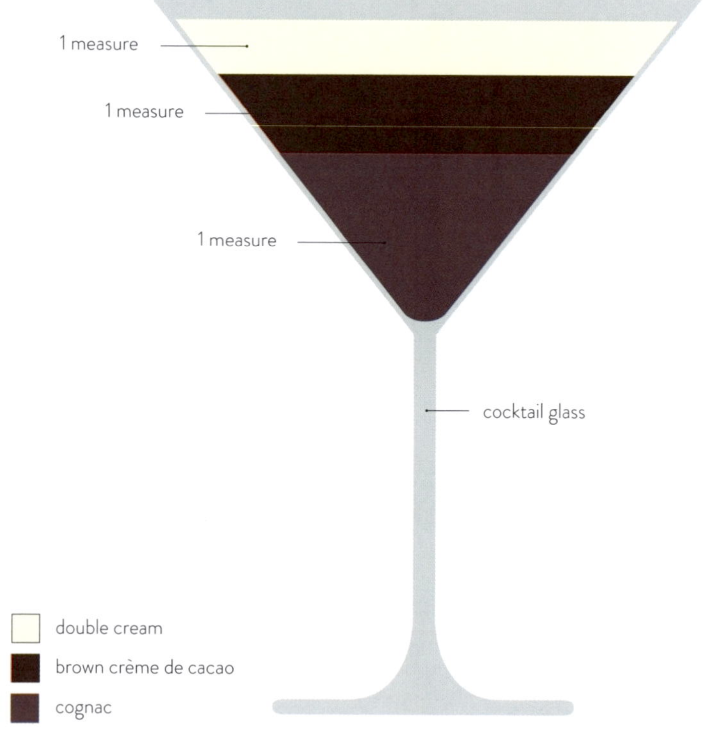

Instructions

1 Mix all the ingredients together in a shaker, then strain into a cocktail glass and serve.

CAIPIRINHA

Instructions

1 Cut the lime into quarters vertically and place them in the base of a chilled Old Fashioned. **2** Add the sugar and crush the lime pieces until the sugar is dissolved. **3** Add the cachaça, then ice cubes, and stir.

COSMOPOLITAN

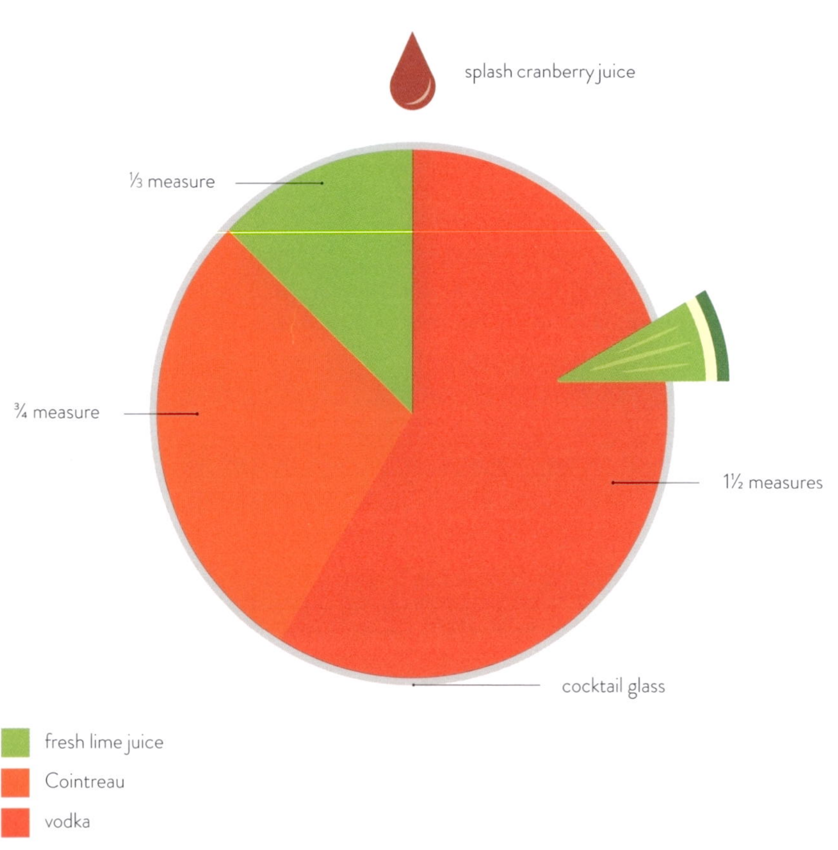

fresh lime juice
Cointreau
vodka

Instructions

1 Shake all ingredients with ice. 2 Strain into a cocktail glass. 3 Garnish with a lime wedge.

DAIQUIRI

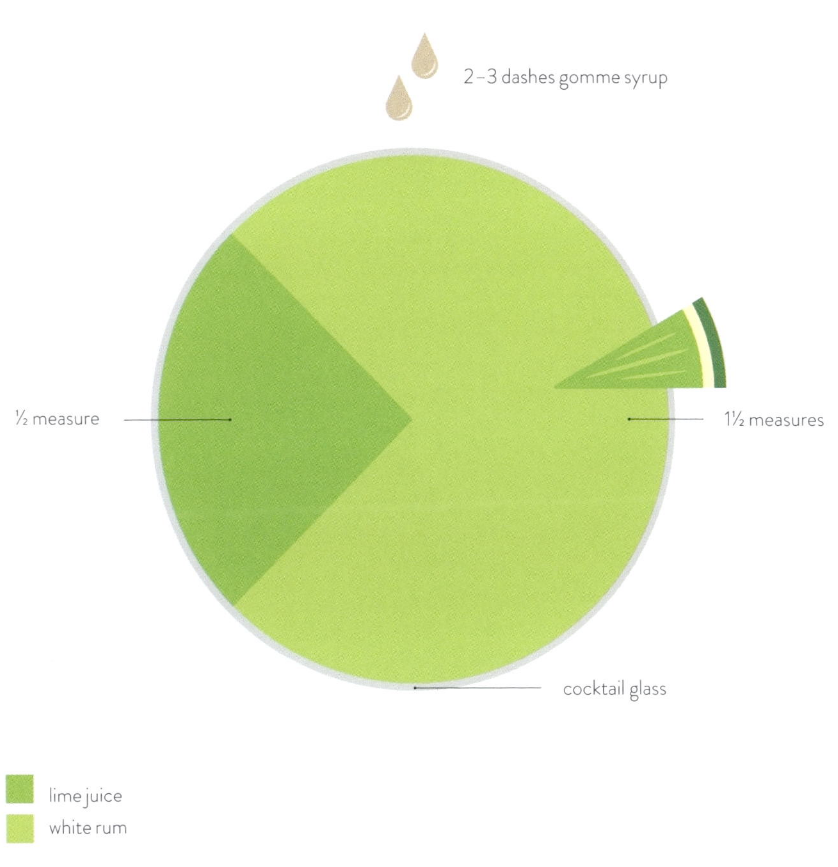

Instructions

1 Pour the ingredients into a shaker with cracked ice. 2 Strain into a chilled cocktail glass and garnish with a lime wedge in the glass.

GIMLET

Instructions

1 Over ice, pour the gin or vodka and lime cordial into a cocktail glass and serve with the lime wedge.

MANHATTAN

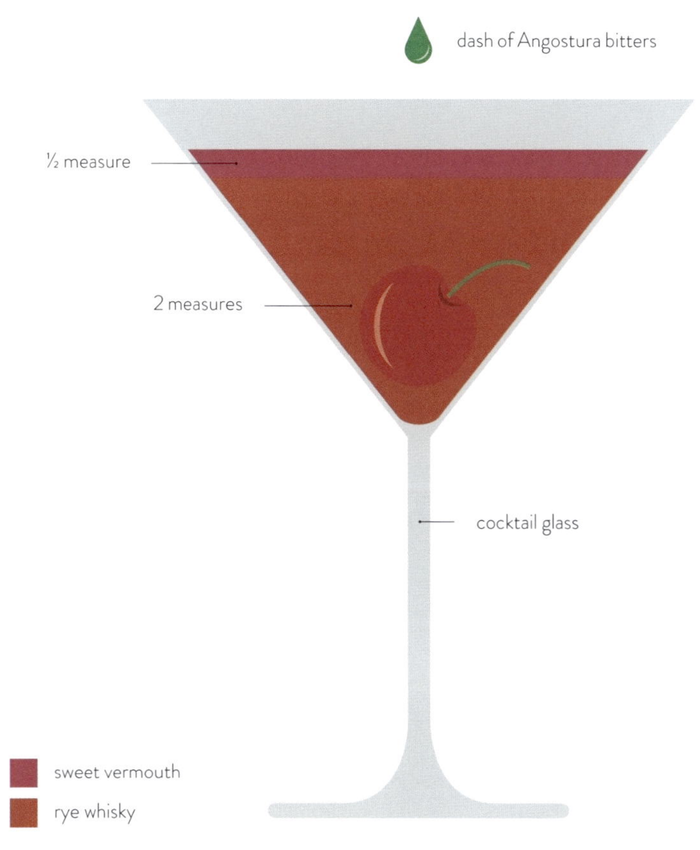

Instructions

1 Pour all the ingredients into a mixing glass and stir. **2** Strain into a cocktail glass. **3** Drop a maraschino cherry in and watch it settle.

LONG ISLAND ICED TEA

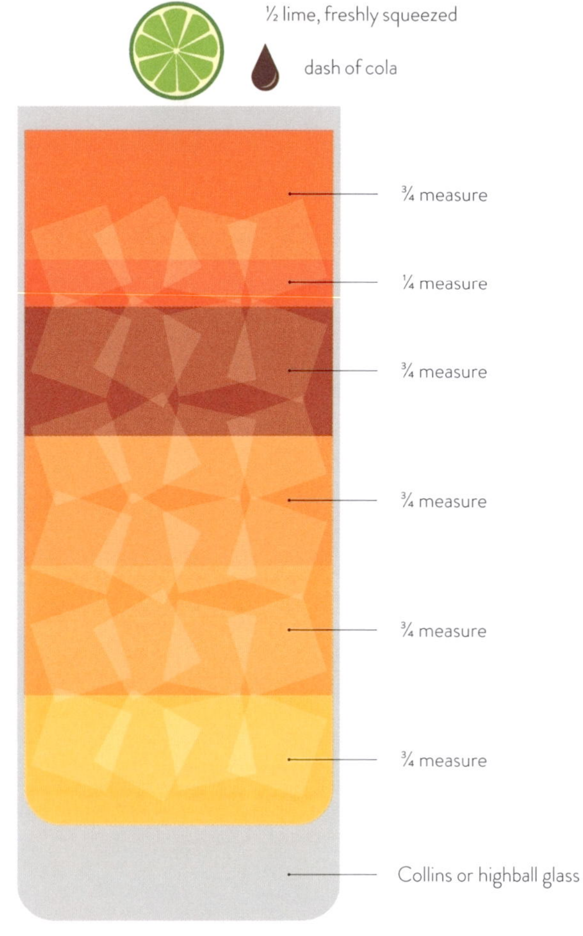

- orange juice
- triple sec
- tequila
- gin
- vodka
- light rum

Instructions

1. Squeeze lime into a Collins or highball glass, add ice cubes, spirits, triple sec and orange juice.
2. Stir and top up with cola.

MAI TAI

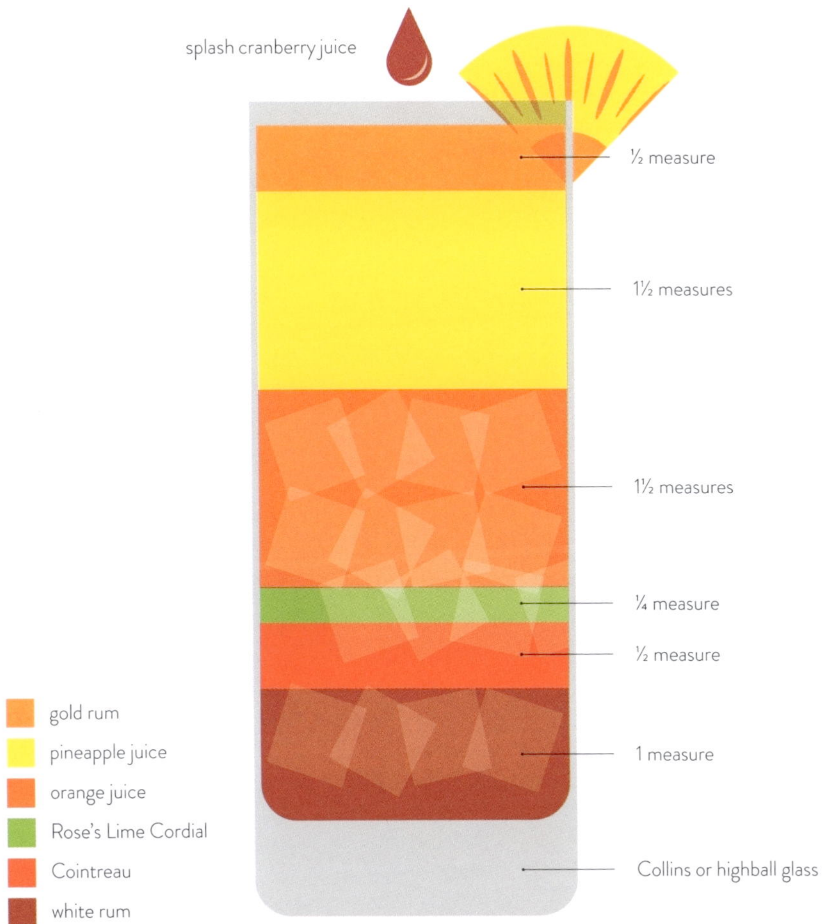

Instructions

1 Shake and strain the white rum, Cointreau, lime cordial and the juices into a Collins or highball glass half-filled with ice. **2** Add the grenadine and gold rum and garnish with a pineapple wedge.

MARGARITA

Instructions

1 Rub a wedge of lime around the rim of a margarita glass and dip the glass into a saucer of salt to create a salt-crusted rim. **2** Pour all the ingredients into a shaker containing cracked ice and shake. **3** Strain into the glass. **4** Garnish with a lime slice.

MARTINI

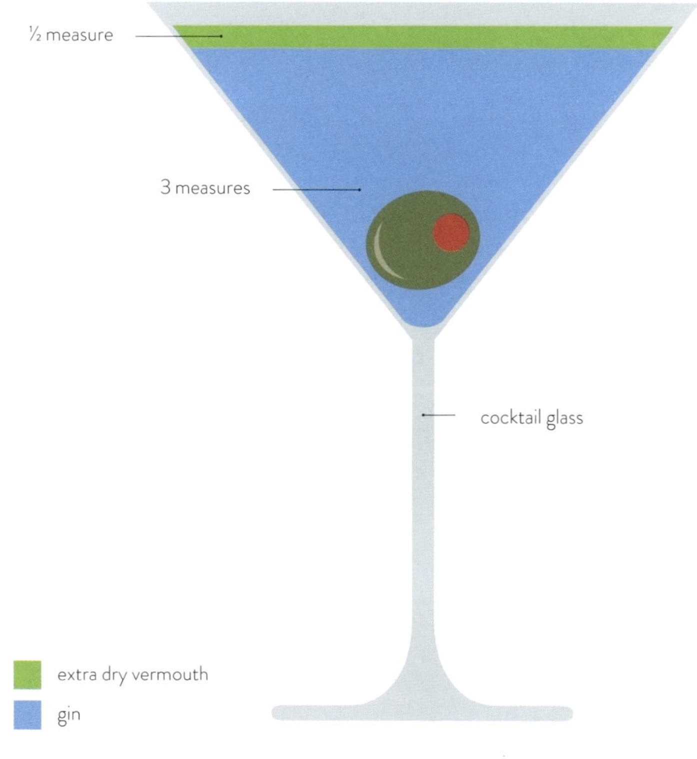

Instructions

1 Pour the vermouth into a mixing glass filled with the coldest ice imaginable. **2** Let it dribble down the ice and then strain it from the mixing glass. **3** Add the chilled gin and stir quickly with a barspoon. **4** Strain onto a chilled cocktail glass. **5** Add a thin twist of lemon or an olive before serving.

MINT JULEP

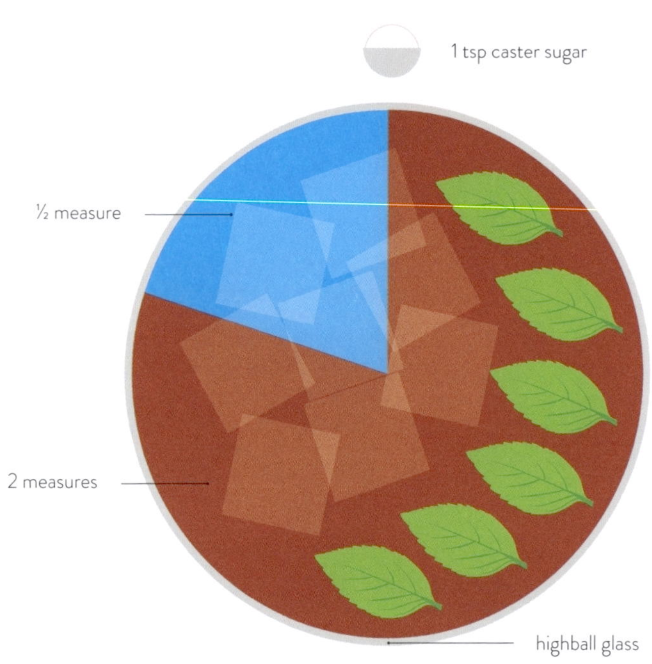

Instructions

1 Place the mint in a highball glass then add the sugar and water. 2 Muddle the mint for about a minute. 3 Add the bourbon. 4 Fill the glass with crushed ice. Stir. 5 Add a sprig of mint as a garnish. 6 Serve with a straw and a stirrer.

NEGRONI

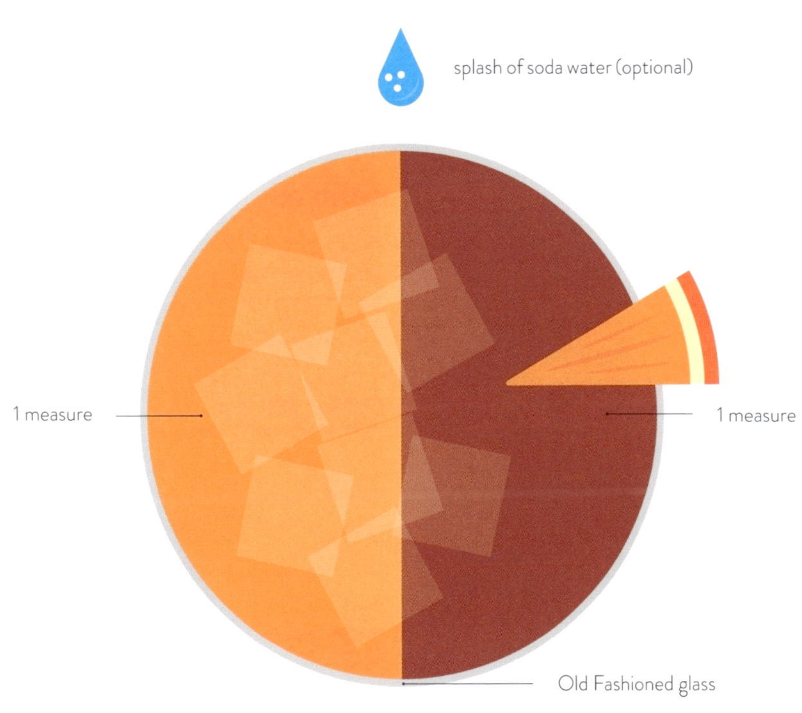

sweet vermouth

Campari

Instructions

1 Pour the Campari and sweet vermouth into an ice-filled Old Fashioned glass and stir. **2** Add the soda, if using, then garnish with the orange slice and serve.

OLD FASHIONED

Instructions

1 Put the bitters, sugar cube, and a dash of the bourbon into an Old Fashioned glass and muddle together. **2** Add 2 ice cubes and 1 measure of the bourbon and stir. **3** Squeeze some of the juice from the orange slice into the glass, then add 2 more ice cubes and 1 measure of bourbon and stir again. **4** Finally add 2 more ice cubes, the remaining bourbon, the orange slice and cherry, then serve.

PISCO SOUR

Instructions

1 Pour all ingredients into a shaker with ice. Shake. **2** Strain into a white wine glass or a champagne saucer.

SIDECAR

Instructions

1 Pour the ingredients into a shaker with cracked ice. 2 Shake and strain into an ice-cold cocktail glass. 3 Garnish with a discreet lemon wedge.

SINGAPORE SLING

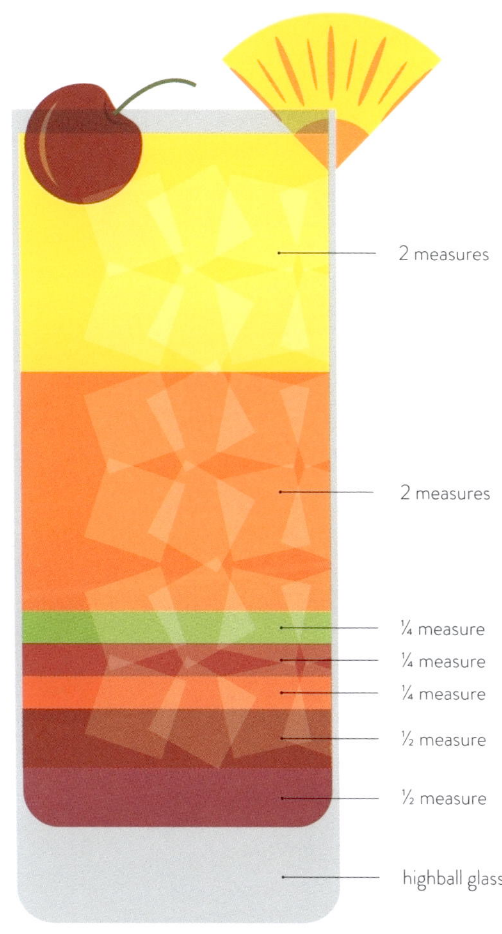

- pineapple juice
- orange juice
- lime juice
- Benedictine
- Cointreau
- cherry brandy
- gin

Instructions

1 Pour the ingredients into a shaker with ice. **2** Shake and strain into a highball with ice. **3** Garnish with a pineapple slice and a maraschino cherry and serve with a straw and a stirrer.

TOM COLLINS

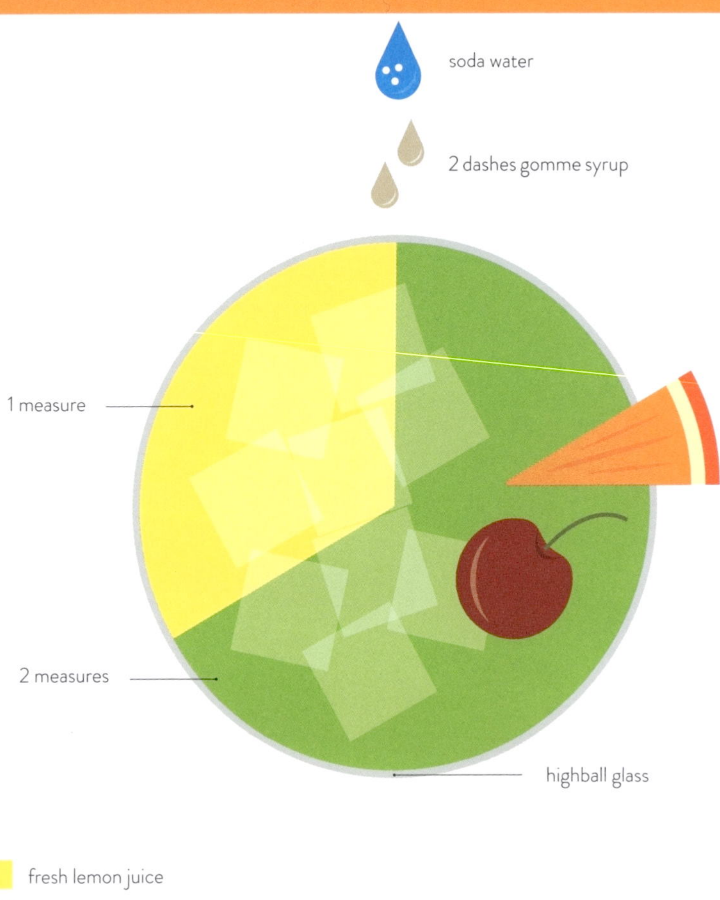

Instructions

1 Add the gin, lemon juice and syrup to a Collins or highball glass filled with lots of ice. 2 Top up with soda. 3 Add a slice of orange and a maraschino cherry, or a cherry and a slice of lime. Serve with a stirrer.

WHISKY SOUR

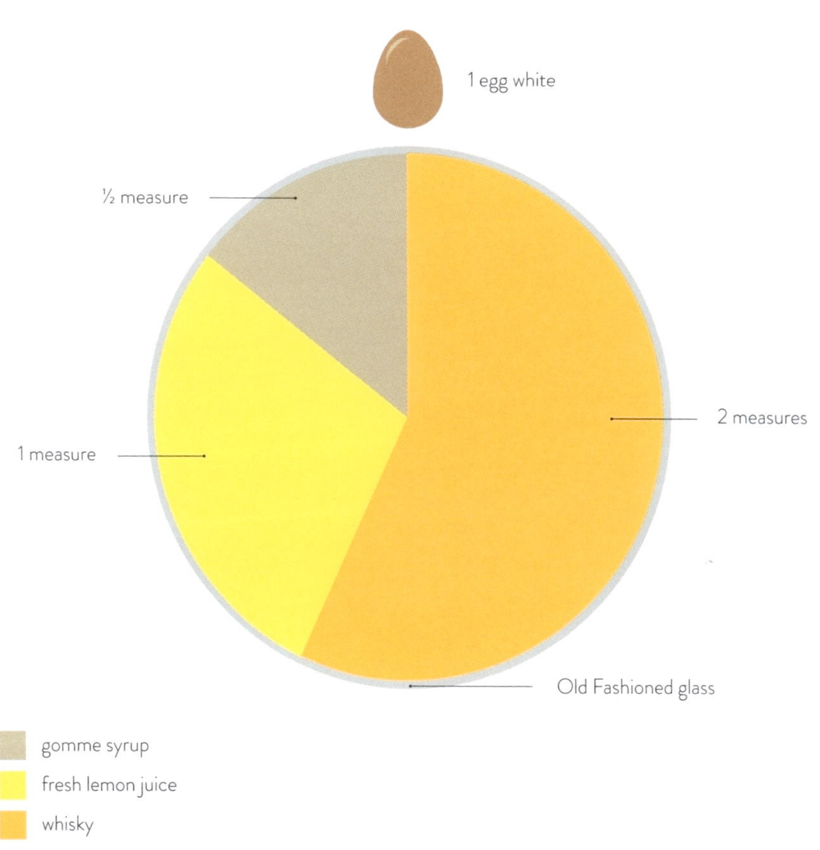

Instructions

1 Mix the whisky, lemon juice, and gomme in a shaker, then pour into an Old Fashioned glass and serve.

VODKA

AVIATION 2

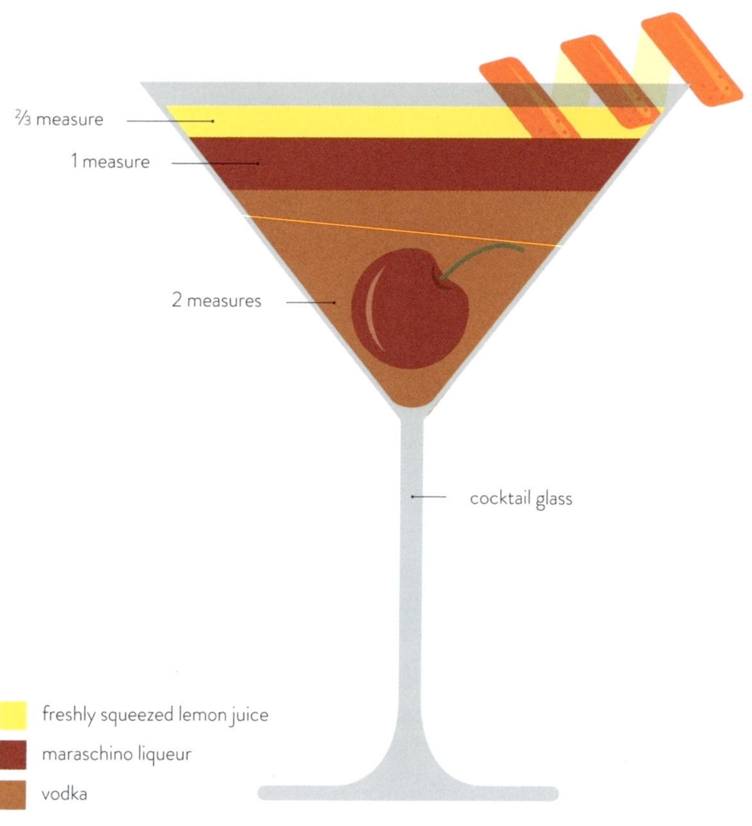

Instructions

1 Shake all the ingredients. Strain into a cocktail glass. **2** Drop a maraschino cherry in the drink and a twist of lemon.

BIKINI

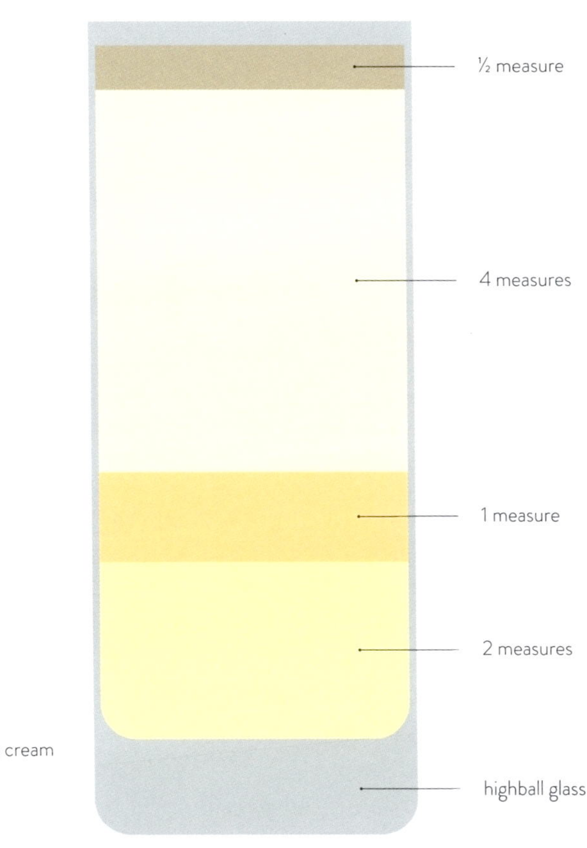

Instructions

1 Shake the ingredients together, then strain into a highball glass and serve.

BLACK MAGIC

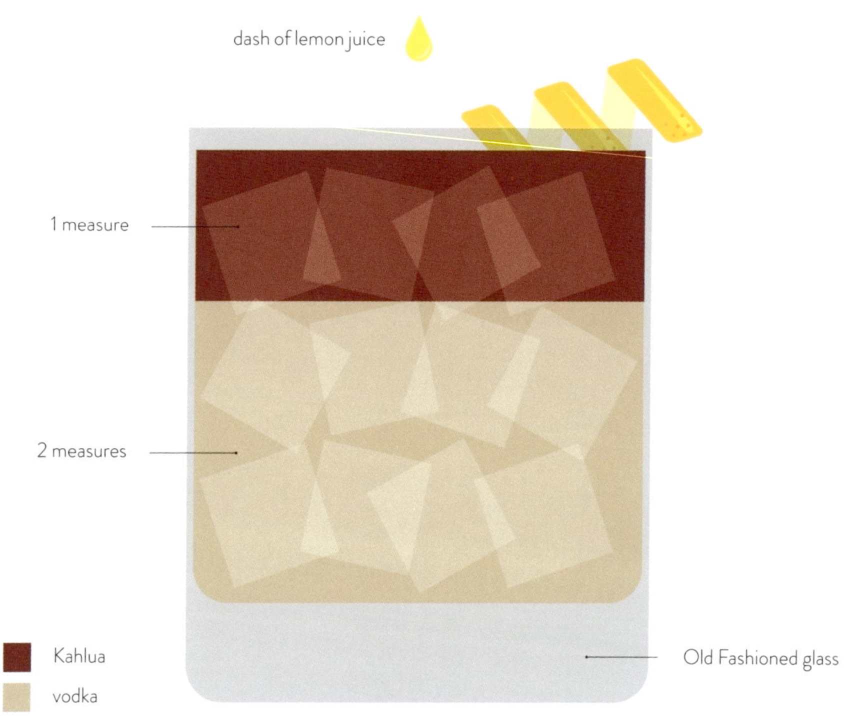

Instructions

1 Stir all the ingredients together, then pour into an ice-filled Old Fashioned glass. **2** Serve with the lemon twist.

BLACK RUSSIAN

Instructions

1 Pour the vodka, then the Kahlua into an Old Fashioned glass straight up or over crushed ice, then serve.

BULLSHOT

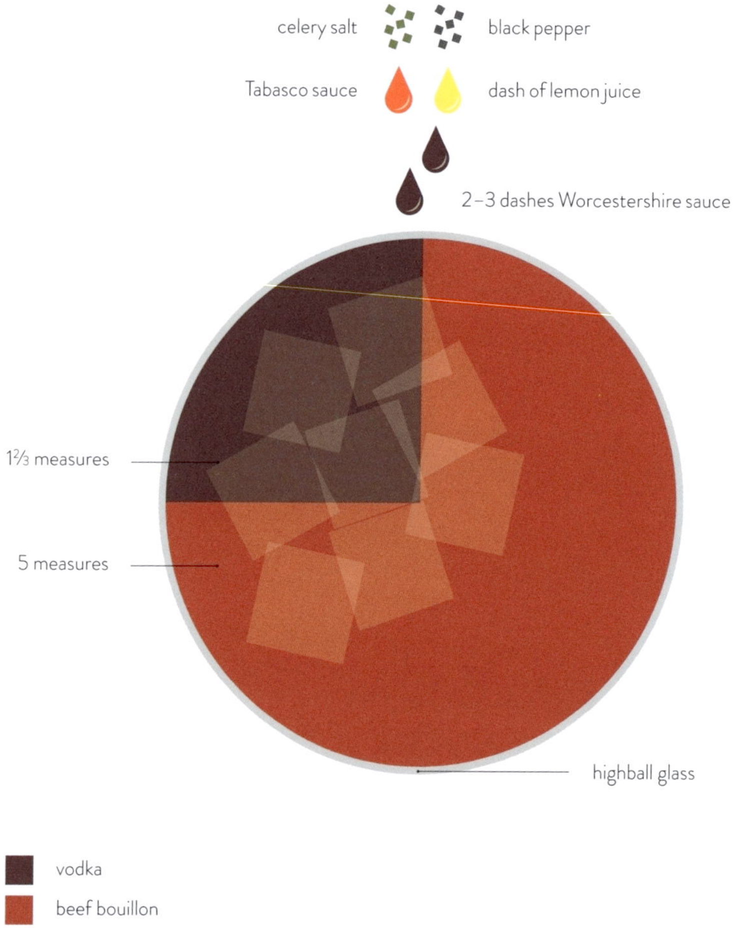

celery salt

black pepper

Tabasco sauce

dash of lemon juice

2–3 dashes Worcestershire sauce

$1\frac{2}{3}$ measures

5 measures

highball glass

vodka

beef bouillon

Instructions

1 Shake bouillon, lemon juice, Tabasco and Worcestershire sauces with vodka. **2** Strain into a highball glass full of ice cubes. **3** Add black pepper. **4** Serve with a stirrer.

CAPE CODDER

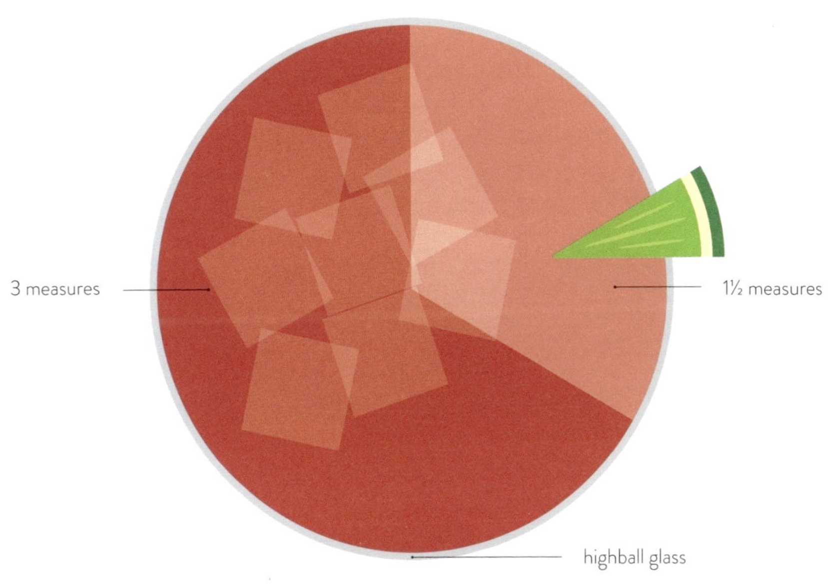

cranberry juice

vodka

Instructions

1 Pour vodka and cranberry juice into a highball glass over ice. **2** Stir well, add the lime and serve.

FRENCH KISS

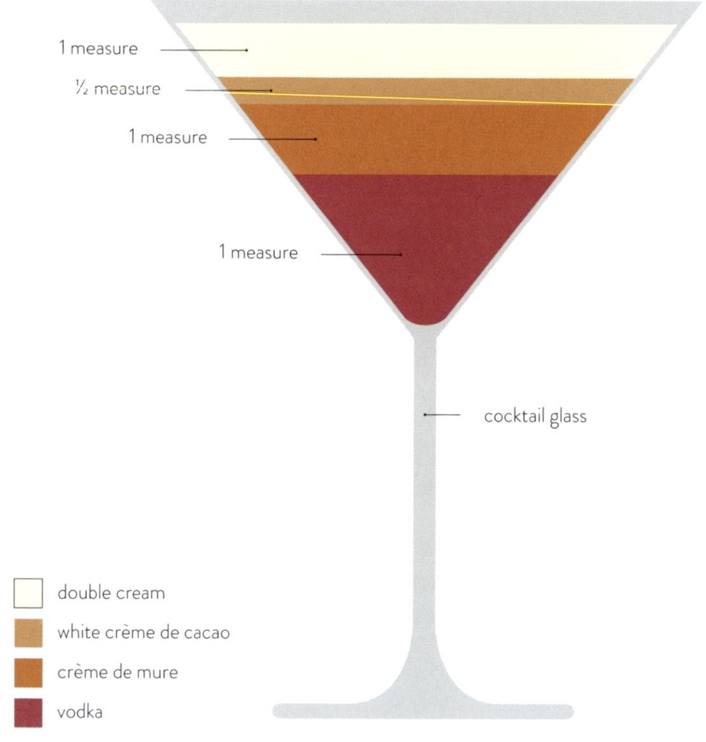

Instructions

1 Mix the ingredients together in a shaker, then strain into a cocktail glass.

FRENCH MARTINI

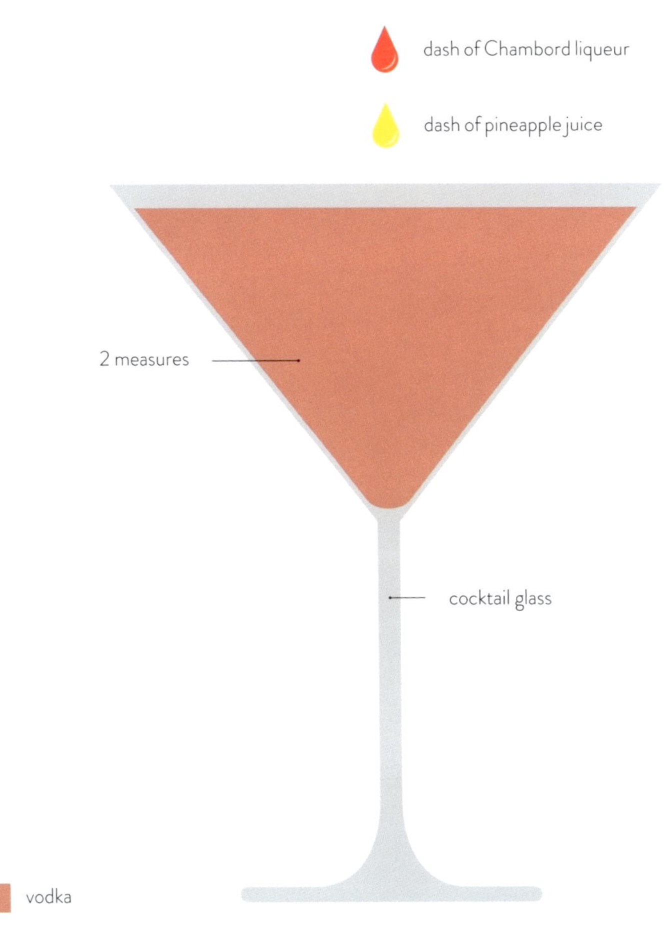

Instructions

1 Shake all the ingredients together and strain into a cocktail glass.

HARVEY WALLBANGER

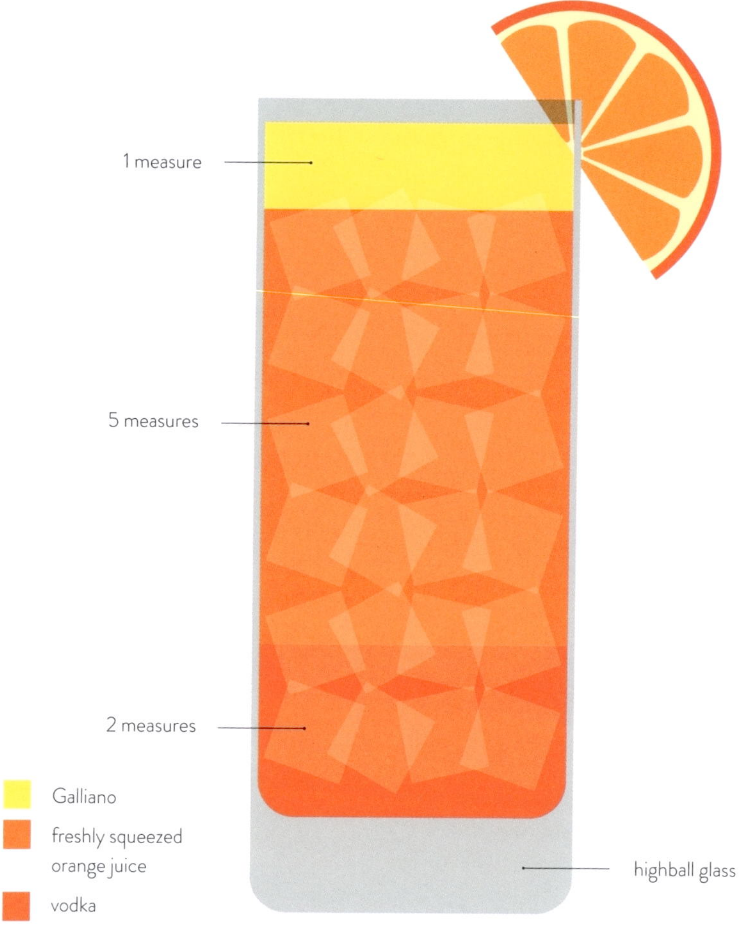

Instructions

1 Pour vodka and orange juice into a highball glass full of ice and stir. **2** Float Galliano on top. **3** Garnish with a slice of orange and serve with a stirrer.

JOE COLLINS

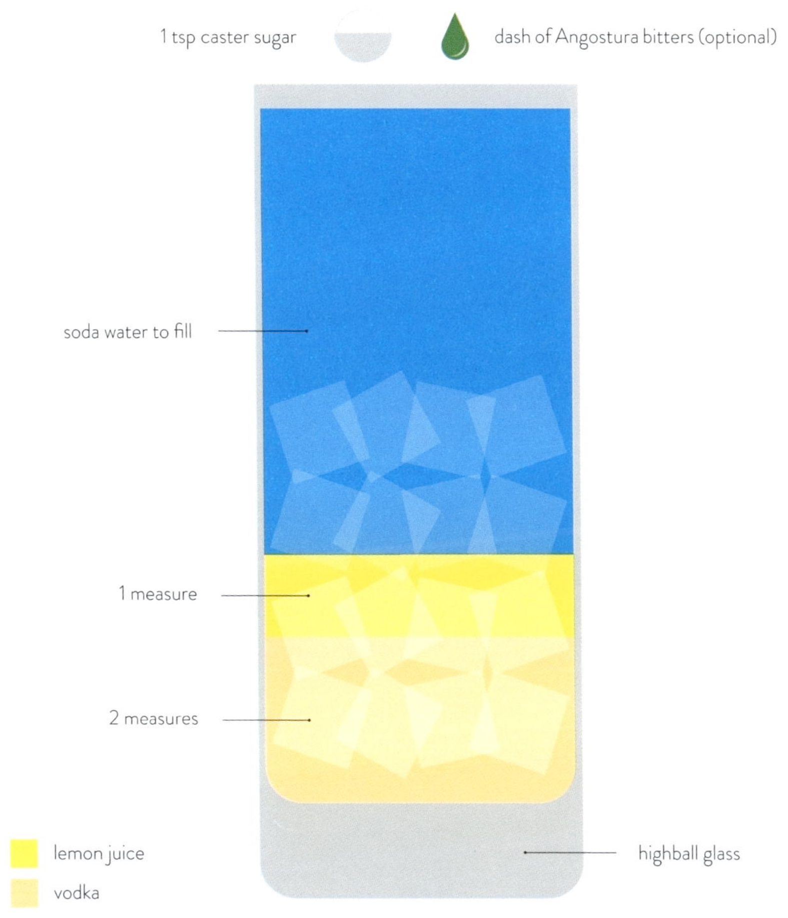

Instructions

1 Place the vodka, juice, sugar and bitters in a tall glass half-filled with ice, and stir to mix. **2** Top up with soda. **3** Stir gently.

LOVE FOR SALE

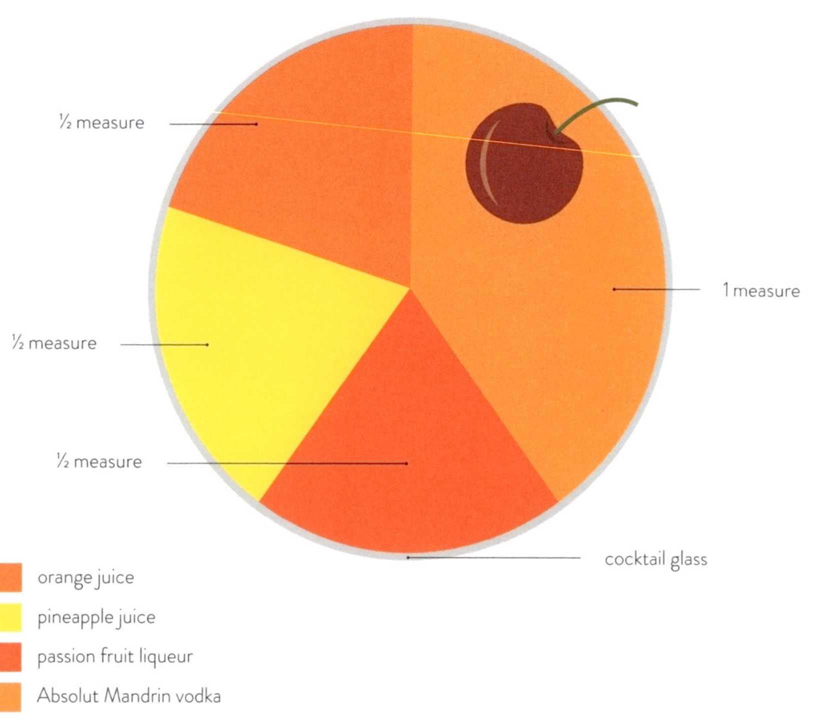

Instructions

1 Shake all the ingredients with ice and strain into a chilled cocktail glass. **2** Garnish with a maraschino cherry.

LYCHEE MARTINI

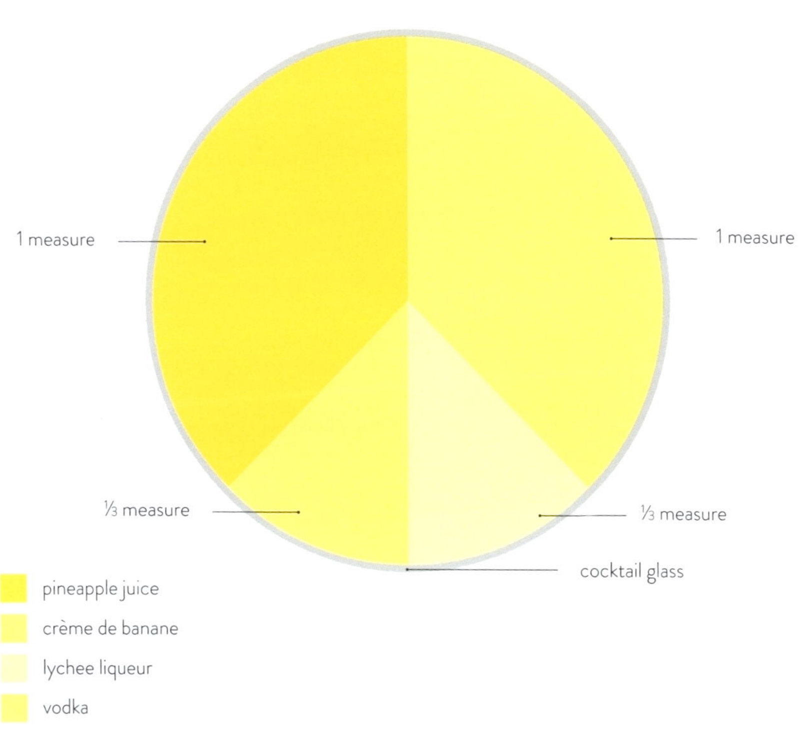

Instructions

1 Shake all the ingredients. **2** Strain into a cocktail glass.

METROPOLIS

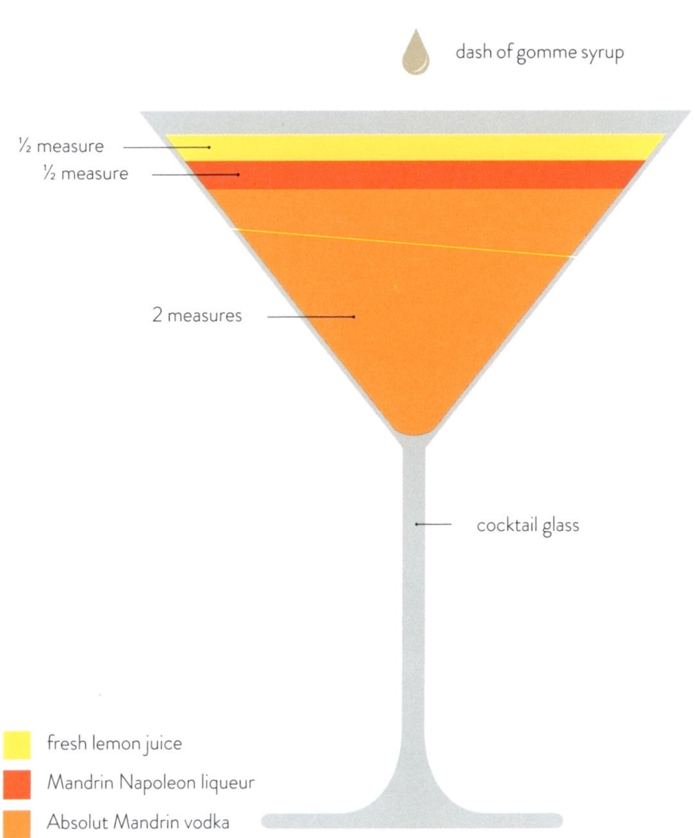

Instructions

1 Shake all ingredients with ice and strain into a cocktail glass.

MUDSLIDE

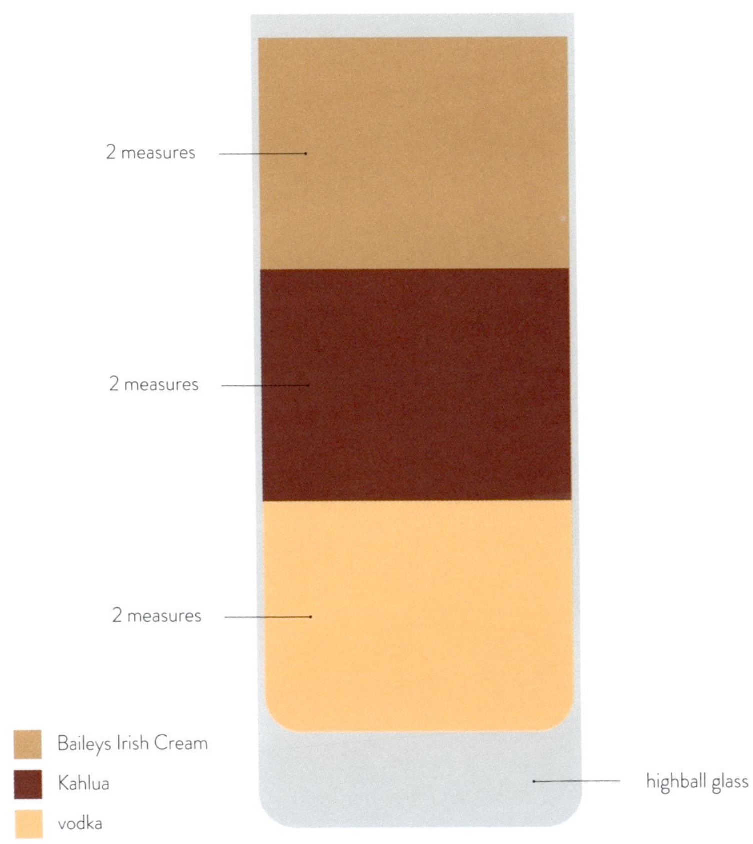

Instructions

1 Mix with cracked ice in a shaker. **2** Strain and serve in a chilled highball glass.

POISON ARROW

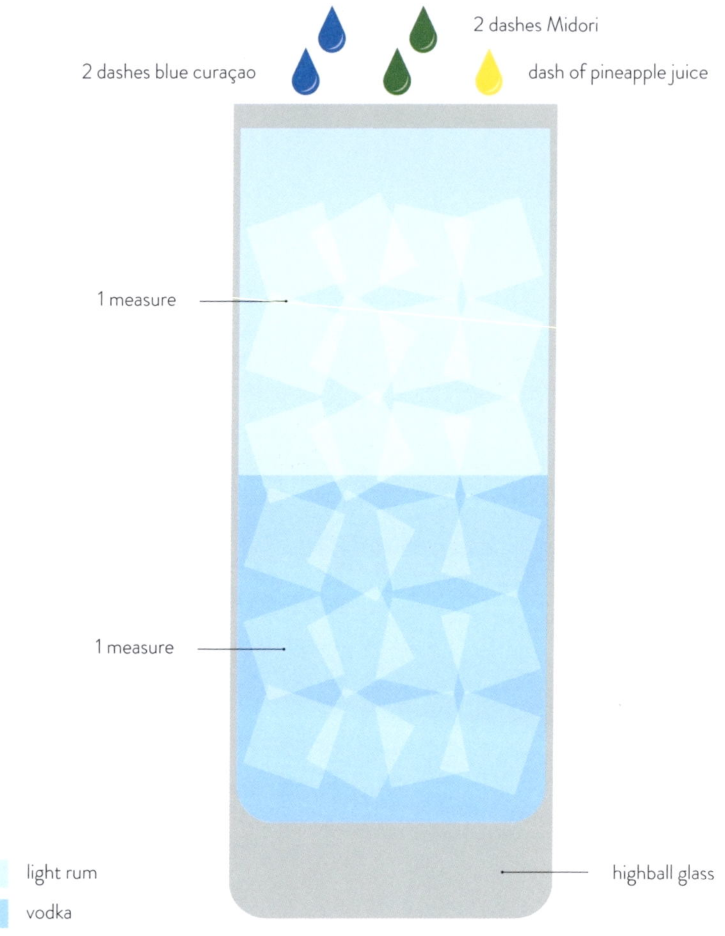

Instructions

1 Shake all the ingredients with ice. **2** Strain into a chilled highball glass filled with crushed ice.

SALTY DOG

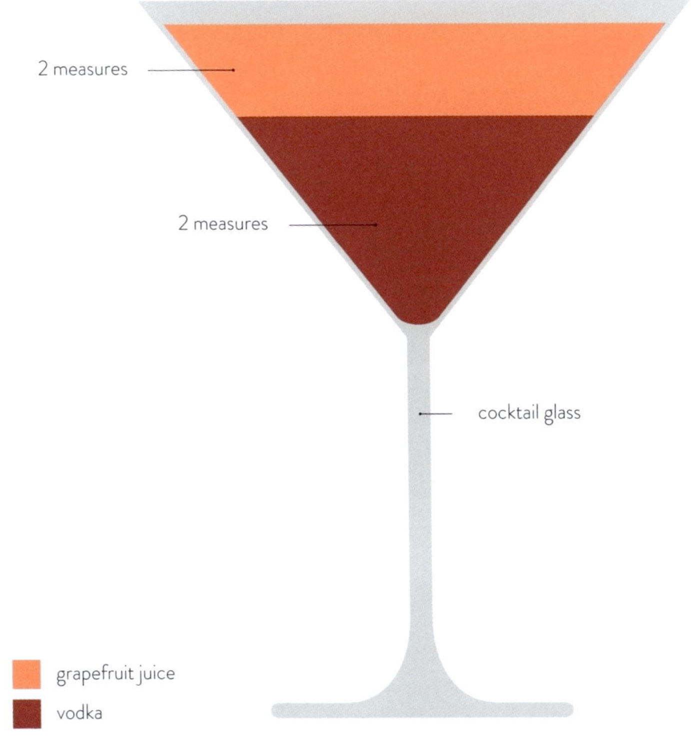

Instructions

1 Mix the vodka with the grapefruit juice in a shaker, then strain into a cocktail glass and serve.

SCREWDRIVER

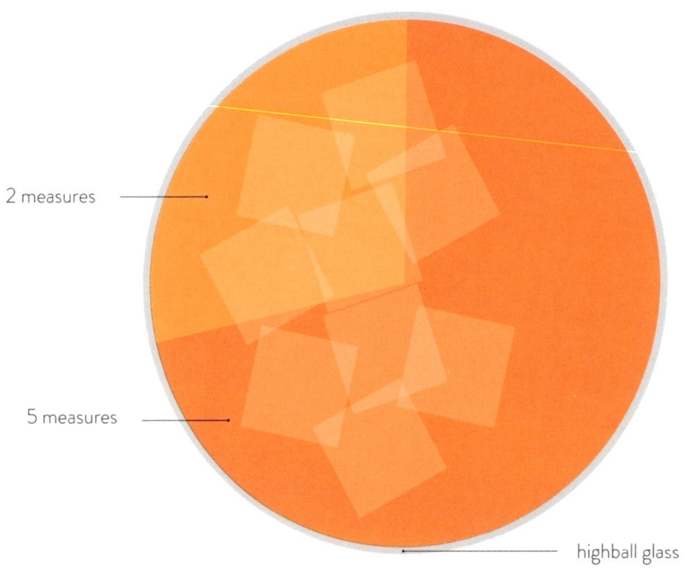

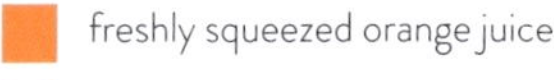

Instructions

1 Pour the vodka into a highball glass with ice. **2** Add orange juice, stir, and serve with a stirrer.

SEA BREEZE

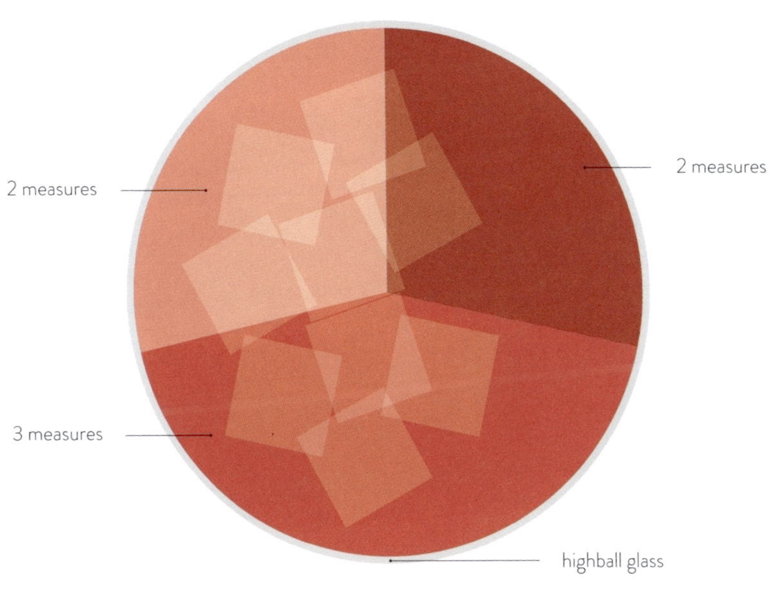

Instructions

1 Pour ingredients over ice into a highball glass. **2** Stir and serve with a stirrer.

SEA HORSE

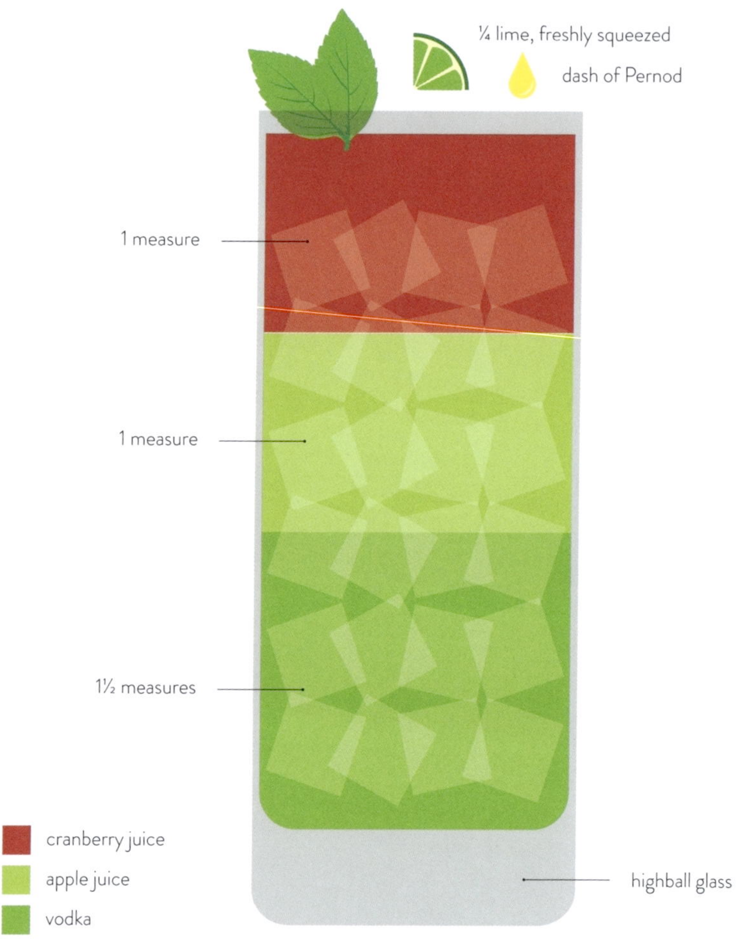

Instructions

1 Pour ingredients into a highball glass filled with ice. **2** Garnish with a sprig of mint.

VESPER

Instructions

1 Vigorously shake ingredients with ice and strain into a chilled cocktail glass. 2 Garnish with a lemon twist.

WHITE RUSSIAN

Instructions

1 Mix the ingredients together in a shaker, then strain into a cocktail glass and serve. **2** Alternatively, layer the ingredients in an ice-filled Old Fashioned glass.

WOO WOO

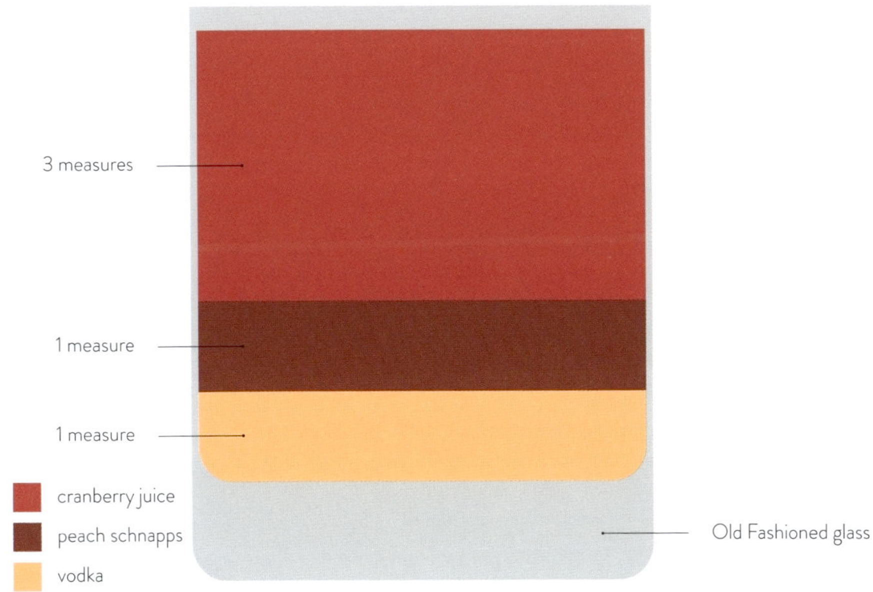

Instructions

1 Shake all the ingredients together, then strain into an Old Fashioned glass and serve.

GIN

ALASKA

gin

Instructions

1 Shake and strain into a cocktail glass. 2 Garnish with a lemon twist.

ASTORIA

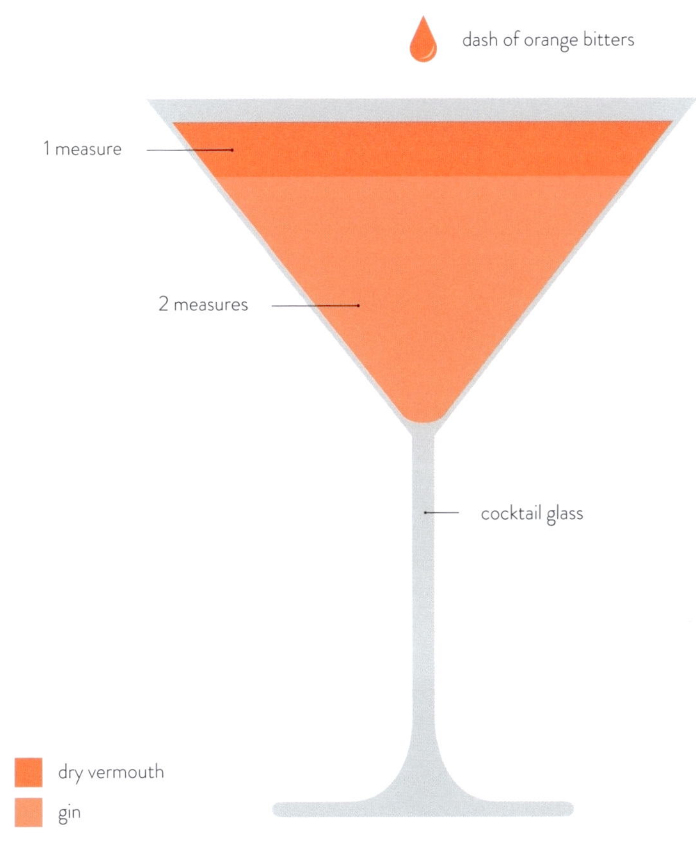

Instructions

1 Shake all the ingredients together and strain into a cocktail glass.

BLUE MONDAY

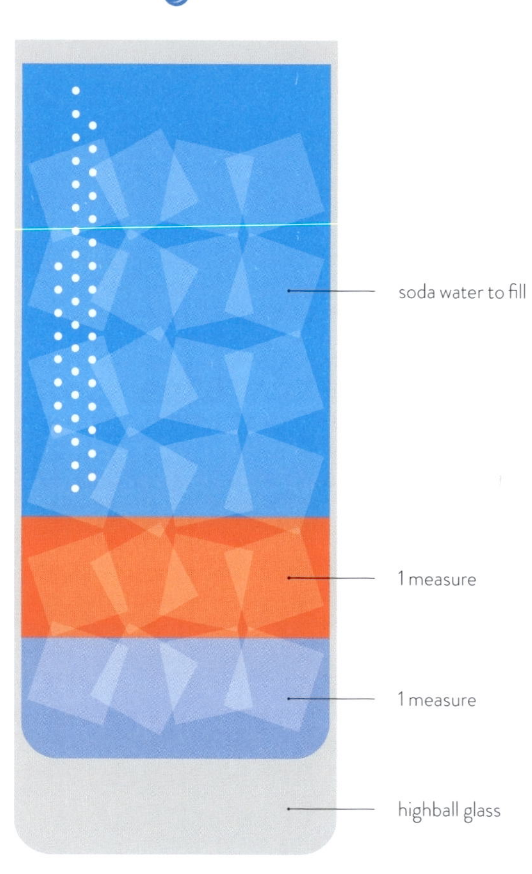

soda water to fill
Cointreau
gin

Instructions

1 Pour the gin and Cointreau into a highball glass filled with ice, then fill with soda water, and stir. 2 Add a few drops of blue curaçao. 3 Stir again and serve with a stirrer in the glass.

BOMBARDIER

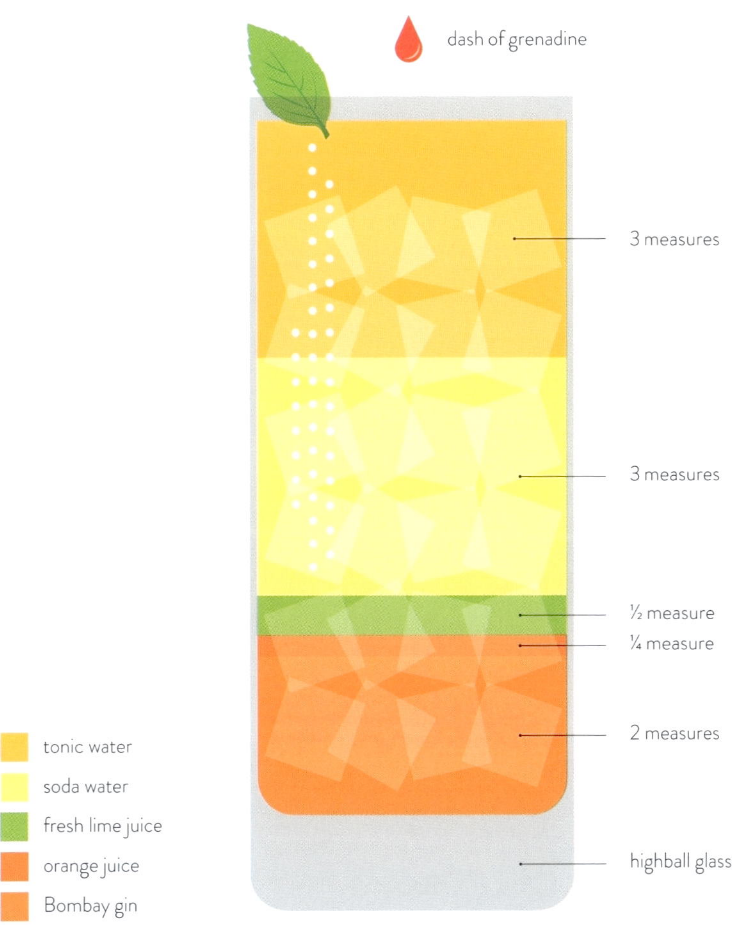

Instructions

1 Shake all the liquid ingredients, except the tonic and soda, with ice and strain into an ice-filled highball glass. **2** Fill up with the tonic and soda waters. **3** Stir, then garnish with a mint leaf.

BROADWAY

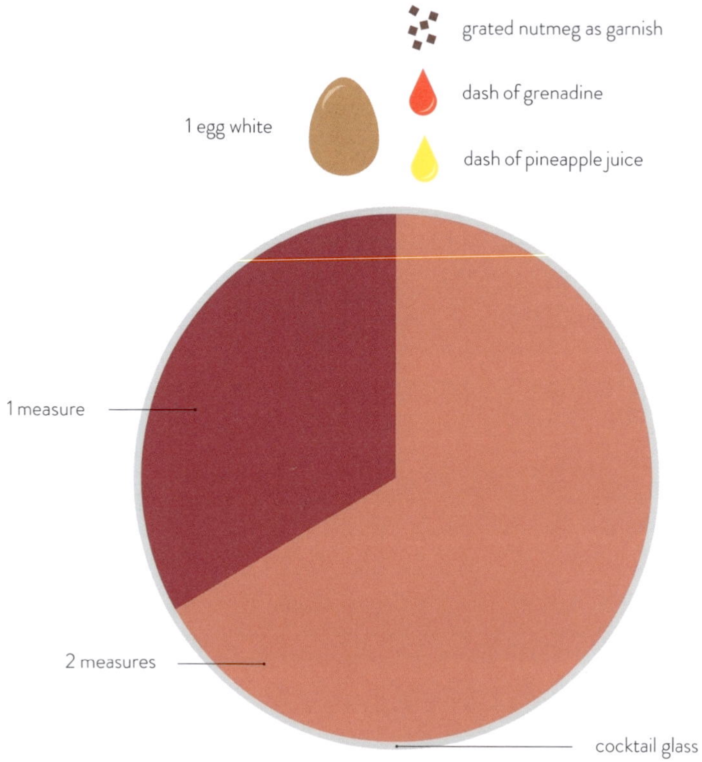

grated nutmeg as garnish
dash of grenadine
1 egg white
dash of pineapple juice
1 measure
2 measures
cocktail glass

sweet vermouth

gin

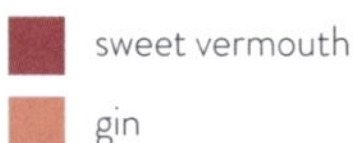

Instructions

1 Shake all the liquid ingredients together, then strain into a cocktail glass. **2** Sprinkle with the nutmeg and serve.

CADILLAC LADY

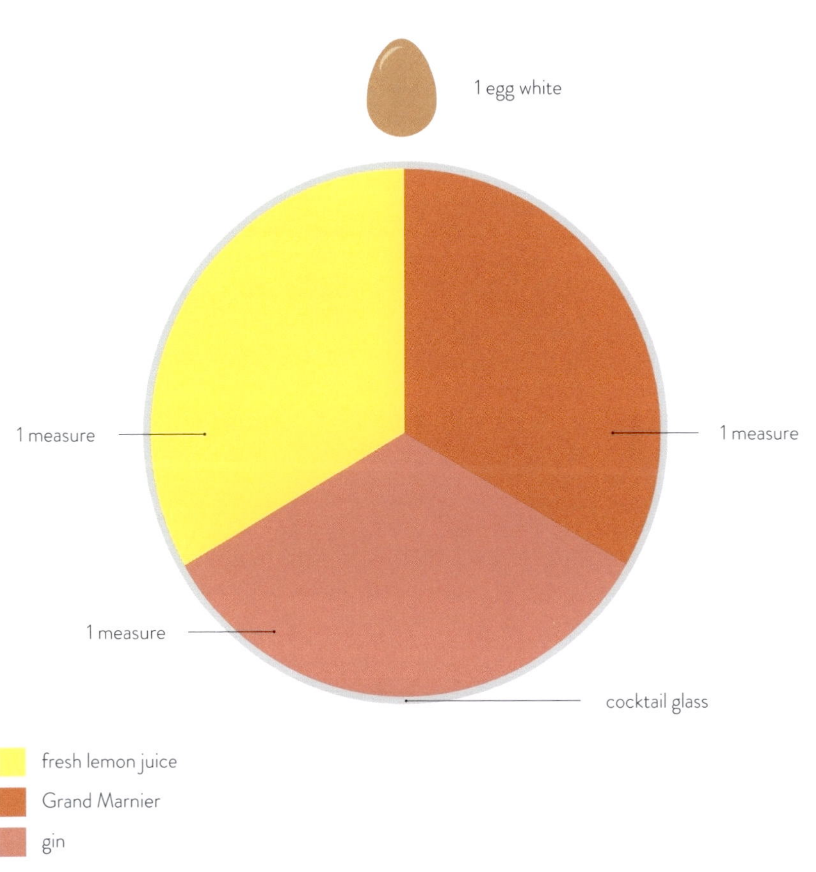

fresh lemon juice
Grand Marnier
gin

Instructions

1 Shake all the ingredients together, then strain into a cocktail glass and serve.

DIRTY MARTINI

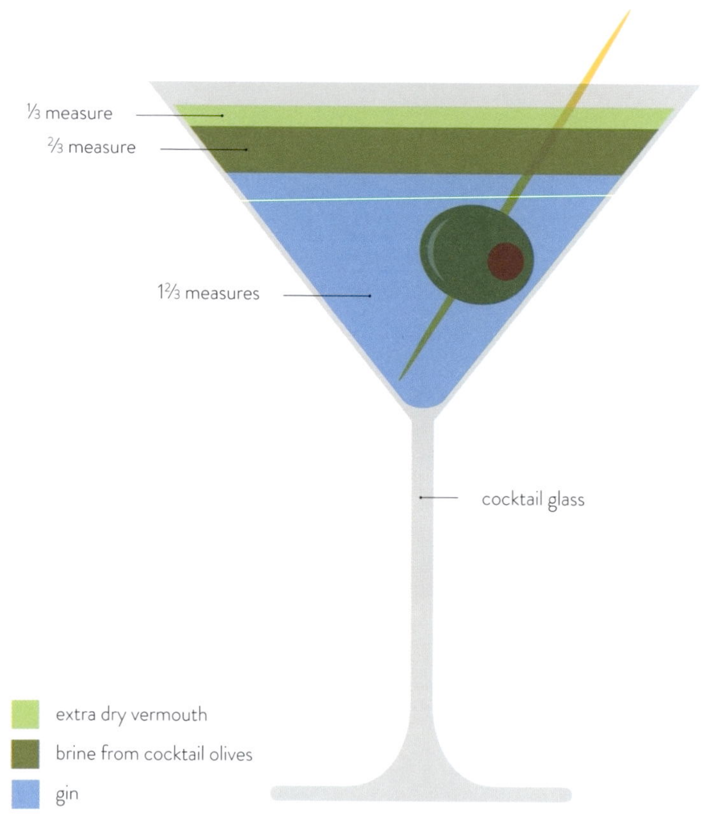

Instructions

1 Pour ingredients into a mixing glass with ice and stir. **2** Strain into a cocktail glass. **3** Add an olive on a cocktail stick.

FLUFFY DUCK

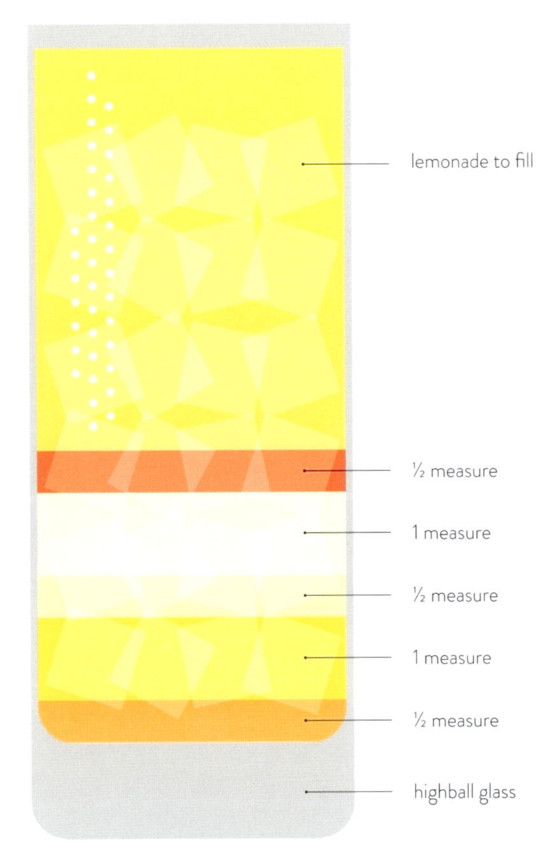

lemonade
Cointreau
cream
vodka
advocaat
gin

Instructions

1 Pour all ingredients, except the lemonde, into a highball glass over ice. **2** Stir, then top up with lemonade.

FRENCH 75

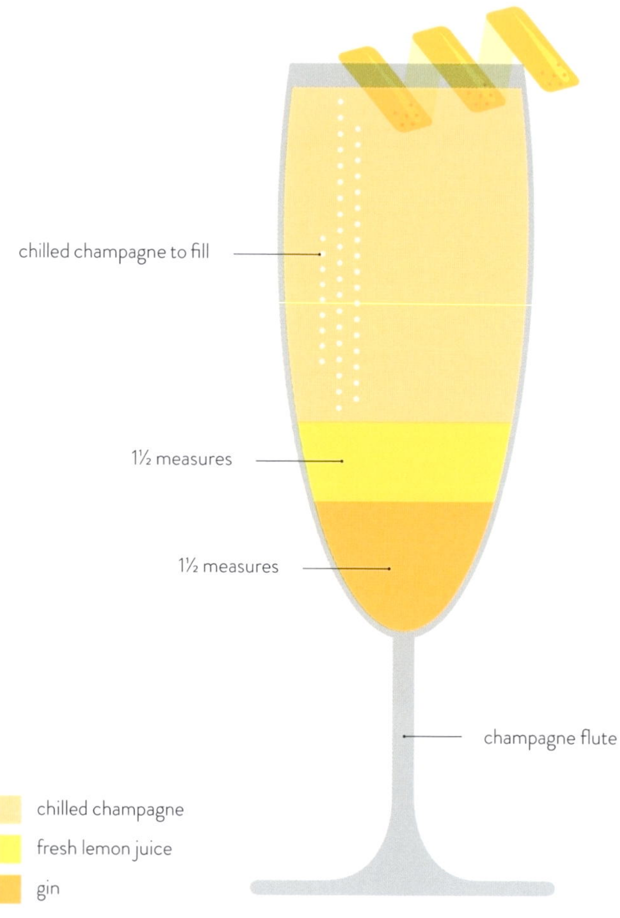

Instructions

1 Mix the gin and lemon juice together in a champagne flute. **2** Top up with champagne, garnish with a lemon twist and serve.

HARRY'S COCKTAIL

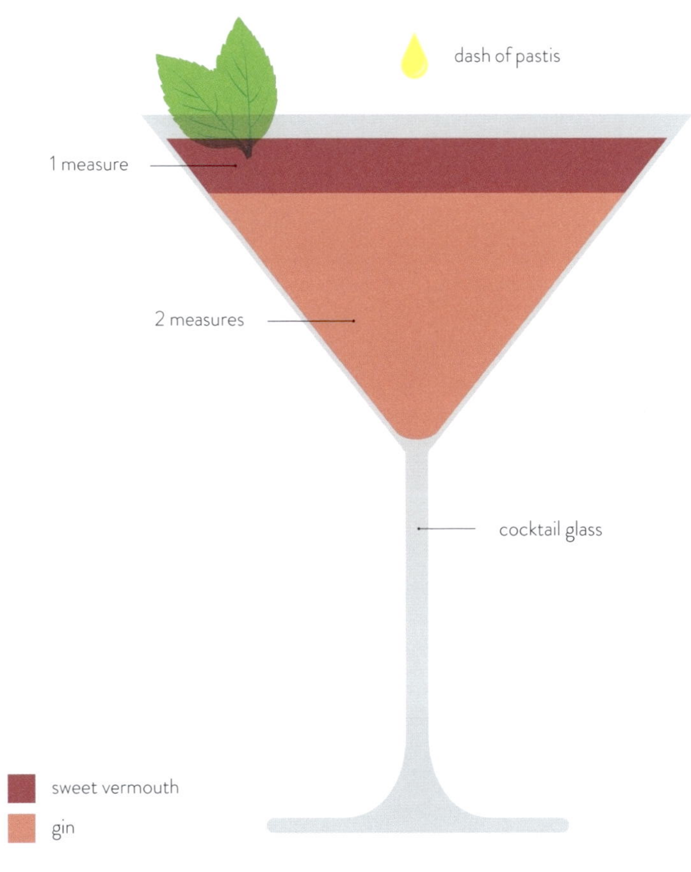

Instructions

1 Shake all the liquids together, then strain into a cocktail glass and serve. **2** Garnish with a sprig of mint.

IMPERIAL

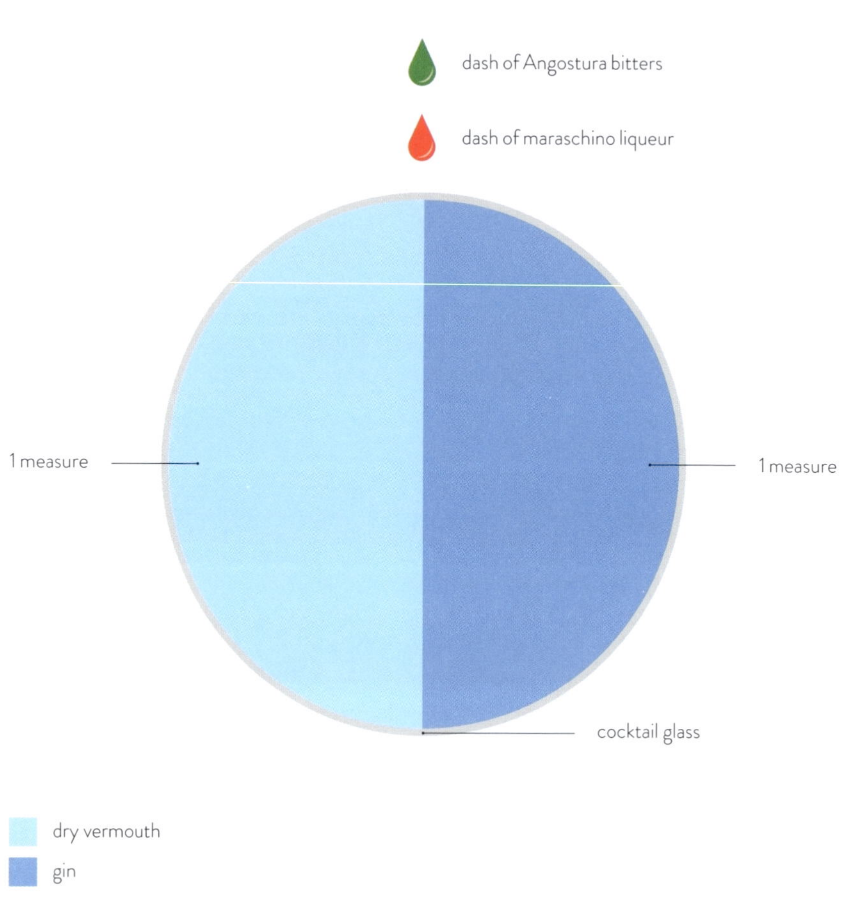

Instructions

1 Shake all the ingredients together, then strain into a cocktail glass and serve.

JACUZZI

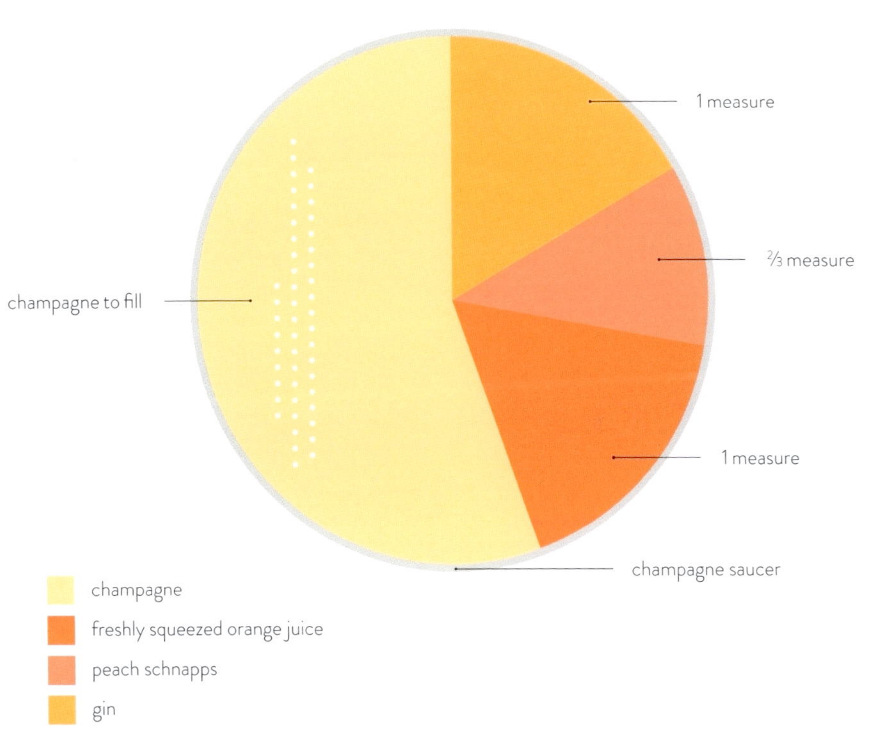

Instructions

1 Pour the gin, schnapps and juice into a shaker with ice. **2** Shake, then strain into a champagne saucer. **3** Stir gently and fill with champagne. Stir again.

JASMINE

Instructions

1 Shake with all the ingredients together with ice and strain into a cocktail glass. **2** Add a lemon twist.

JUNIPER ROYALE

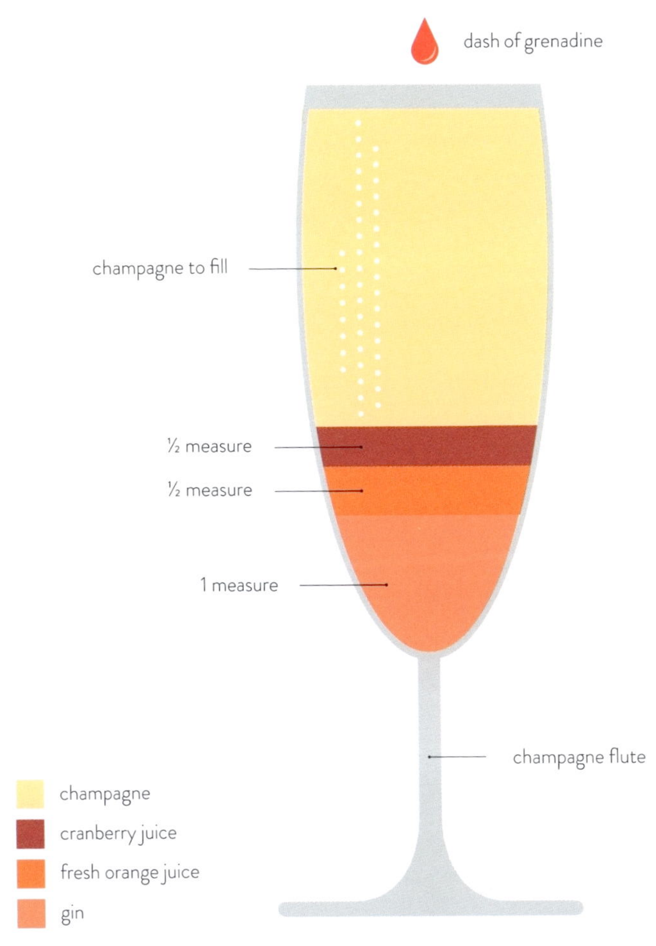

Instructions

1 Pour the gin, juices, and grenadine into a shaker with ice and shake. **2** Strain into a champagne flute and stir gently. **3** Top up with champagne and stir again.

KAISER

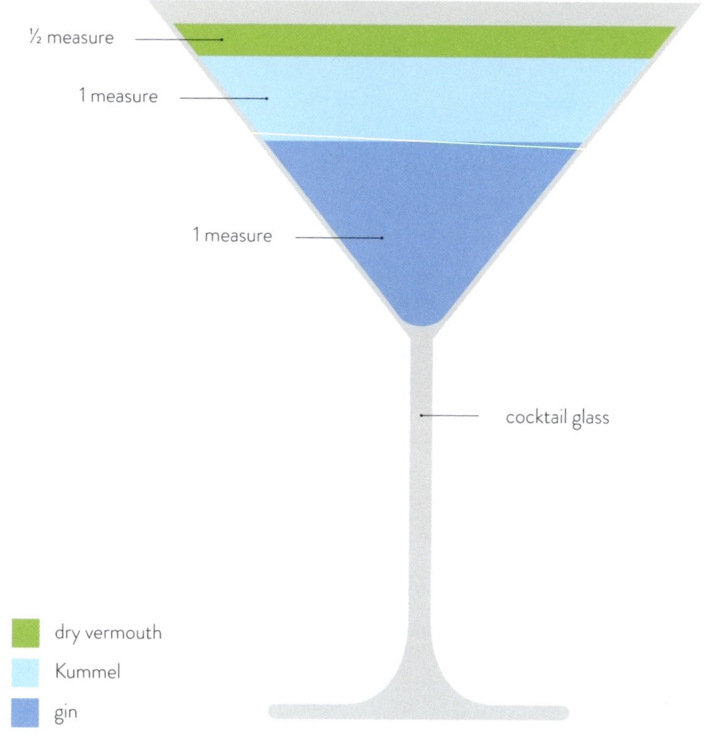

Instructions

1 Stir all the ingredients together, then strain into a cocktail glass and serve.

LEAP YEAR

Instructions

1 Shake all ingredients with ice and strain into a chilled cocktail glass. **2** Garnish with a twist of lemon or orange.

MOULIN ROUGE

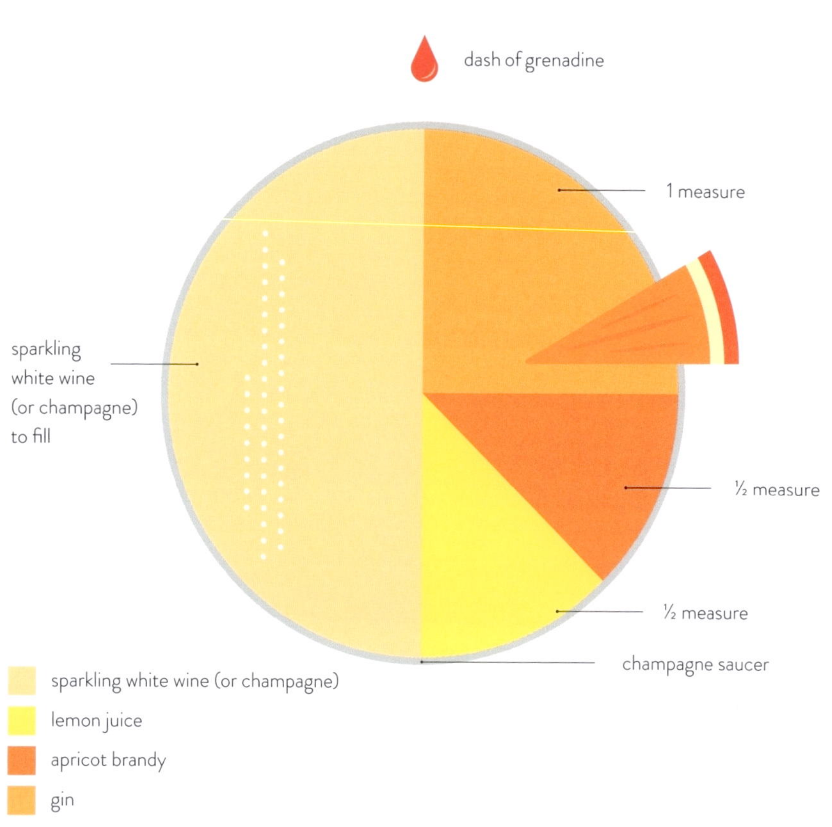

Instructions

1 Shake all the ingredients, except the sparkling wine (or champagne), together, and strain into a champagne saucer. **2** Top with sparkling wine. **3** Garnish with an orange slice.

OLD VERMOUTH

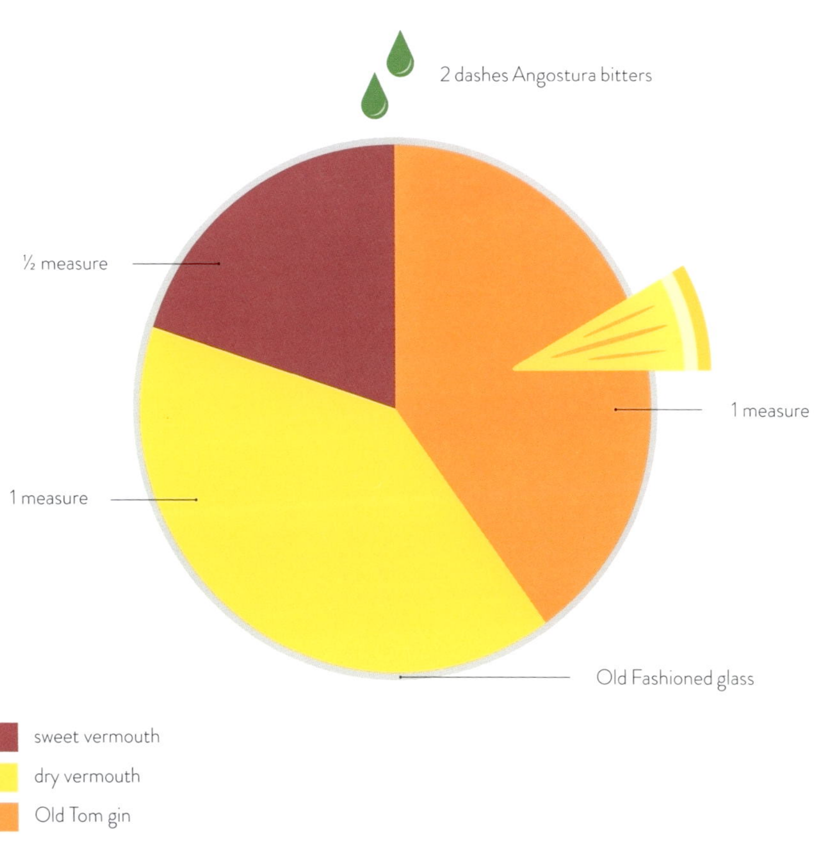

Instructions

1 Pour the gin, vermouths and bitters into an Old Fashioned glass. **2** Garnish with the lemon slice and serve.

RED SNAPPER

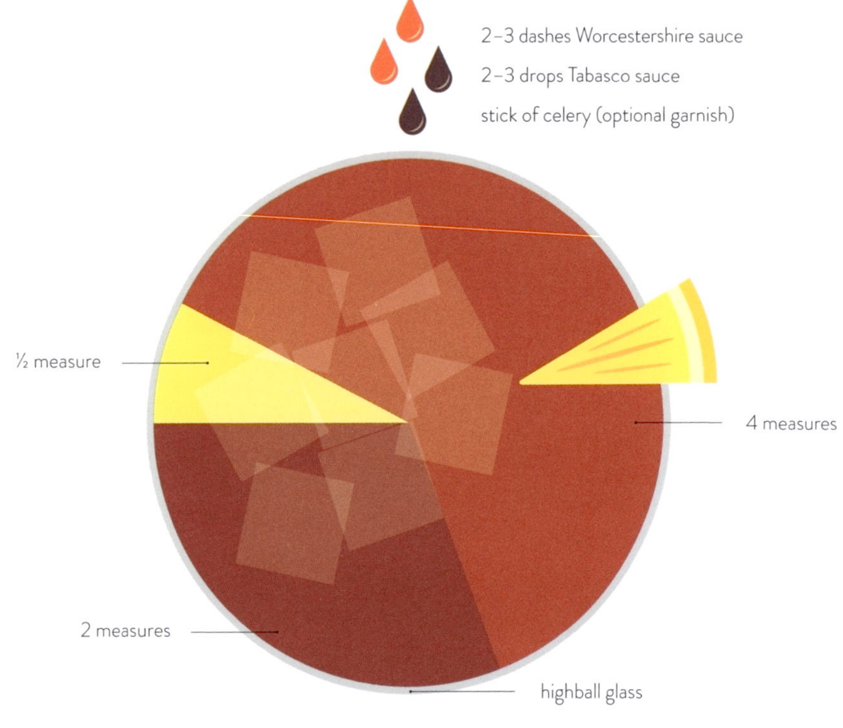

lemon juice

tomato juice

gin

Instructions

1 Shake the gin, tomato juice, and lemon juice with ice and strain into a chilled highball glass filled with ice. 2 Stir in the Worcestershire, Tabasco, and salt and pepper. 3 Add a stick of celery (if needed) and a lemon slice.

THE SWINGER

Instructions

1 Fill a shaker with ice, add sugar, squeezed lemon wedges, and gin. **2** Shake and strain into a cocktail glass. **3** Top up with champagne and garnish with a lemon twist.

TOM FIZZ

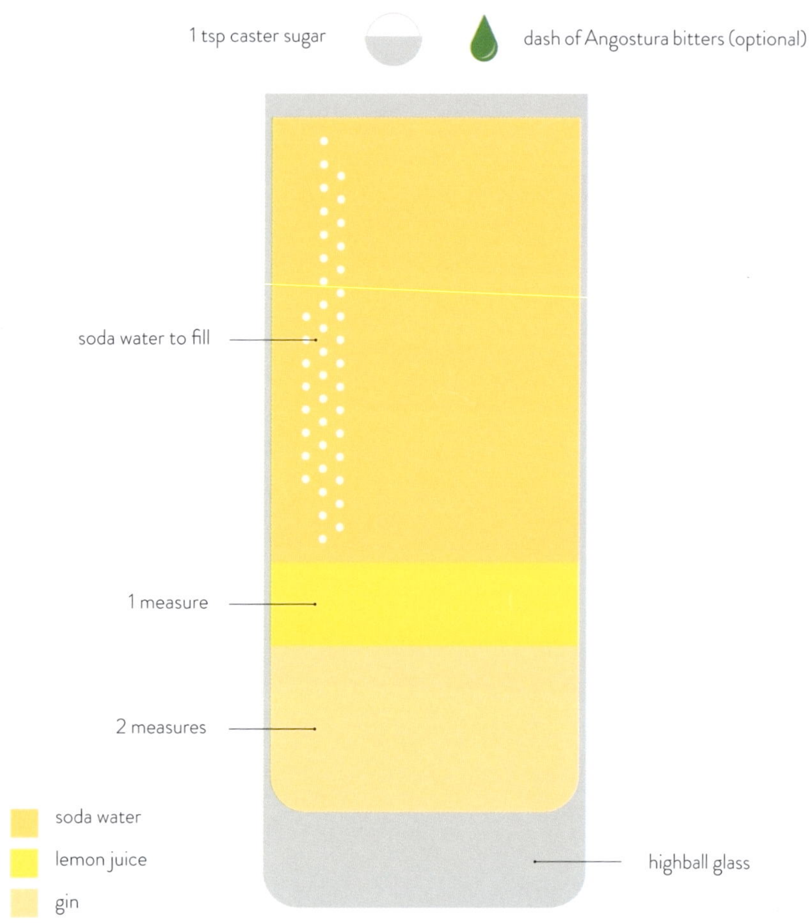

Instructions

1 Shake the gin, juice, sugar and bitters, strain into a tall glass, and top up with soda.

UNION JACK

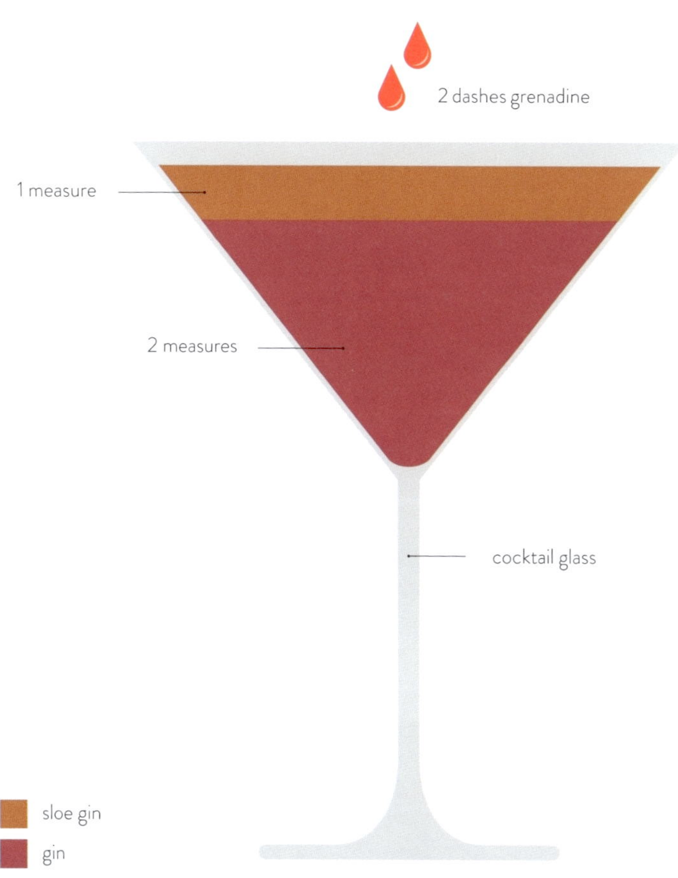

Instructions

1 Mix the gins and grenadine together in a shaker, then strain into a cocktail glass and serve.

WHITE VELVET

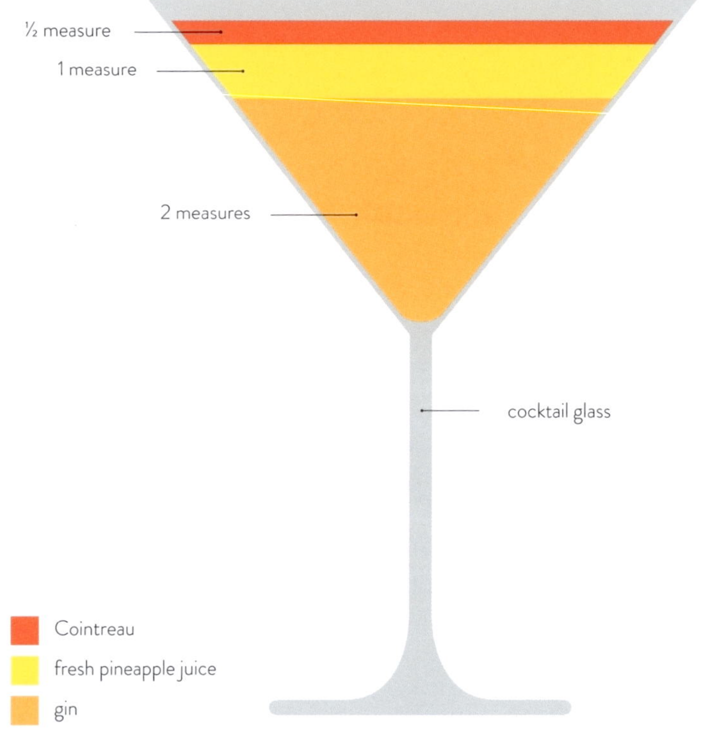

Instructions

1 Pour all the ingredients together, then strain into a cocktail glass and serve.

WOODSTOCK

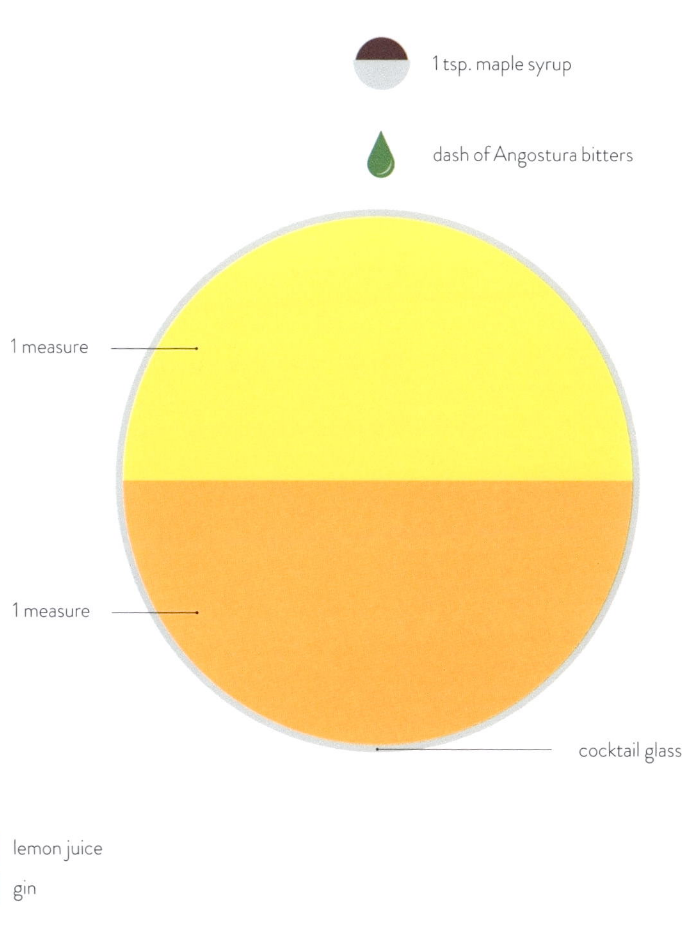

Instructions

1 Shake all the ingredients together, then strain into a cocktail glass and serve.

BRANDY

ADAM AND EVE

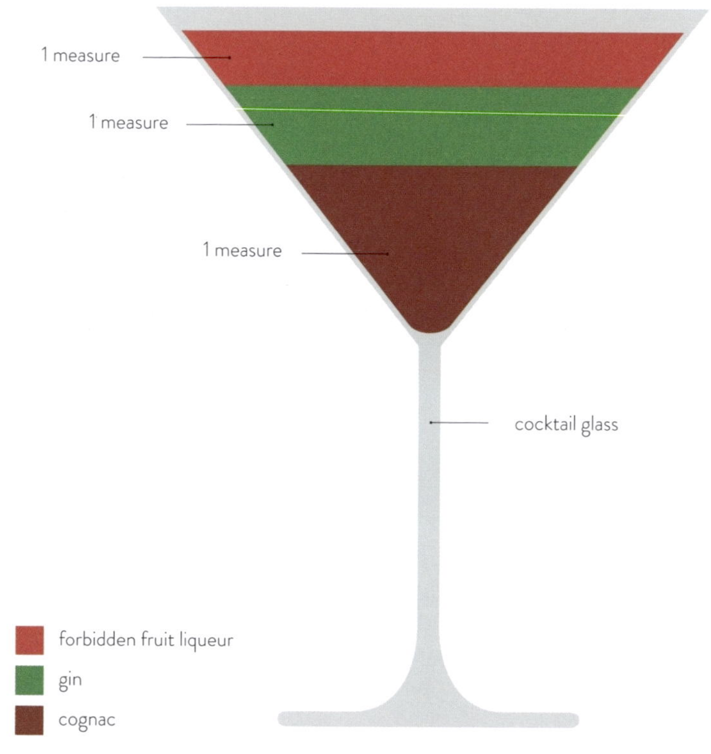

Instructions

1 Shake all the liquids together, then strain into a cocktail glass and serve.

AMERICAN BEAUTY

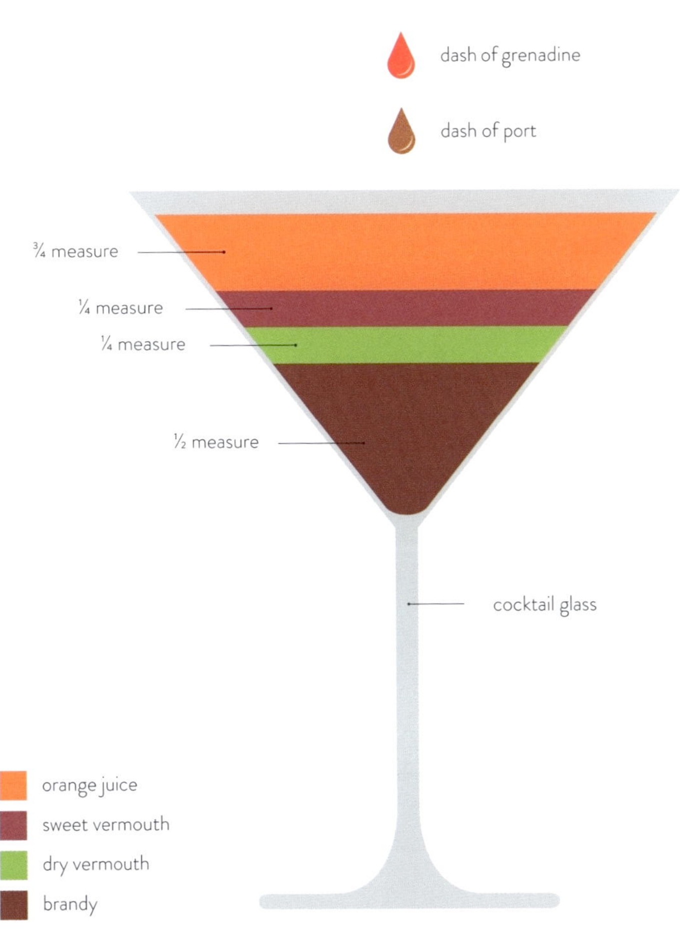

Instructions

1 Shake and strain all the ingredients, except the port, into a cocktail glass. **2** Float the port on top.

APRIL SHOWER

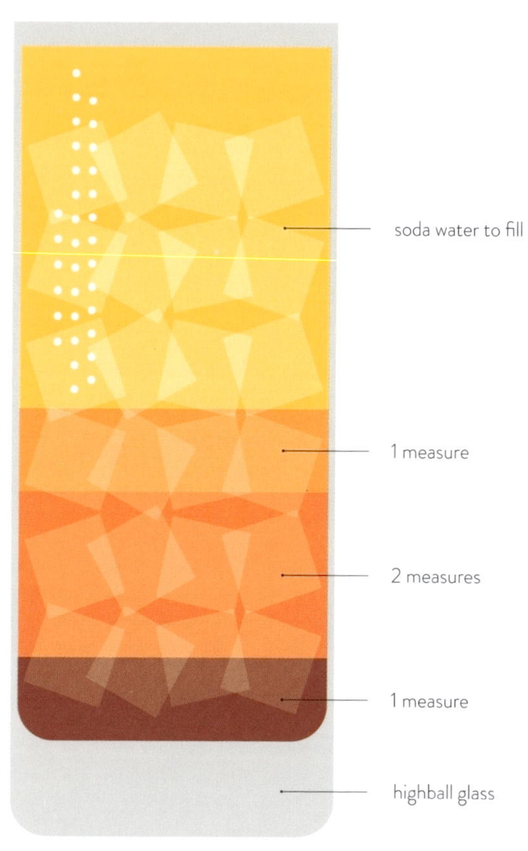

soda water
Benedictine
orange juice
brandy

Instructions

1 Pour the brandy, orange juice, and Benedictine into a highball glass with ice. 2 Stir and top up with soda.

B & B

Instructions

1 Pour the brandy and Benedictine into a brandy glass and serve.

BETWEEN THE SHEETS

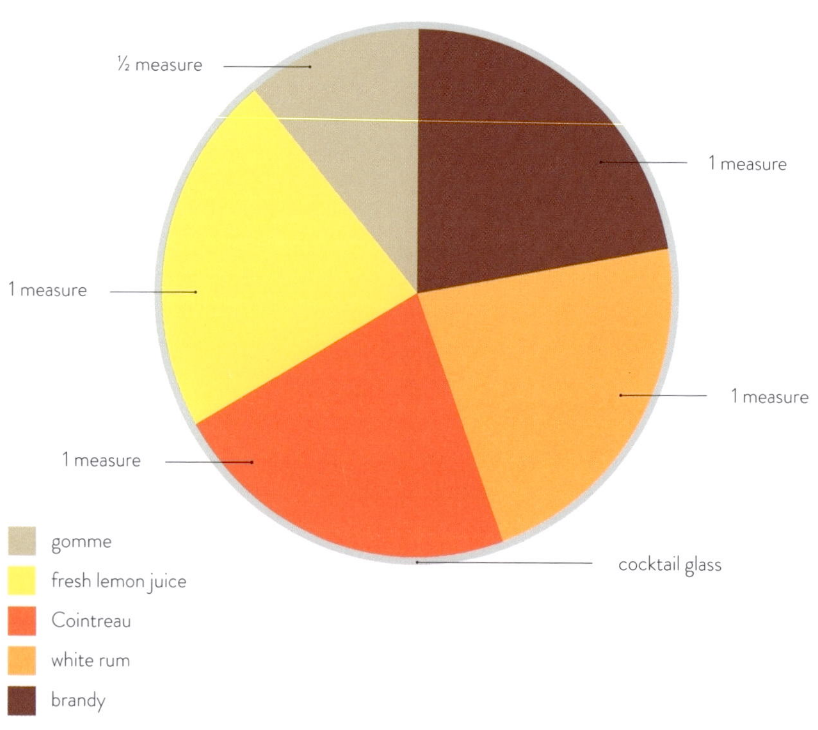

Instructions

1 Shake all the ingredients together, then strain into a cocktail glass, and serve.

BRANDY COCKTAIL

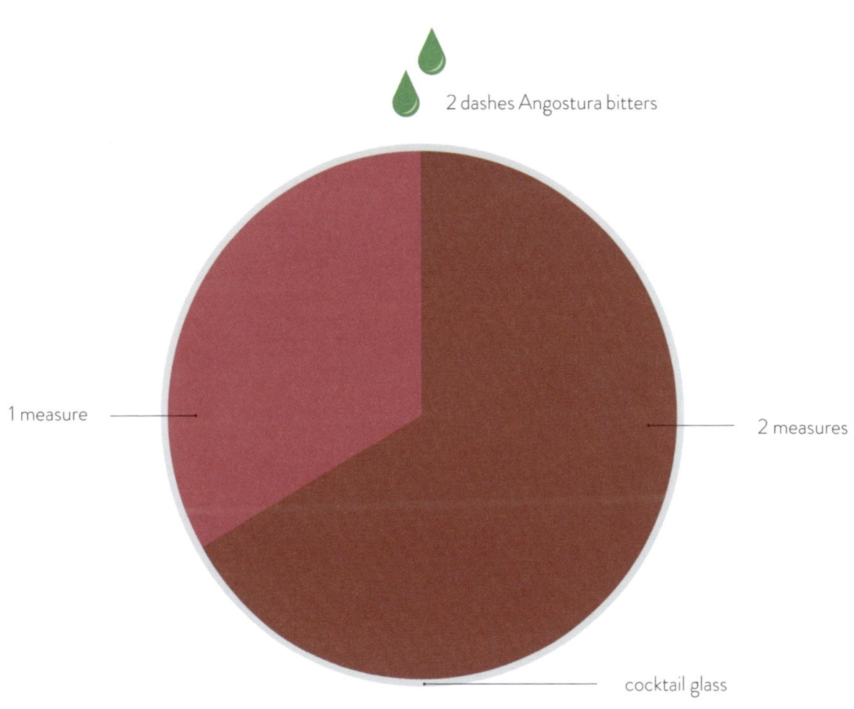

sweet vermouth

cognac

Instructions

1 Stir the cognac, vermouth, and bitters together, then strain into a cocktail glass and serve.

BRANDY DAISY

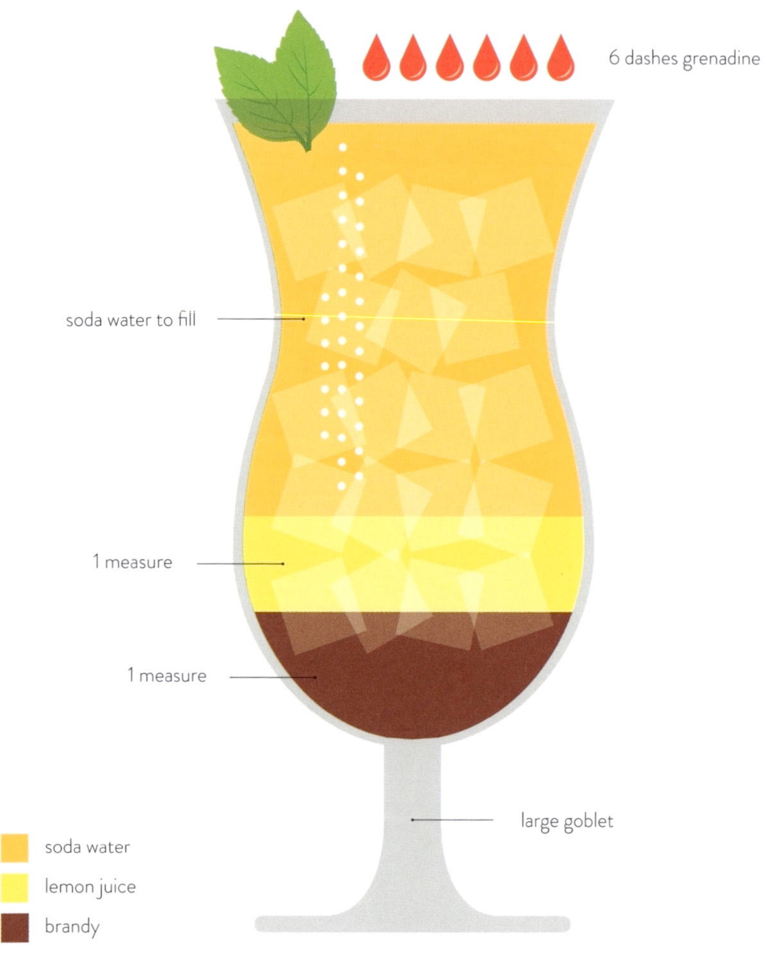

Instructions

1 Shake the brandy, lemon juice, and grenadine and strain into a goblet over ice. **2** Top up with soda and garnish with a sprig of mint.

BRANDY KISS

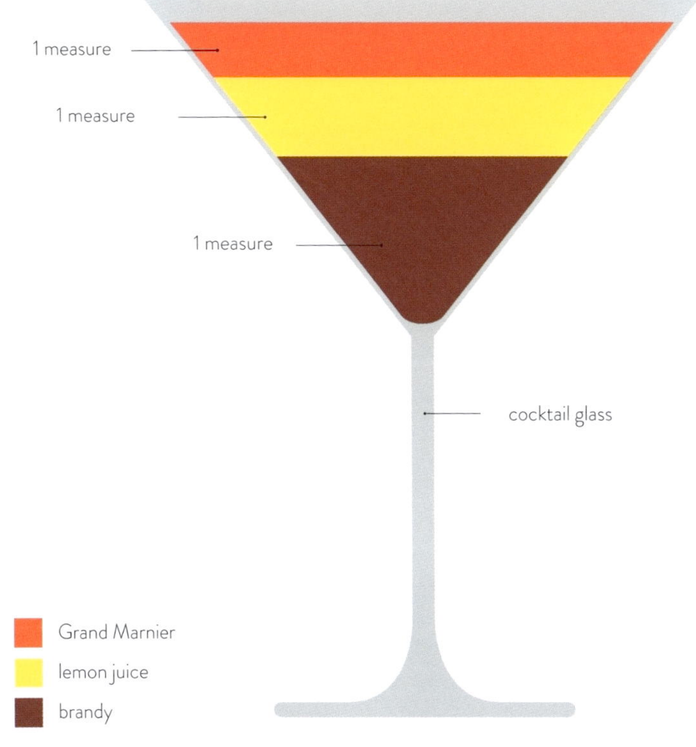

Instructions

1 Shake all the ingredients together with ice and strain into a cocktail glass.

CHERRY PICKER

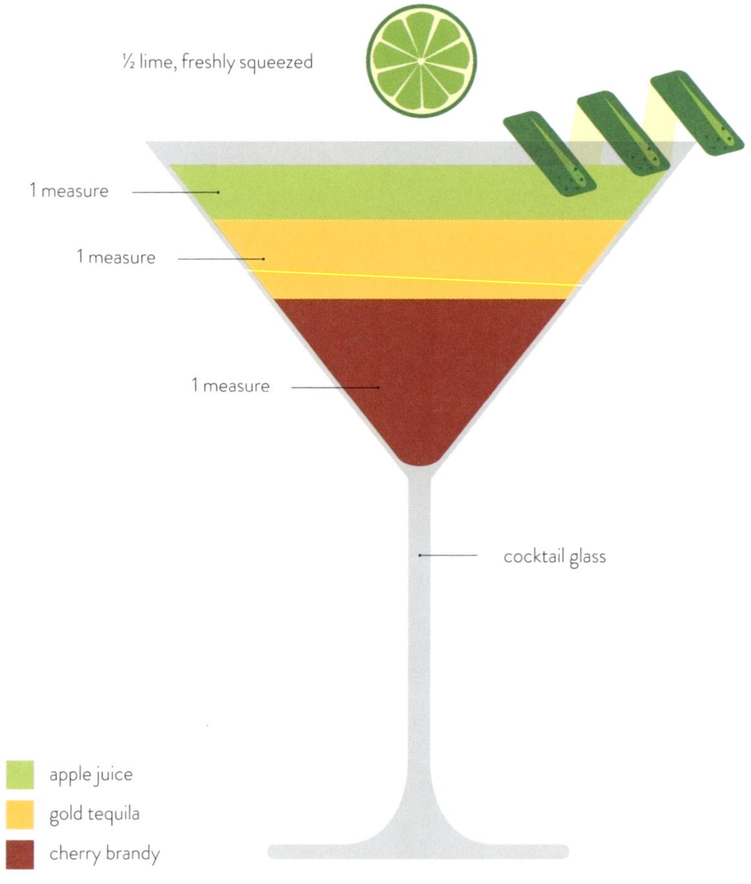

Instructions

1 Put all the ingredients in a shaker. **2** Shake, then strain into a cocktail glass and add a twist of lime to serve.

CHICAGO

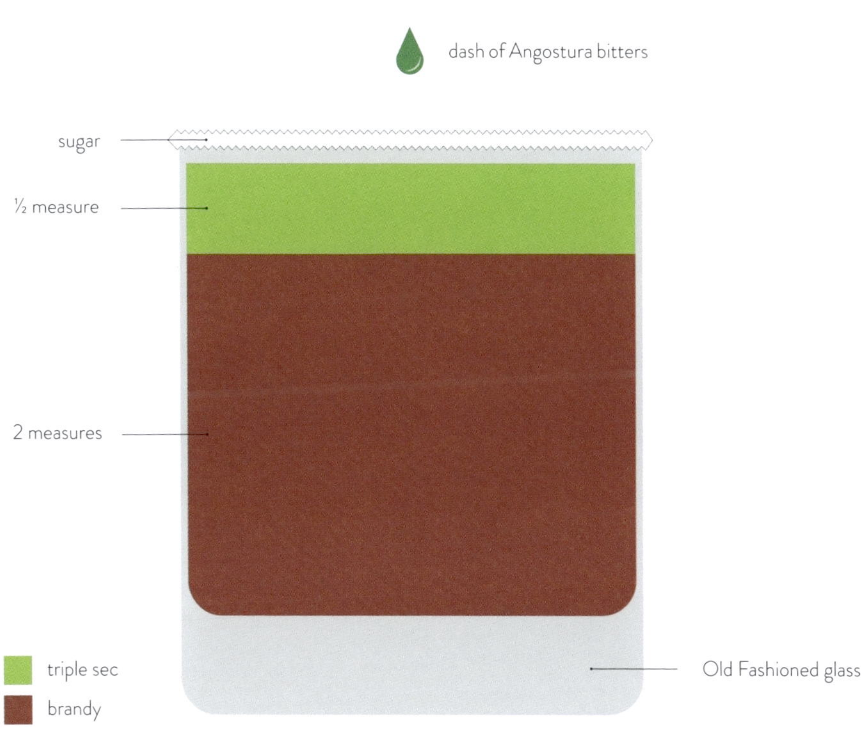

Instructions

1 Shake all the ingredients together, then pour into a sugar-rimmed Old Fashioned glass and serve.

CORPSE REVIVER

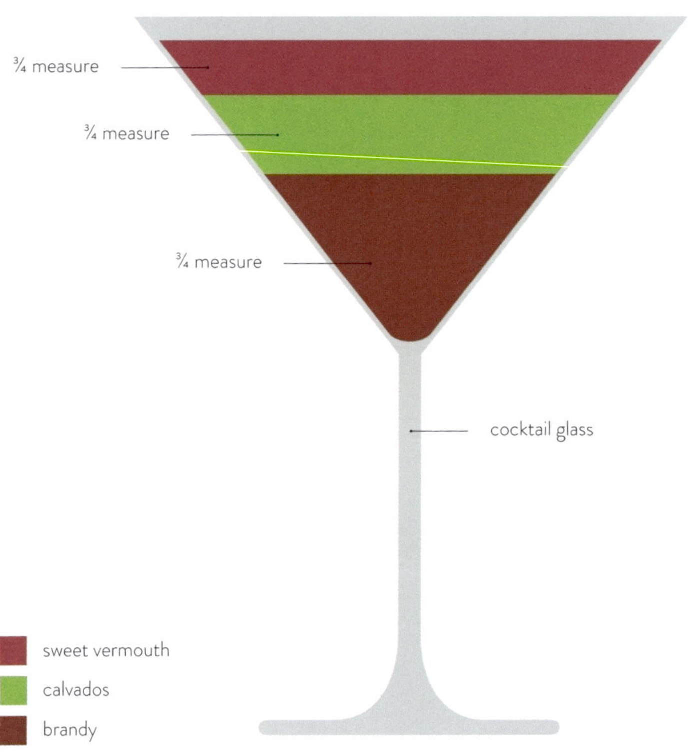

Instructions

1 Shake all the ingredients together and strain into a cocktail glass.

DIZZY DAME

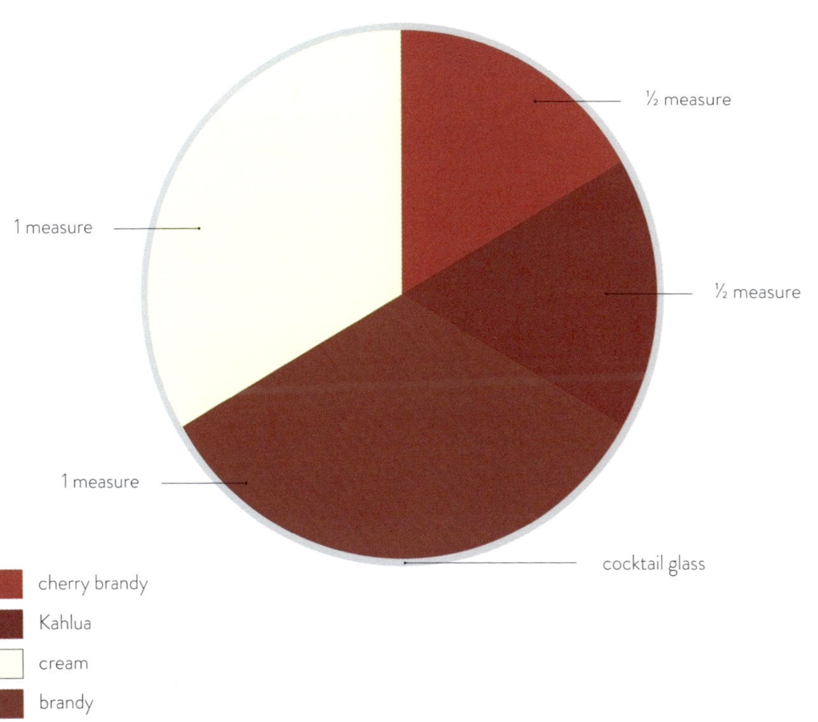

Instructions

1 Shake all the ingredients together with ice and strain into a cocktail glass.

EGGNOG

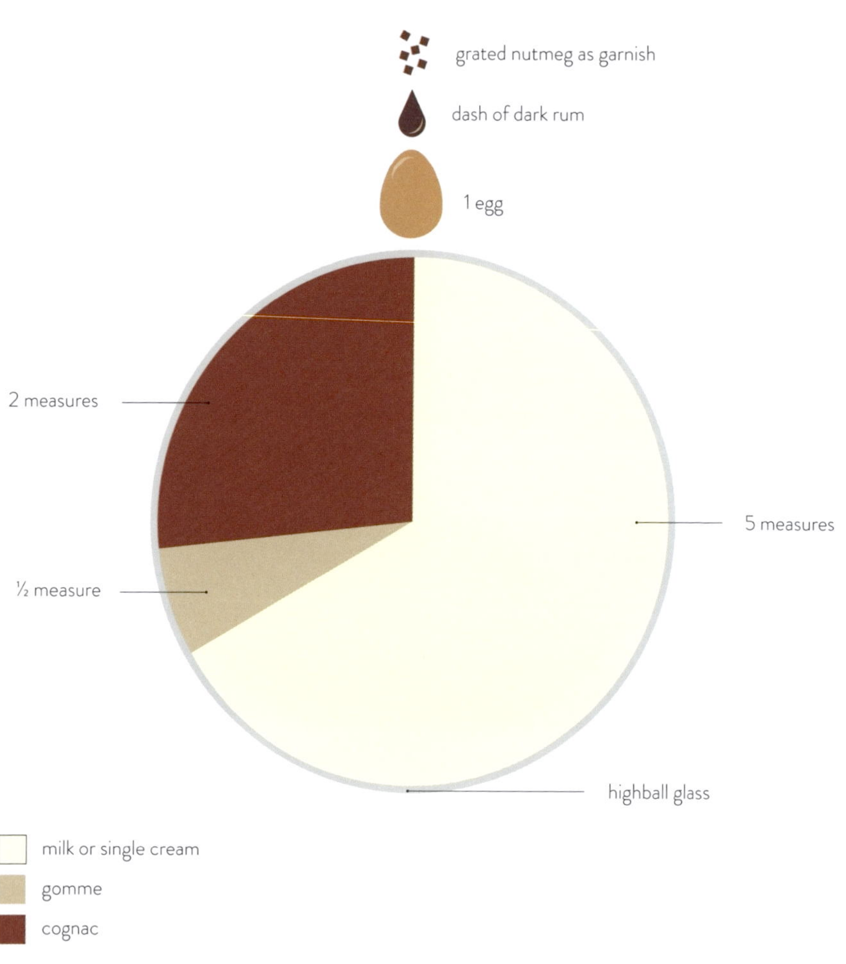

Instructions

1 Mix the ingredients together in a shaker, then pour into a highball glass. **2** Sprinkle on the grated nutmeg and serve.

FRENCHIE

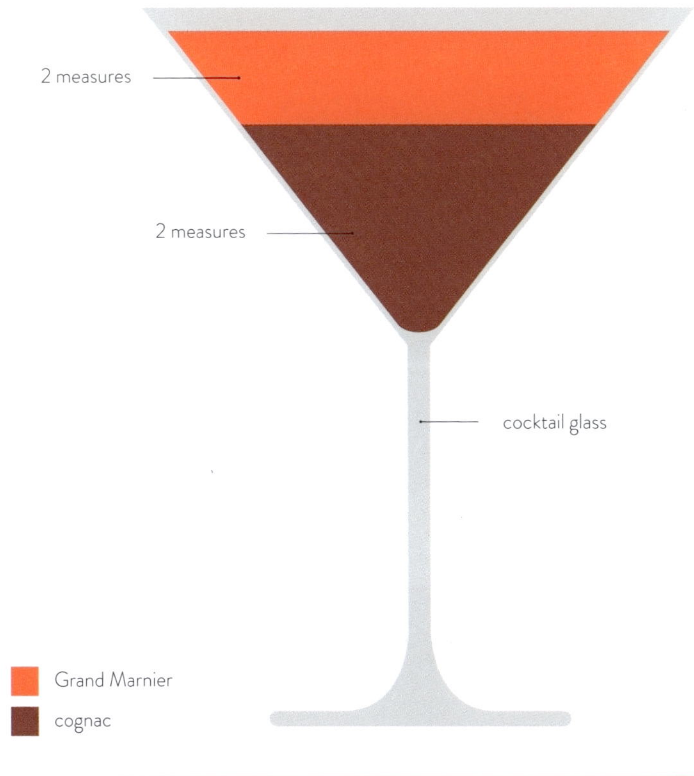

Instructions

1 Pour the ingredients into a cocktail glass and stir.

JACK ROSE

Instructions

1 Shake ingredients with ice and strain into a cocktail glass. 2 Garnish with a slice of lime.

LIEUTENANT

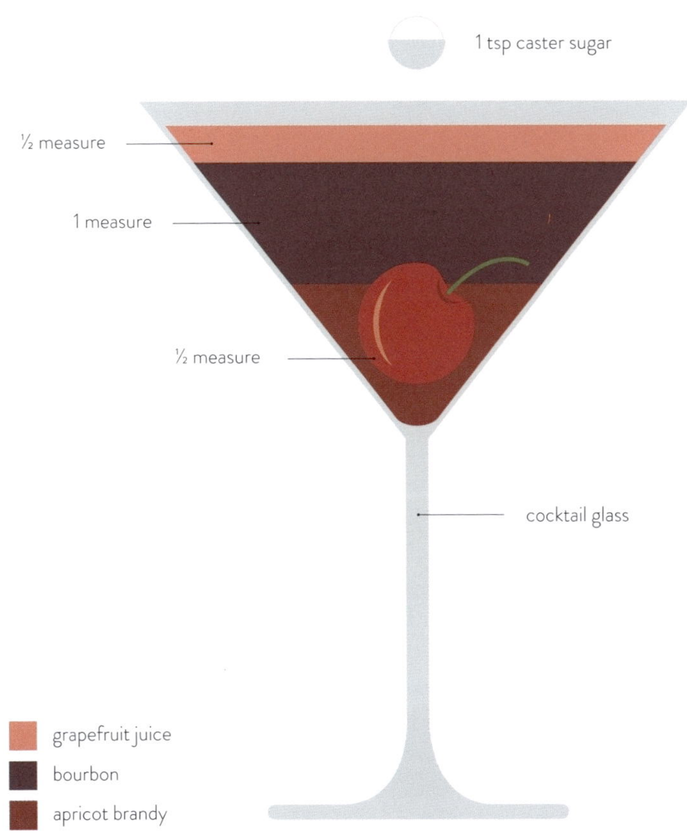

Instructions

1 Shake all the ingredients together with ice and strain into a cocktail glass. **2** Garnish with a cherry and serve.

MIKADO

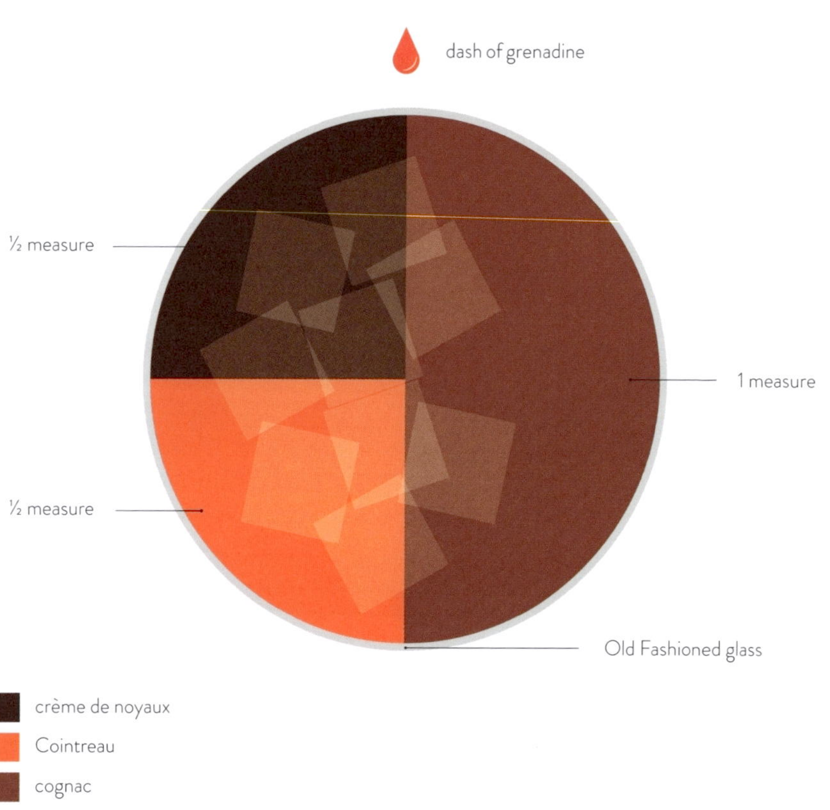

Instructions

1 Stir all the ingredients together, then strain into an ice-filled Old Fashioned glass and serve.

NICKY FINN

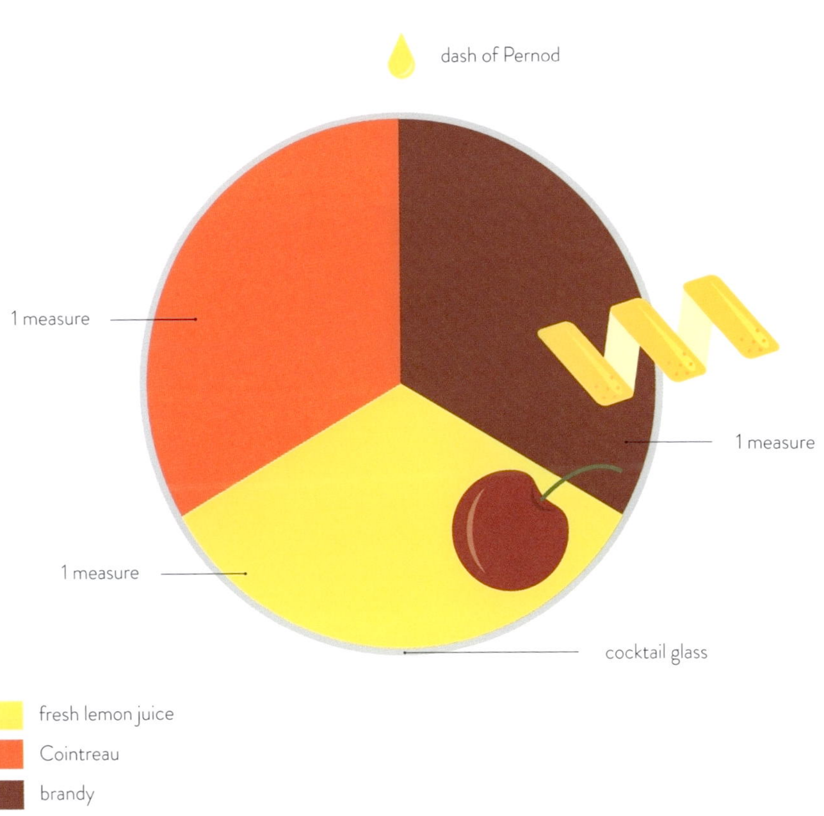

Instructions

1 Shake with ice and strain into a chilled cocktail glass. **2** Garnish with a lemon twist or a maraschino cherry.

RAJA

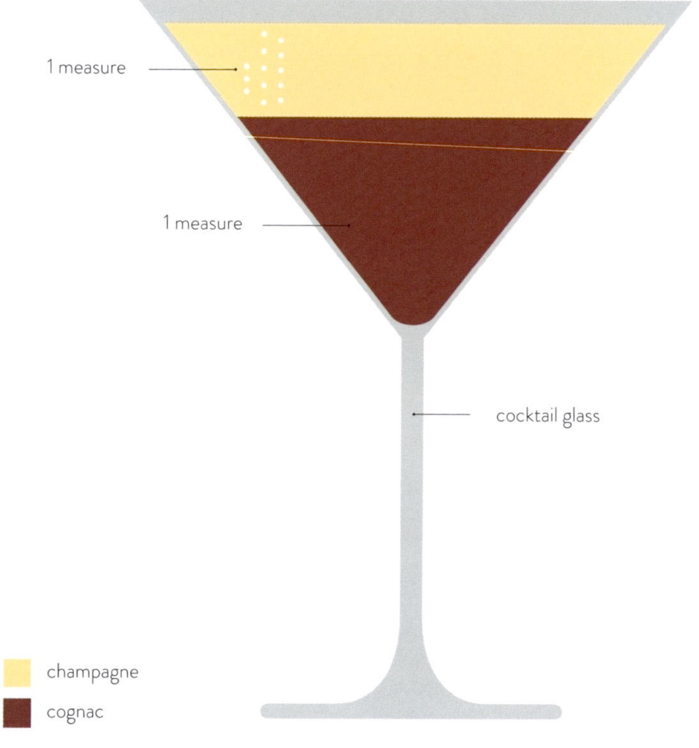

Instructions

1 Stir the cognac and champagne together, then strain into a cocktail glass and serve.

TULIP

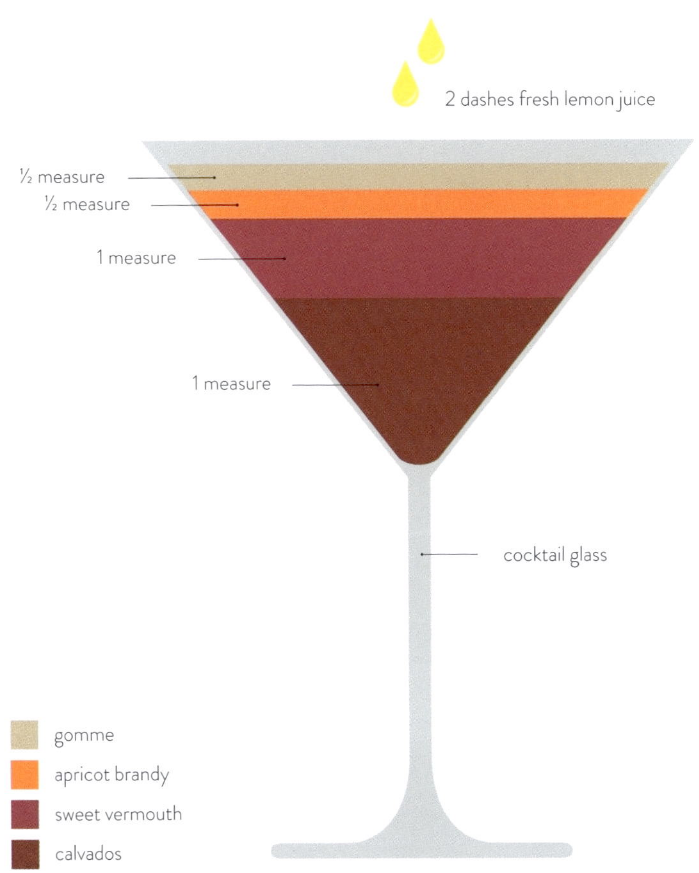

Instructions

1 Shake all the ingredients together, then strain into a cocktail glass and serve.

RUM

AFTERNOON DELIGHT

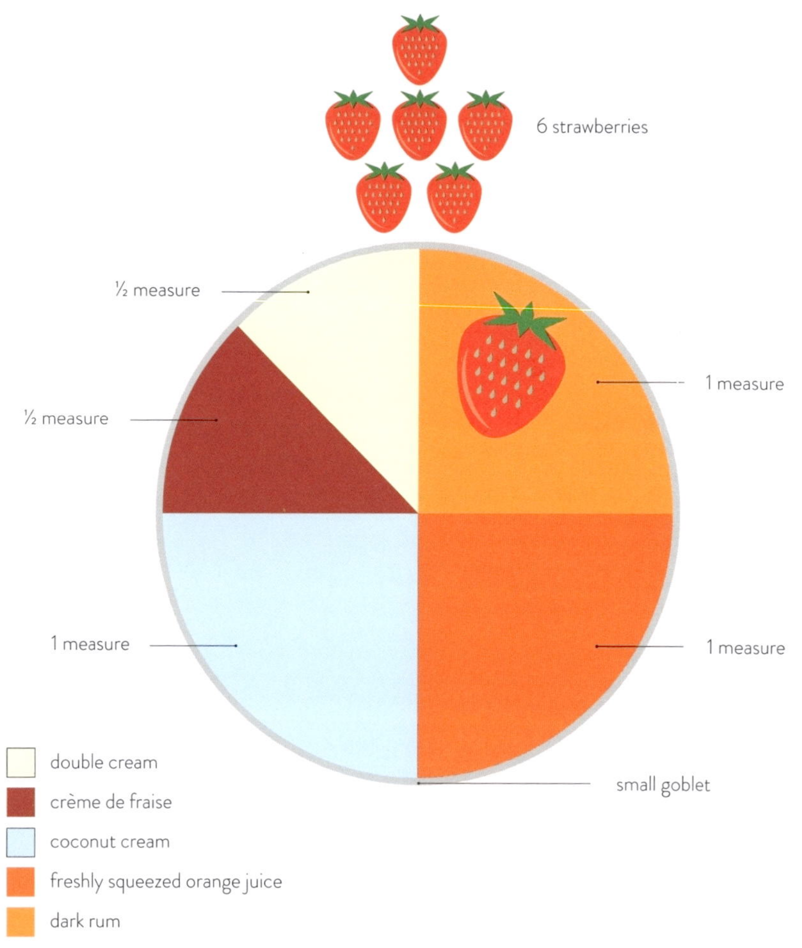

Instructions

1 Place all the ingredients, except one strawberry, into a blender. **2** Add crushed ice and blend. Pour into a goblet. **3** Garnish with a strawberry and serve with a straw.

APOLLO 13

Instructions

1 Shake all the ingredients together with ice and strain into a champagne saucer. **2** Garnish with a maraschino cherry.

BAHIA

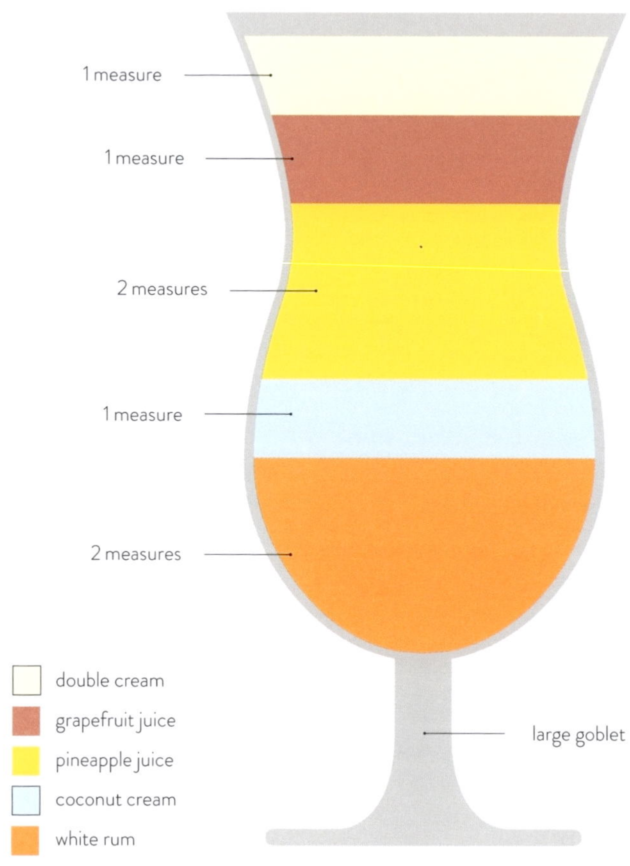

Instructions

1 Blend all the ingredients together and pour into a large goblet.

BARRACUDA

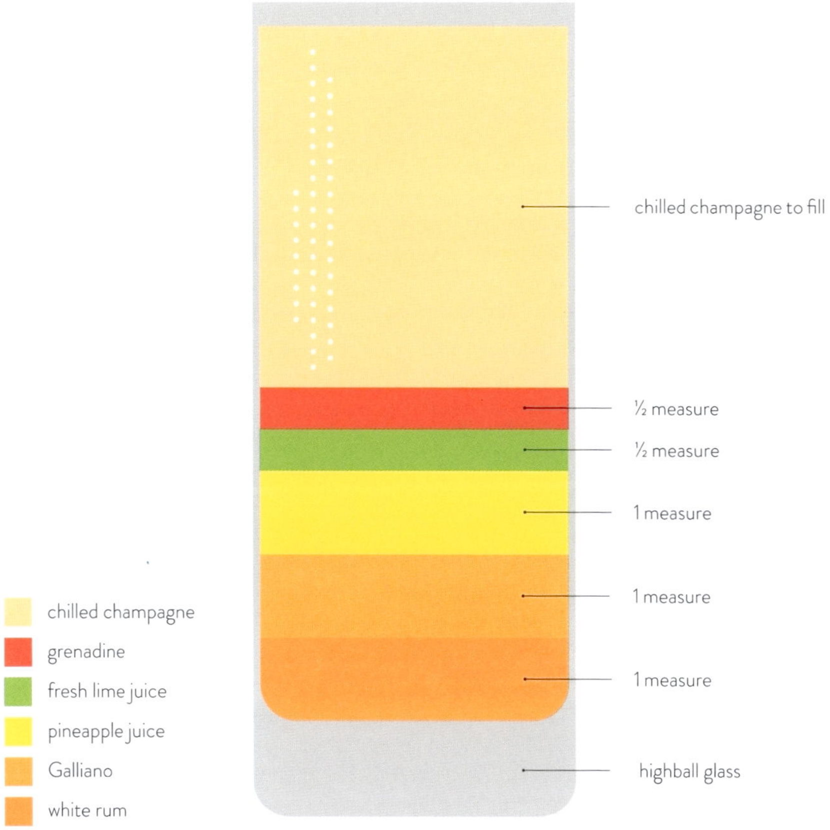

chilled champagne to fill

½ measure

½ measure

1 measure

1 measure

1 measure

highball glass

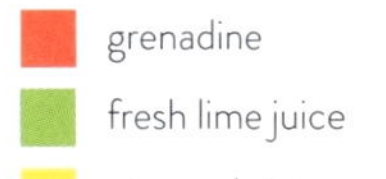

chilled champagne

grenadine

fresh lime juice

pineapple juice

Galliano

white rum

Instructions

1 Pour each of the ingredients into a highball glass, top up with champagne and serve.

BEE'S KISS

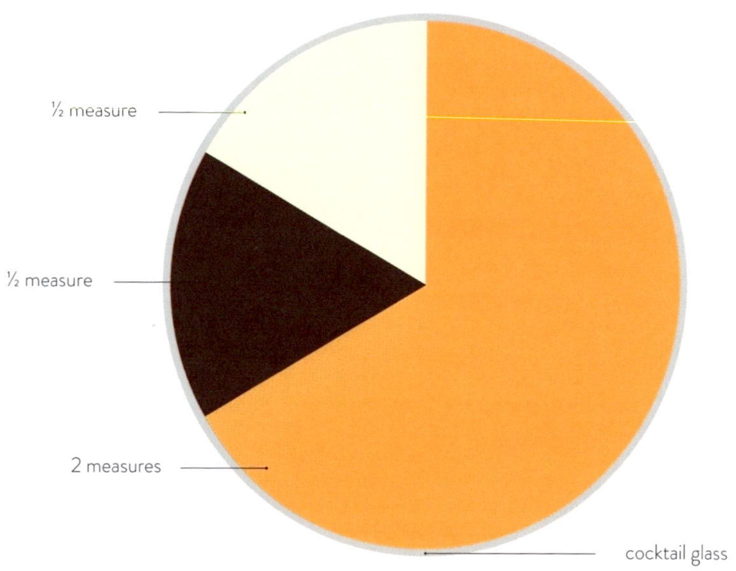

Instructions

1 Shake all the ingredients well and strain into a cocktail glass.

BELLA DONNA

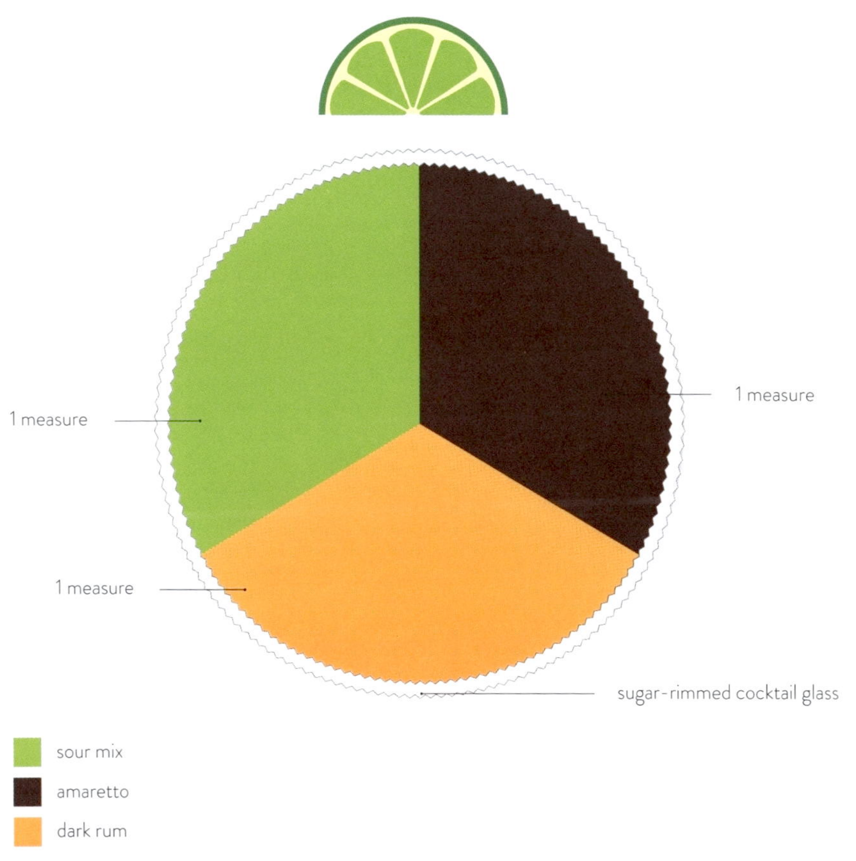

sour mix

amaretto

dark rum

Instructions

1 Rub the rim of a cocktail glass with a wedge of lime and then dip it into a saucer of sugar to coat the rim. **2** Shake all ingredients with ice and strain into the glass.

BLUE HAWAIIAN

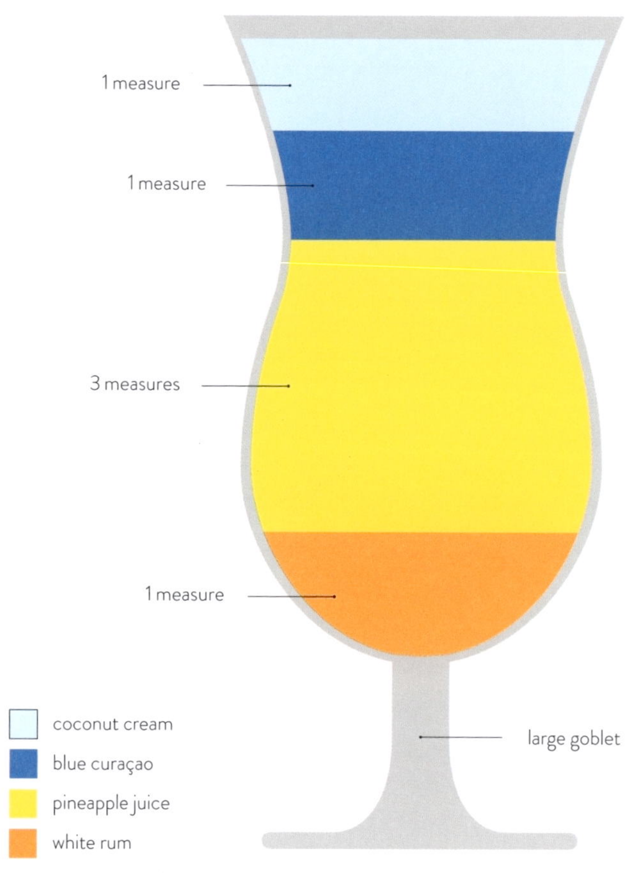

Instructions

1 Blend all the ingredients together and pour into a large goblet.

CASABLANCA

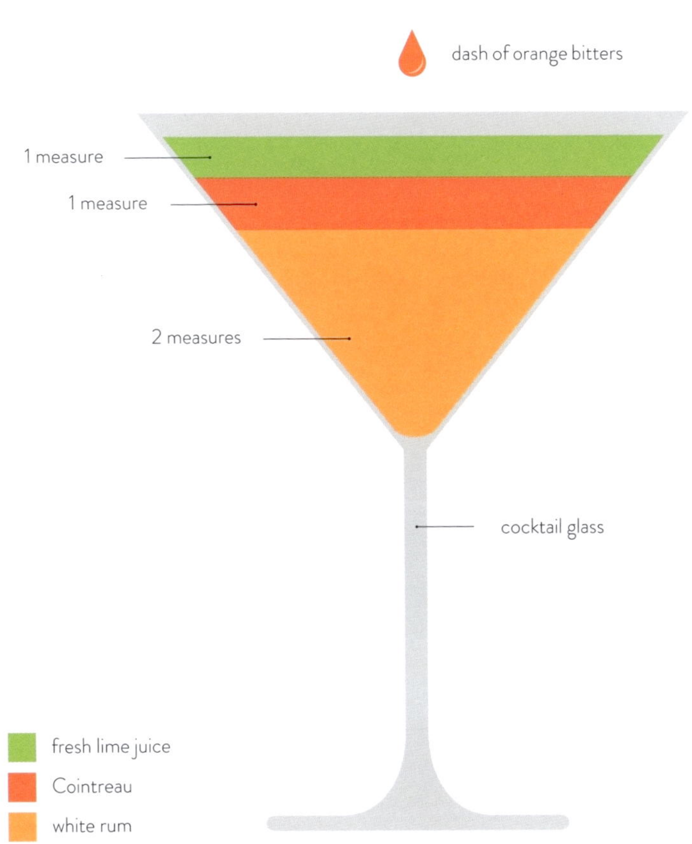

Instructions

1 Shake all the ingredients together, then strain into a cocktail glass, and serve.

COCOLOCO

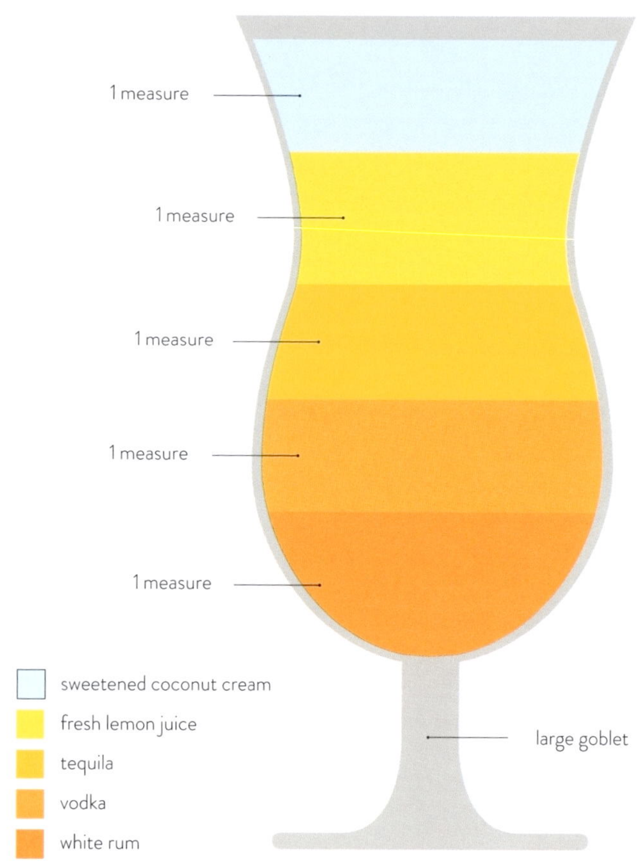

Instructions

1 Blend all the ingredients together until smooth, then pour into a large goblet.

CUBA LIBRE

Instructions

1 Pour the juice, then the rum into a highball glass filled with ice. **2** Top up with cola, add a wedge of lime, then serve with a stirrer.

DIZZY GILLESPIE

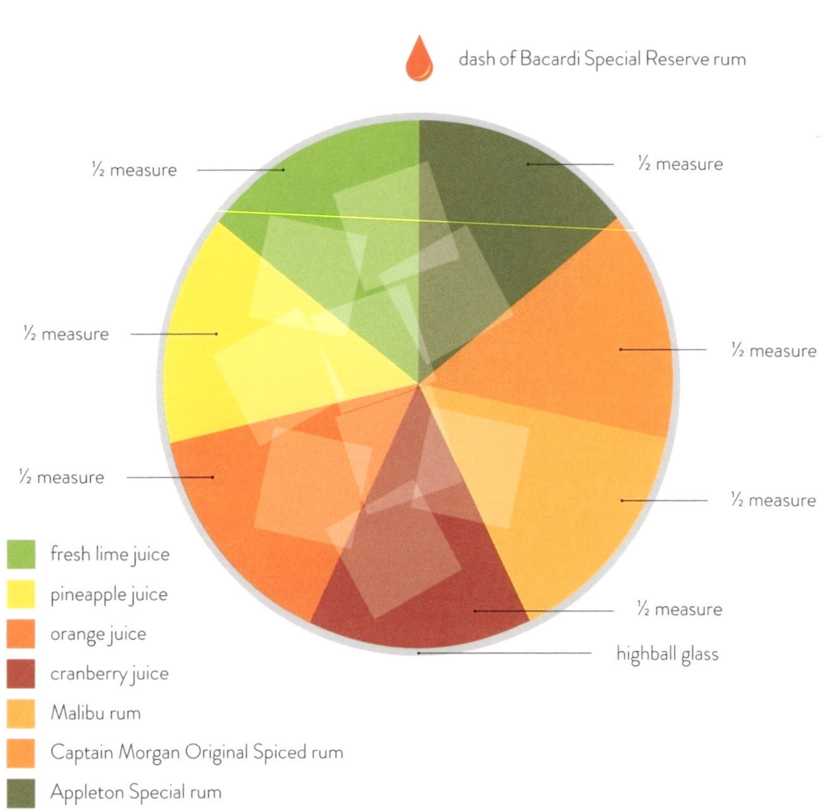

Instructions

1. Shake all the ingredients, except the Bacardi, with ice and strain into a highball glass with ice.
2. Float the Bacardi Special Reserve.

EL PRESIDENTE

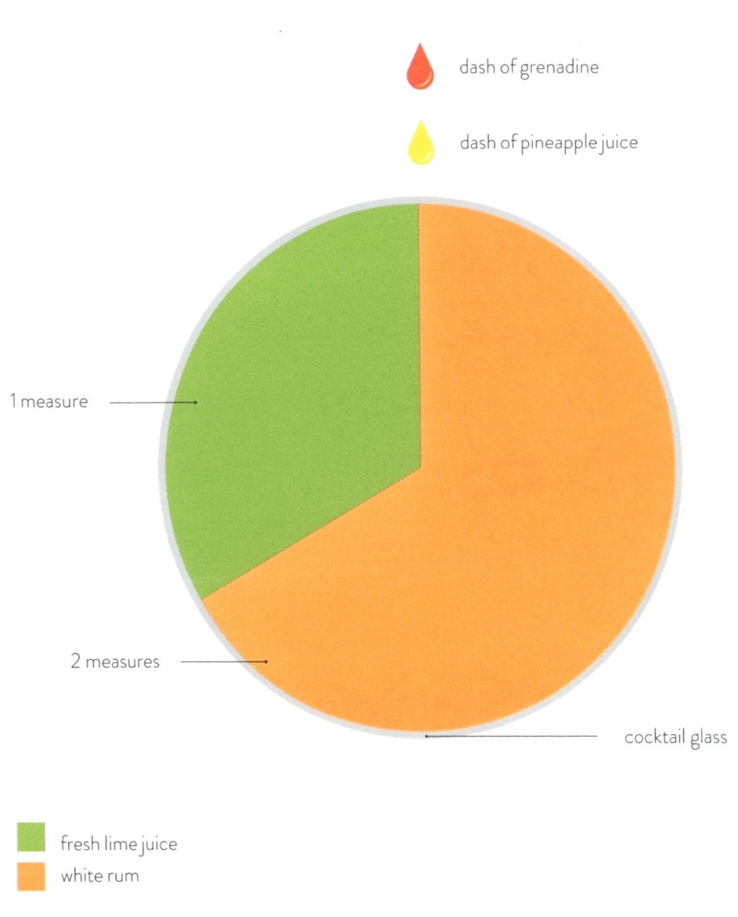

Instructions

1 Pour the grenadine into a cocktail glass. In an ice-filled shaker, mix the rum and the lime and pineapple juices, then strain into the glass and serve.

FLORIDITA

Instructions

1 Shake all the ingredients over ice cubes and strain into a cocktail glass.

HURRICANE

Instructions

1 Shake all the ingredients together and strain into a highball glass filled with ice. **2** Add a pineapple wedge to decorate.

JUNGLE JUICE

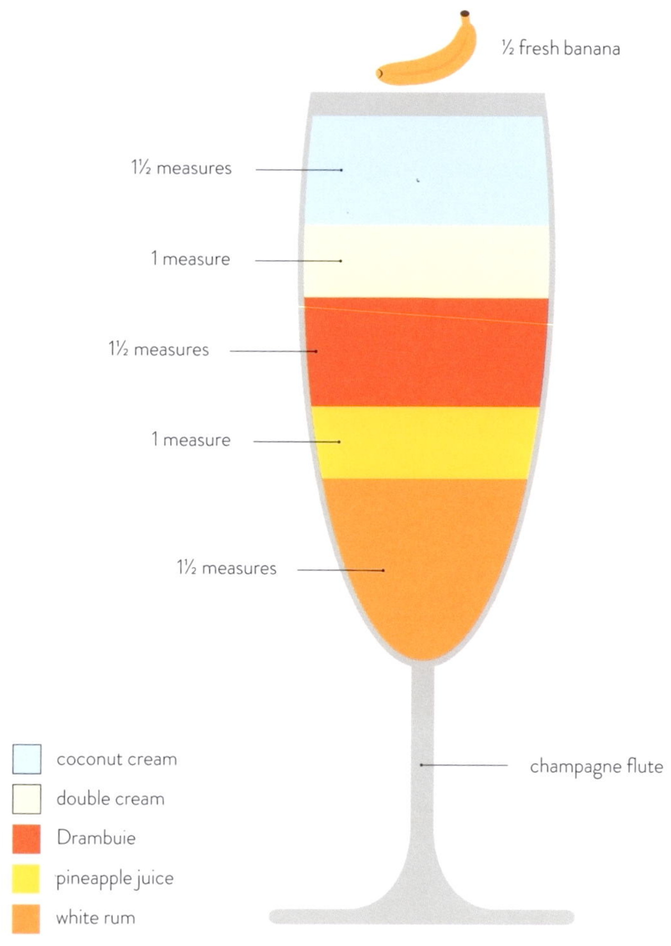

Instructions

1 Blend all the ingredients together until smooth, then pour into a champagne flute.

MADONNA

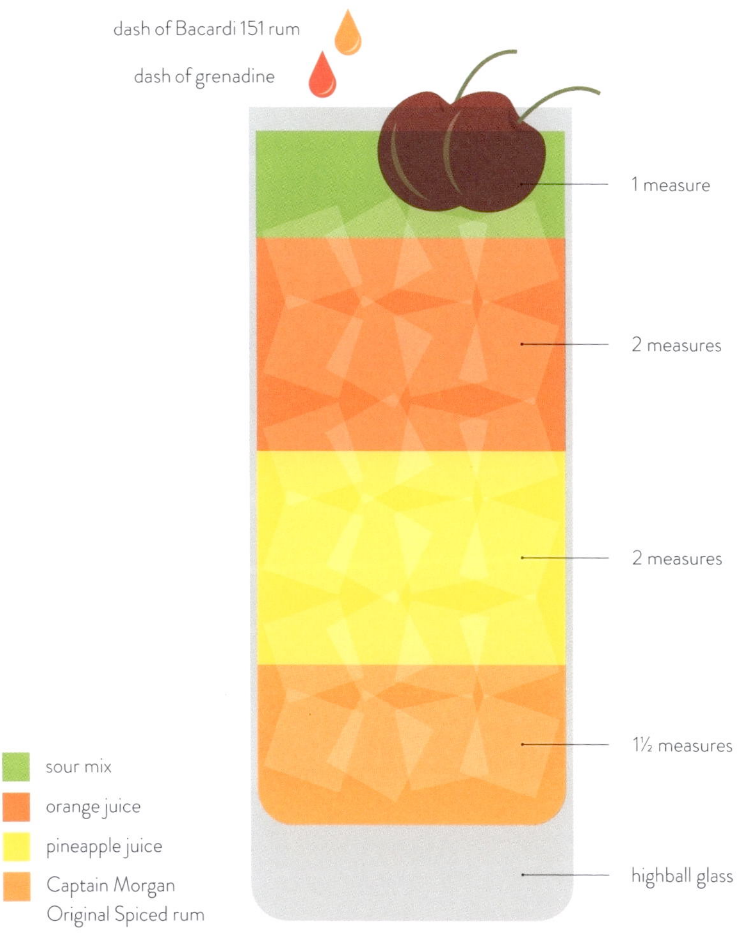

Instructions

1 Shake the Captain Morgan, pineapple juice, orange juice and sour mix with ice and strain into an ice-filled highball glass. **2** Float the Bacardi over the top, then the grenadine and garnish with two maraschino cherries.

MOJITO

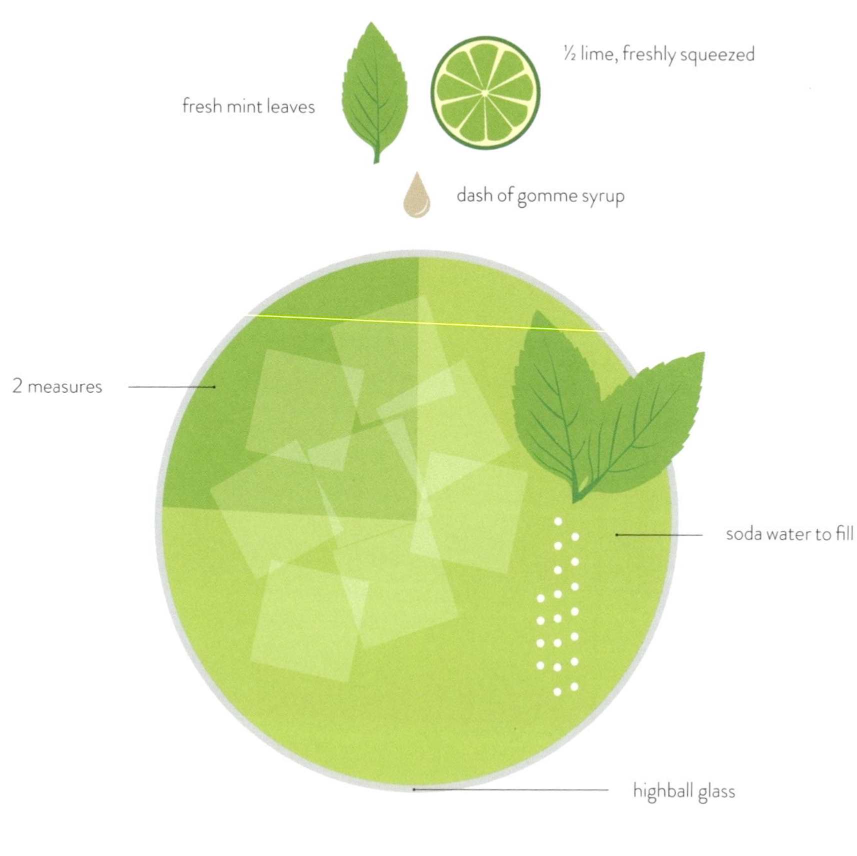

soda water

white rum

Instructions

1 In a large highball glass, muddle the mint leaves and gomme. **2** Squeeze lime juice into the glass and add lime half. **3** Then add the rum and some ice. **4** Stir, then add the soda, stir again briefly, and garnish with a sprig of mint.

NAKED LADY

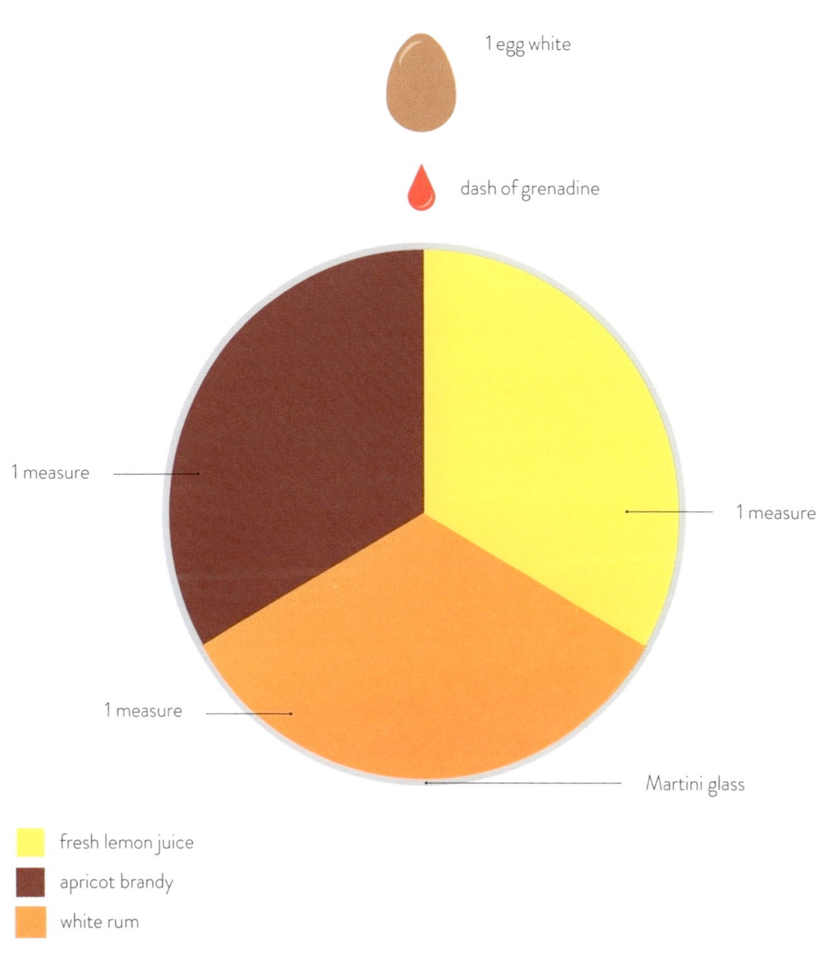

fresh lemon juice
apricot brandy
white rum

Instructions

1 Shake all the ingredients together, then strain into a cocktail glass and serve.

PAINKILLER

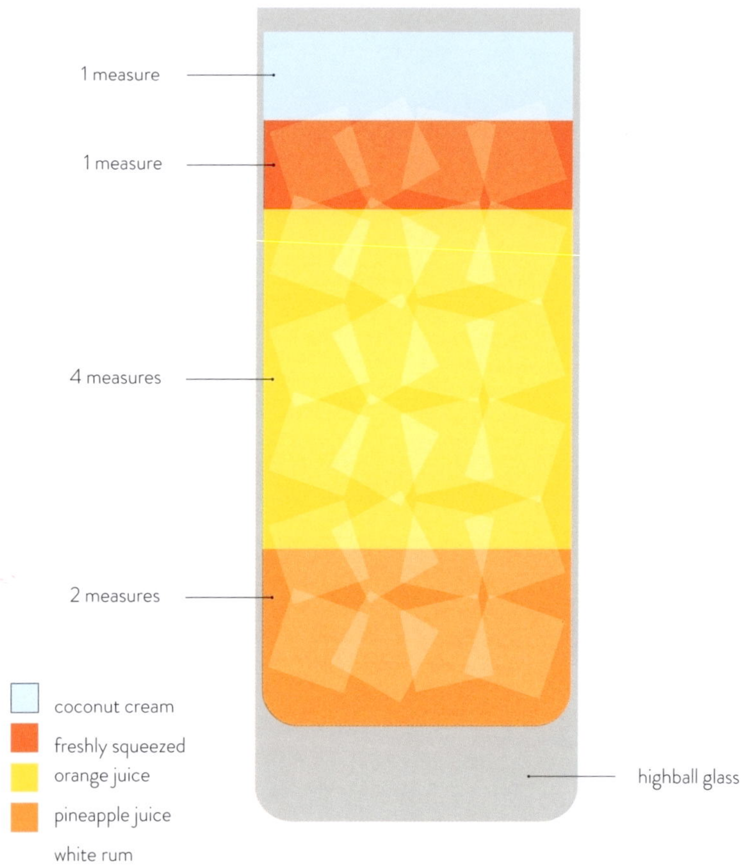

Instructions

1 Shake all the ingredients together and strain into a highball glass filled with ice.

PIÑA COLADA

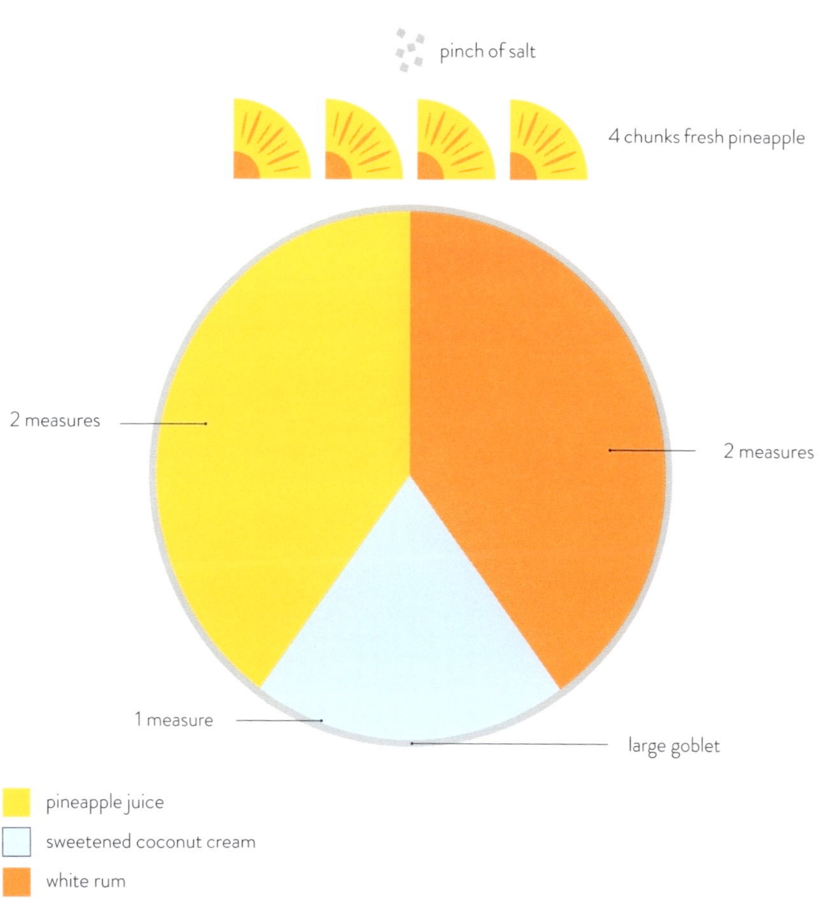

Instructions

1 Blend all the ingredients together until smooth, then pour into a large goblet.

PUSSY FOOT

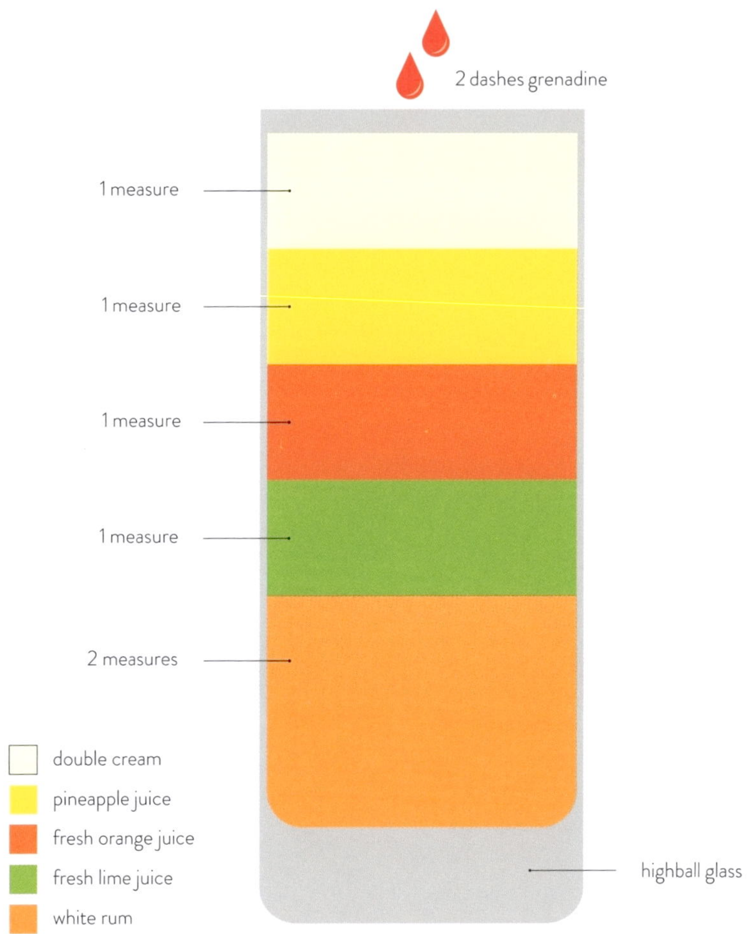

Instructions

1 Mix all the ingredients together in a shaker, then pour into a highball glass and serve.

ZOMBIE

Instructions

1 Shake all the ingredients together and strain into a large highball glass half-filled with ice.

WHISKY

ALGONQUIN

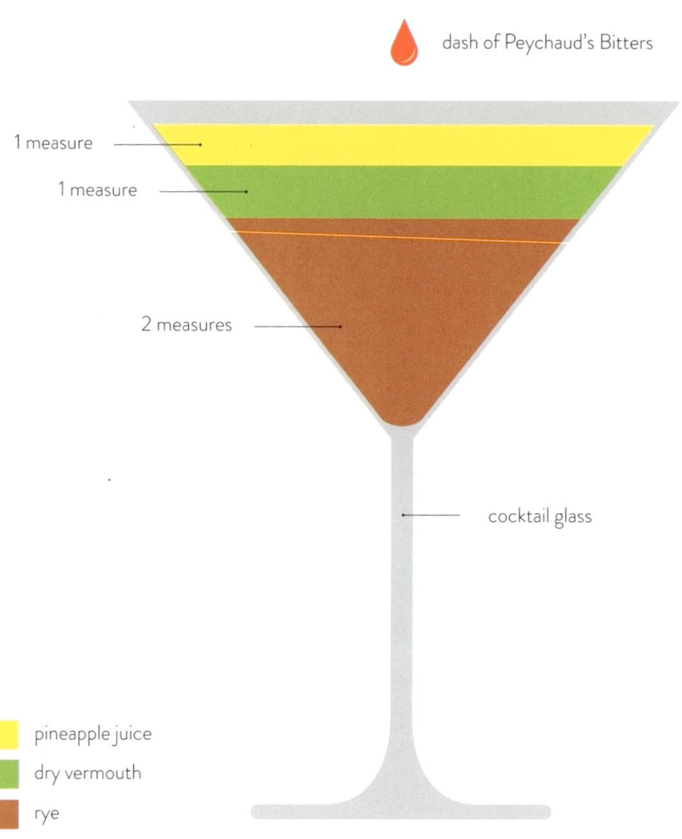

Instructions

1 Shake all the ingredients together and strain into a cocktail glass.

ANGELIC

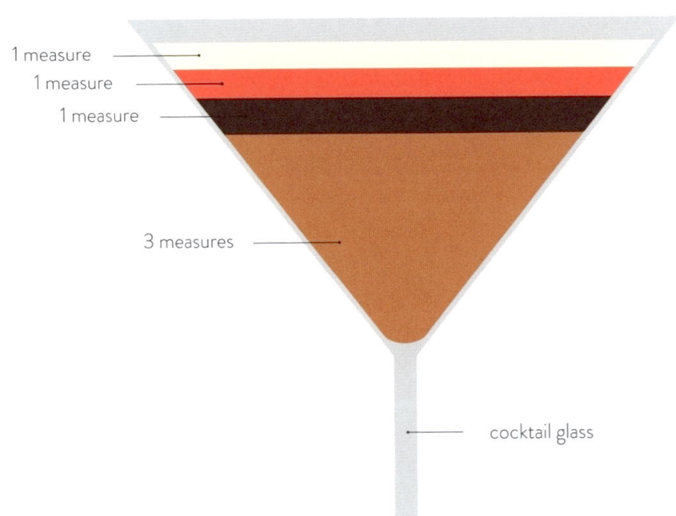

double cream

grenadine

crème de cacao

bourbon

Instructions

1 Mix the ingredients together in a shaker, then strain into a cocktail glass. **2** Sprinkle on the nutmeg and serve.

BALLANTINE'S

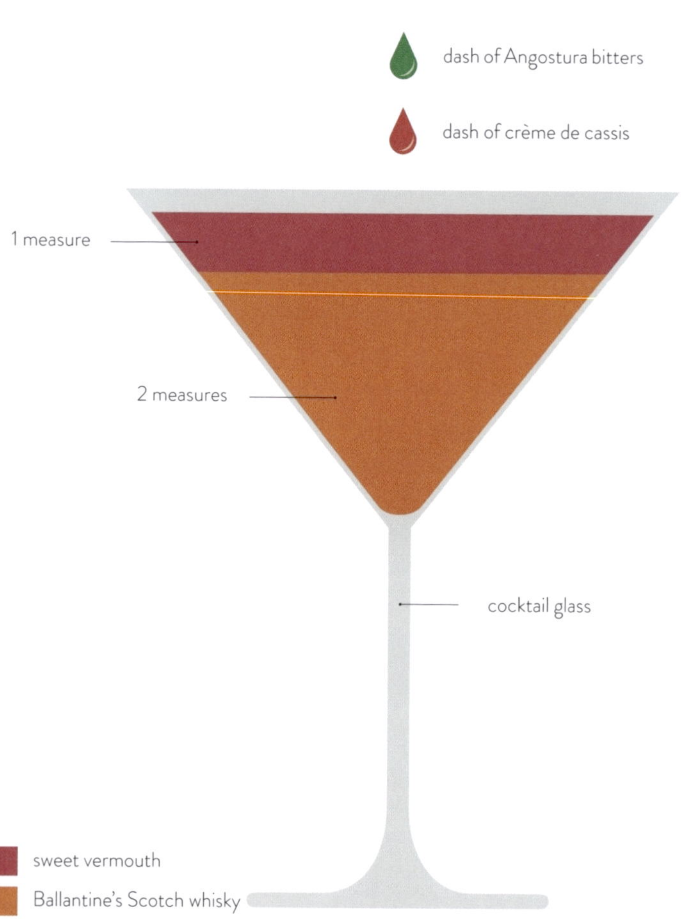

Instructions

1 Pour all the ingredients into a shaker and shake. **2** Strain into a cocktail glass and serve.

BLOOD AND SAND

Instructions

1 Mix ingredients with ice in a mixing glass, then strain into a champagne saucer. **2** Garnish with an orange twist.

BROOKLYN

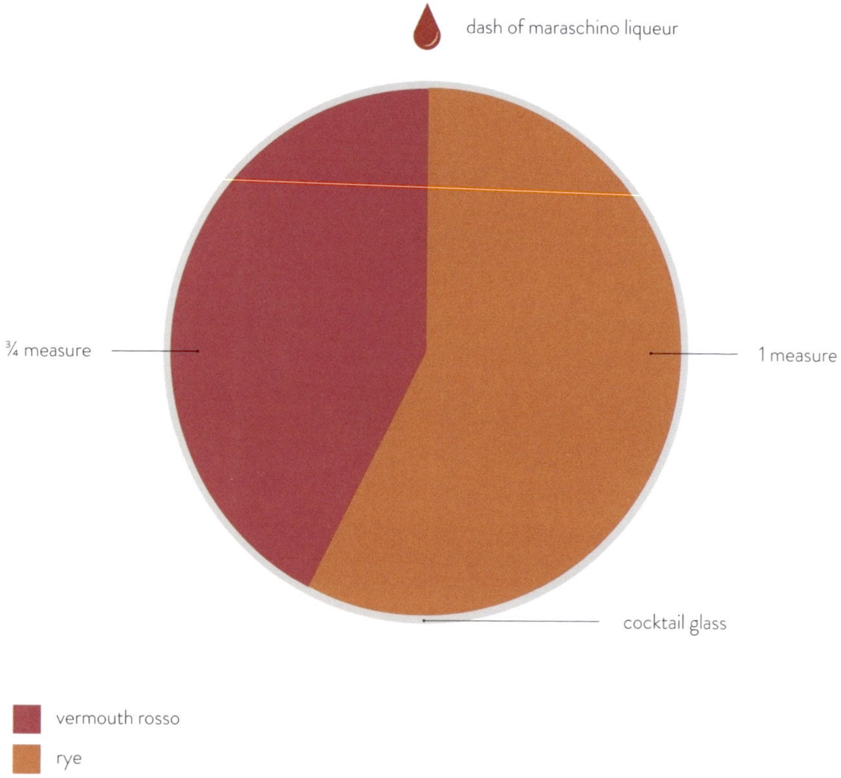

dash of maraschino liqueur

¾ measure

1 measure

cocktail glass

vermouth rosso

rye

Instructions

1 Stir all the ingredients together, then strain into a cocktail glass.

CANADIAN SHERBET

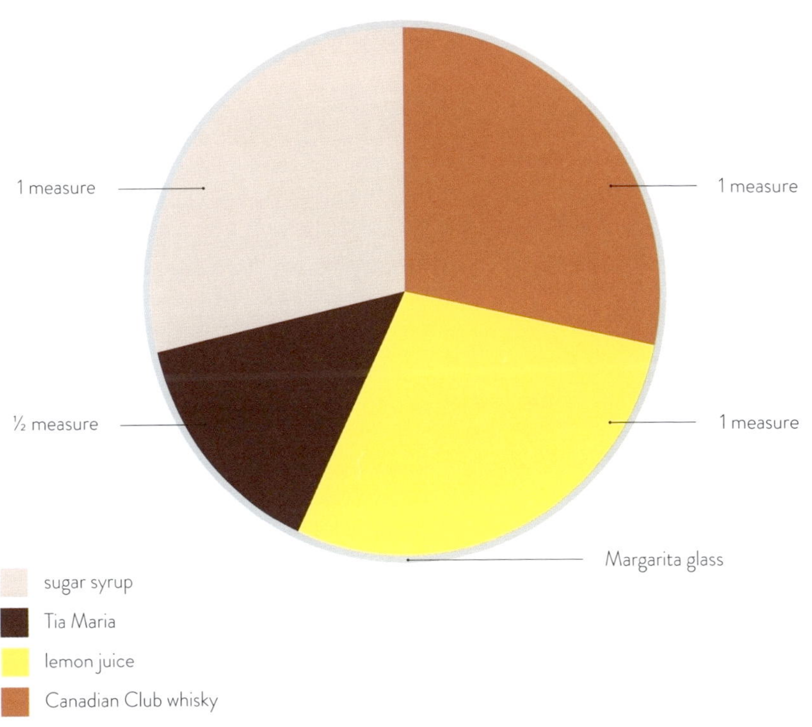

Instructions

1 Blend ingredients with ice and pour into a margarita glass.

CHAPEL HILL

Instructions

1 Shake all the liquids together, then strain into a cocktail glass and serve with an orange twist.

COLONEL FIZZ

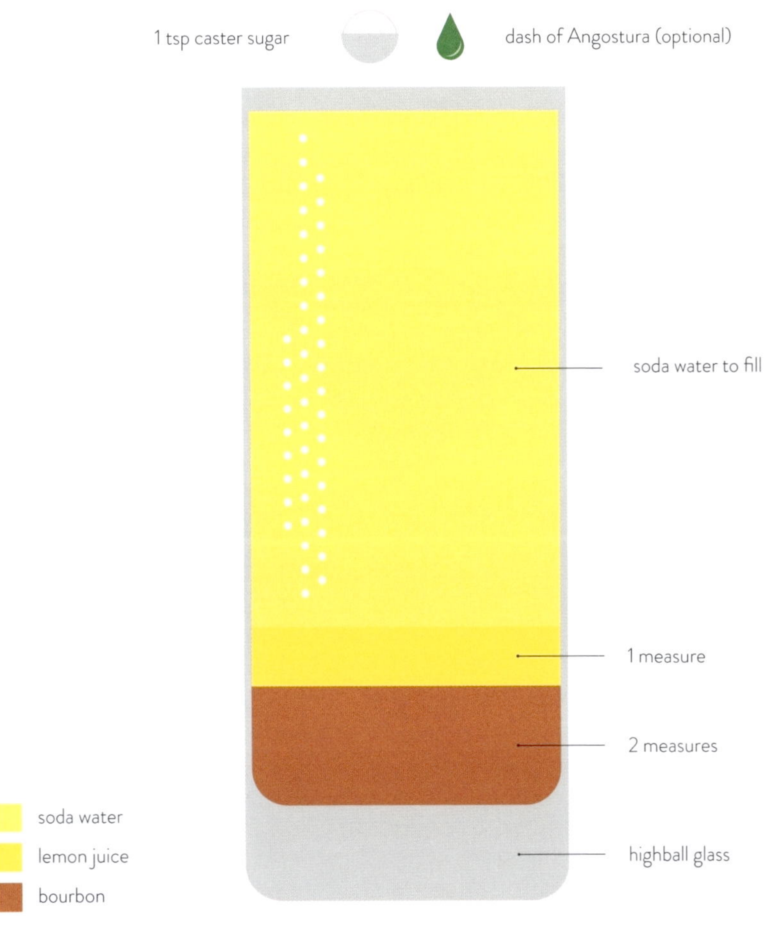

Instructions

1 Shake the juice, bourbon, sugar and Angostura and strain into a tall glass. **2** Top up with soda.

FRISCO

Instructions

1 Shake all ingredients with ice and strain into a cocktail glass. **2** Garnish with a slice of lemon.

GODFATHER

Instructions

1 Pour the Scotch and amaretto into an Old Fashioned glass and serve.

GUMDROP

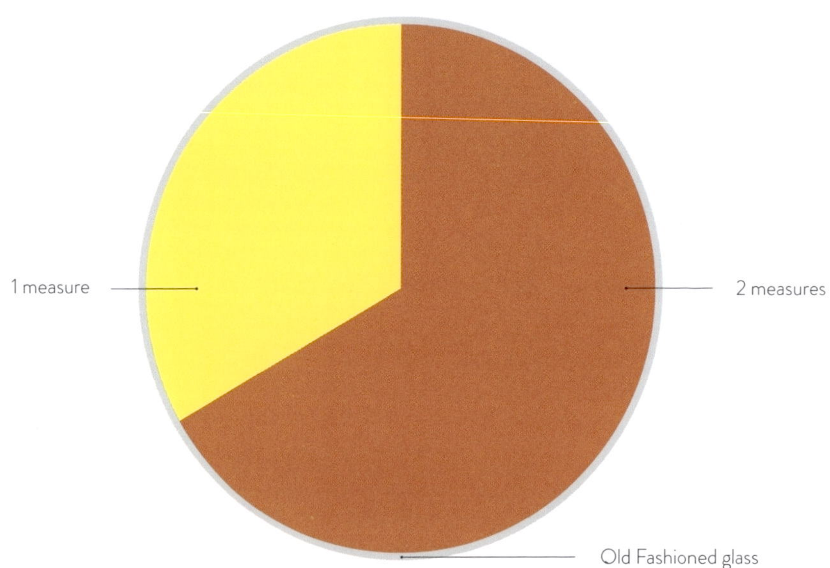

Instructions

1 Pour the Scotch and Galliano into an Old Fashioned glass and serve.

KENTUCKY SUNSET

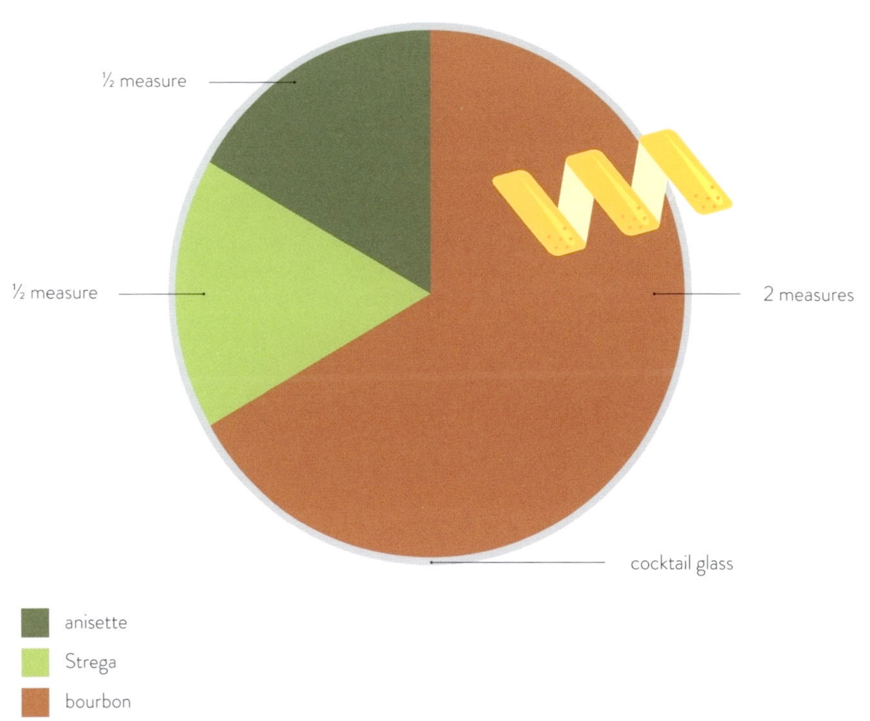

Instructions

1 Stir the bourbon, Strega, and anisette together, then strain into a cocktail glass. **2** Serve, garnished with a lemon twist.

LAST EMPEROR

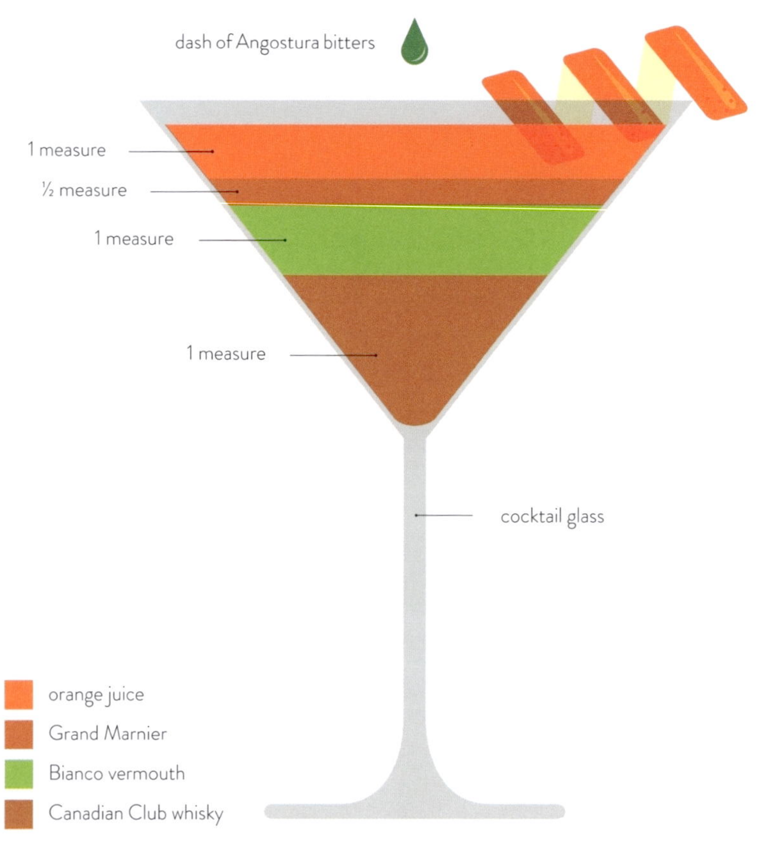

Instructions

1 Place ingredients in a mixing glass with ice and stir well. **2** Strain into a cocktail glass and stir again. **3** Add a strip of orange peel.

LIBERTY BELL

Instructions

1 Stir all the ingredients together, then strain into a cocktail glass and serve.

MILK PUNCH

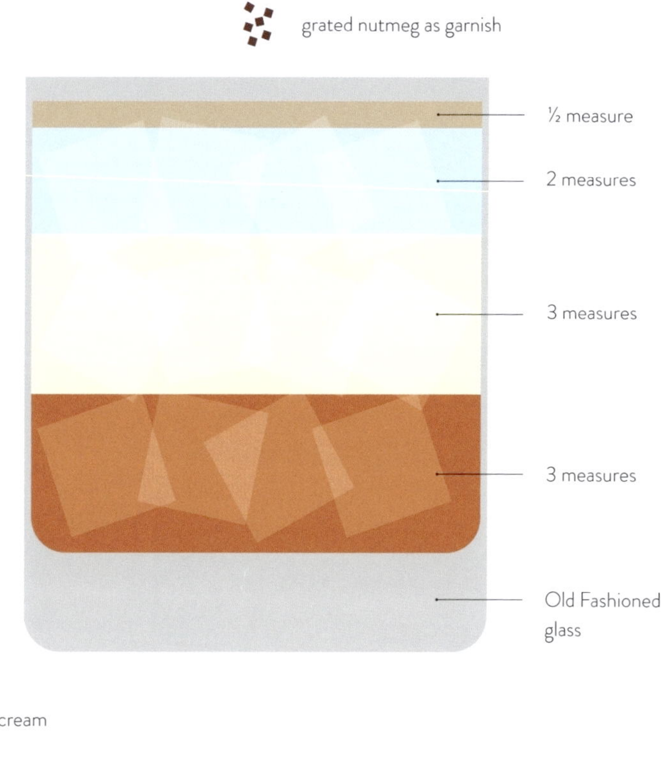

gomme
single cream
milk or single cream
bourbon

Instructions

1. Shake all the liquid ingredients with ice and strain into a ice-filled Old Fashioned glass.
2. Shake grated nutmeg over the drink.

ROB ROY

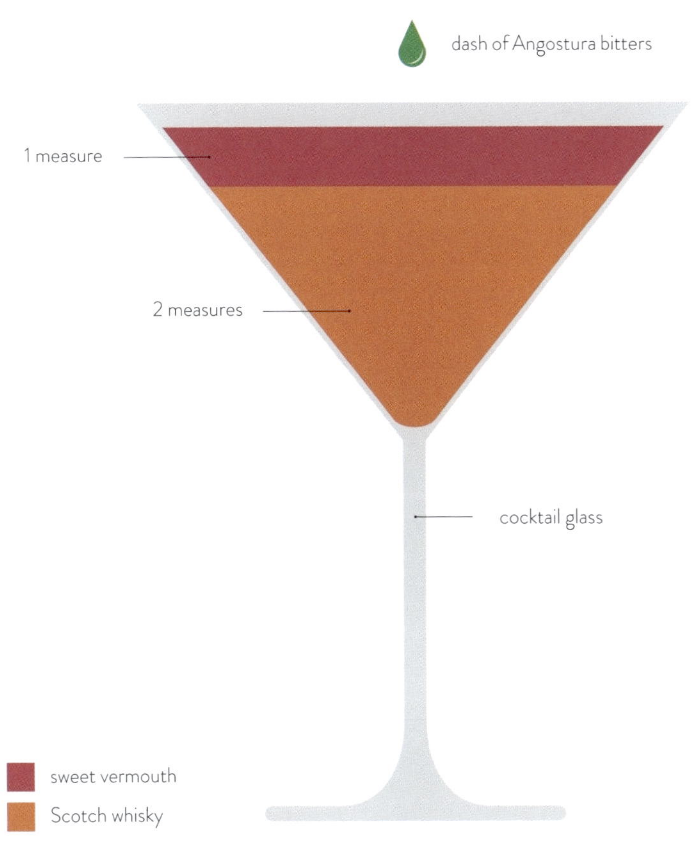

Instructions

1 Stir all the ingredients together, then strain into a cocktail glass and serve.

RUSTY NAIL

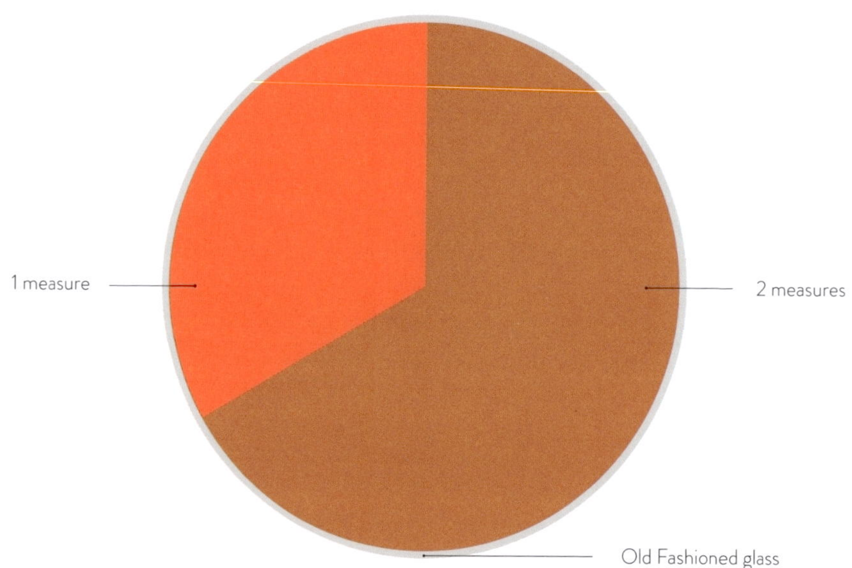

Instructions

1 Pour the Scotch and Drambuie into an Old Fashioned glass and serve.

SAZERAC

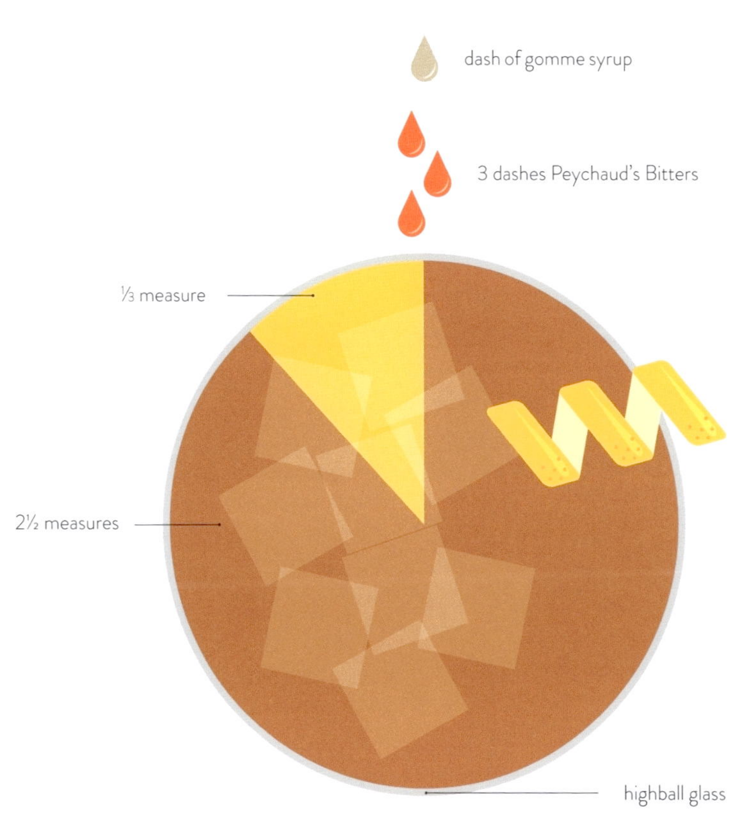

absinthe or Pernod

bourbon

Instructions

1 Pour the absinthe (Pernod) into a highball glass, coat and discard the excess. **2** Shake the other ingredients and pour over ice into the glass.

SHAMROCK

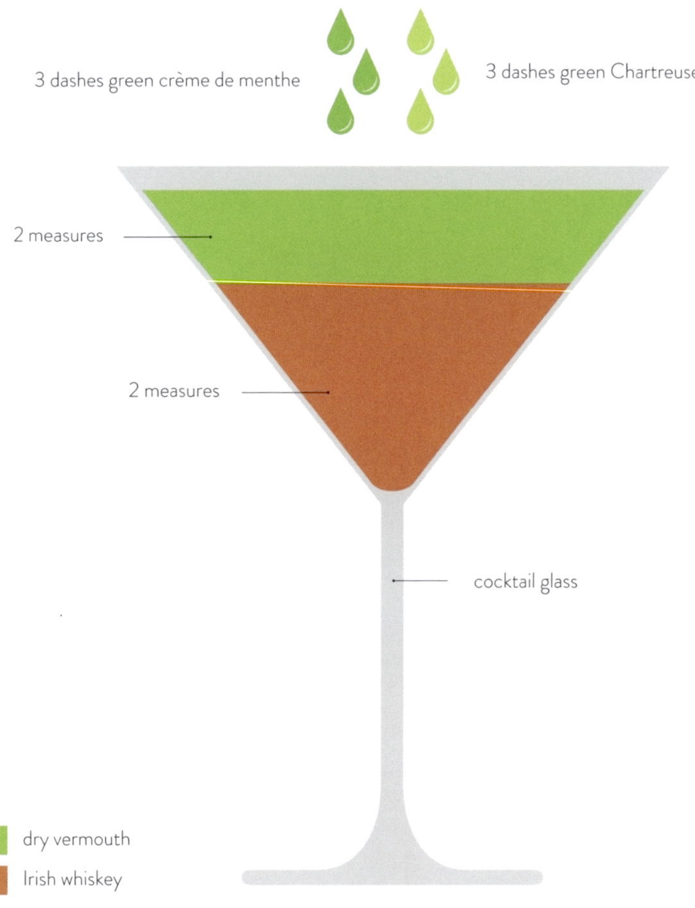

Instructions

1 Mix all the ingredients together in a shaker, strain, and serve in a cocktail glass.

VIP

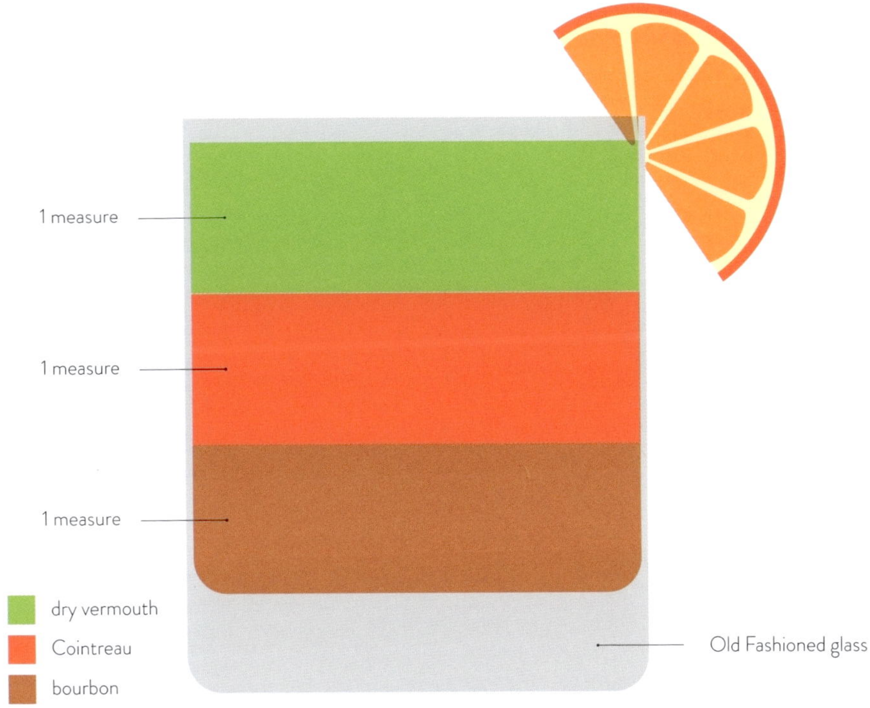

1 measure

1 measure

1 measure

- dry vermouth
- Cointreau
- bourbon

Old Fashioned glass

Instructions

1 Pour the ingredients into an Old Fashioned glass, garnish with the orange slice and serve.

WHISKY MAC

Stones Ginger Wine
Scotch whisky

Instructions

1 Pour the Scotch and ginger wine into an Old Fashioned glass, stir, and serve.

WHIZZ DOODLE

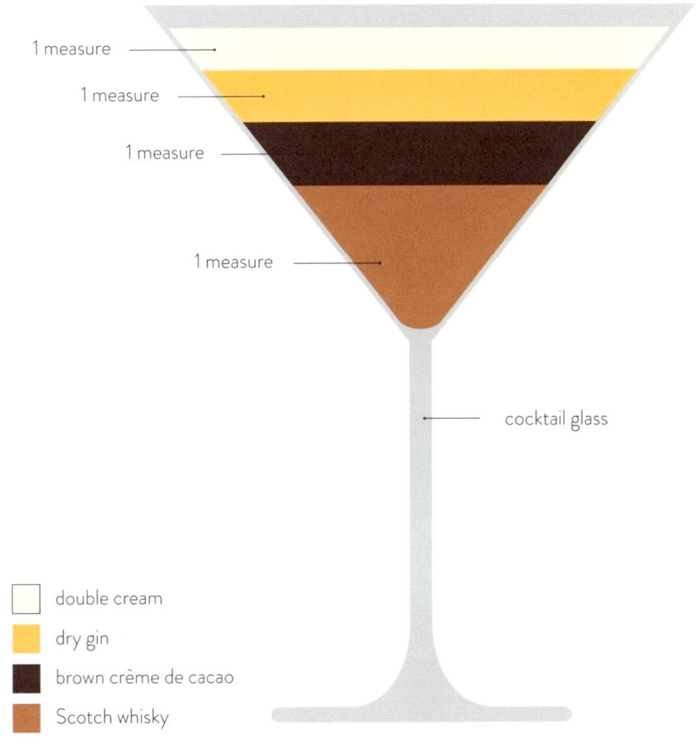

Instructions

1 Mix all the ingredients together in a shaker with ice, strain and pour into a cocktail glass.

TEQUILA

ACAPULCO

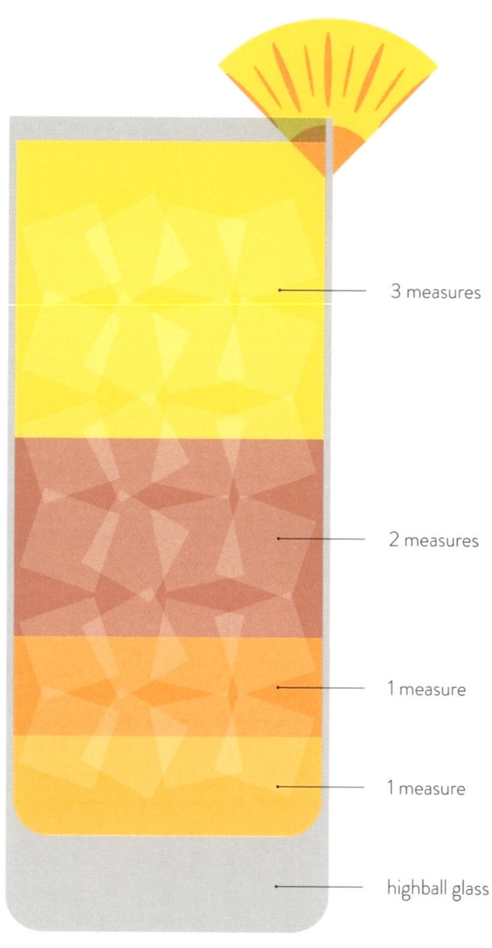

pineapple juice
grapefruit juice
gold rum
gold tequila

Instructions

1 Shake all the ingredients and strain into a highball filled with ice. **2** Garnish with a pineapple wedge.

ALL NIGHT

Instructions

1 Shake all ingredients with ice and strain into a chilled cocktail glass. **2** Garnish with a maraschino cherry.

CHAPALA

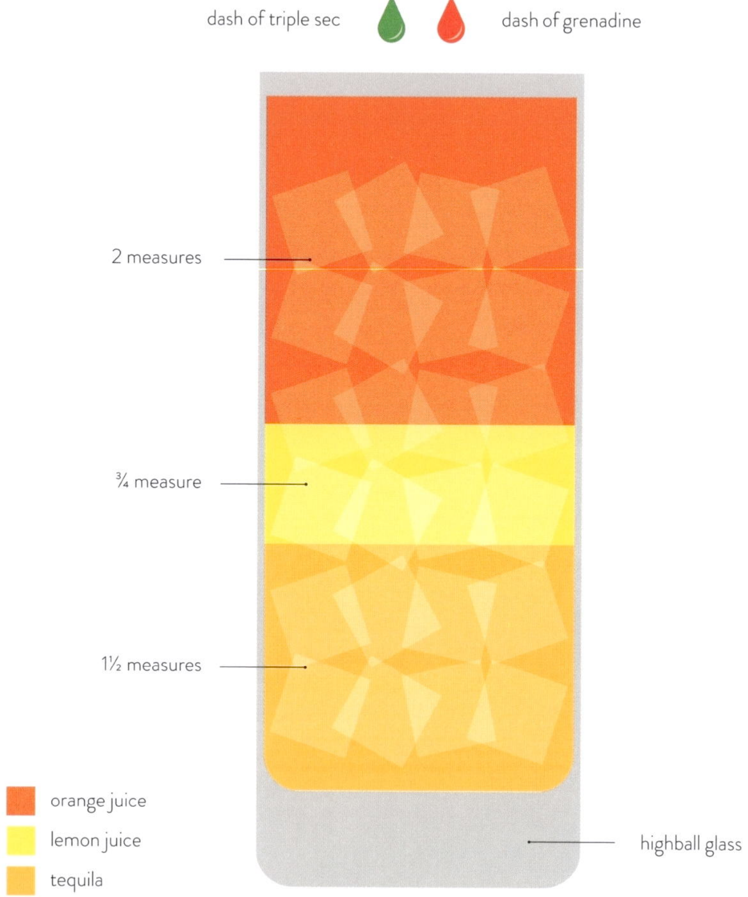

Instructions

1 Stir all the ingredients together over ice in a highball glass.

CLAM DIGGER

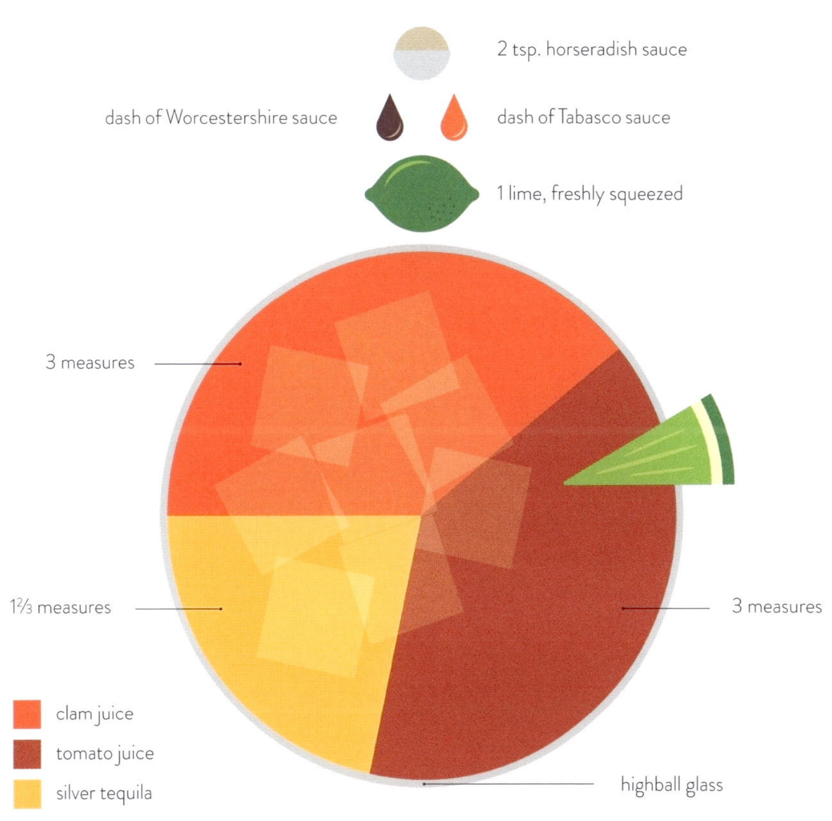

Instructions

1 Shake all the liquid ingredients together and strain into a highball with ice. **2** Garnish with a lime wedge.

COOL GOLD

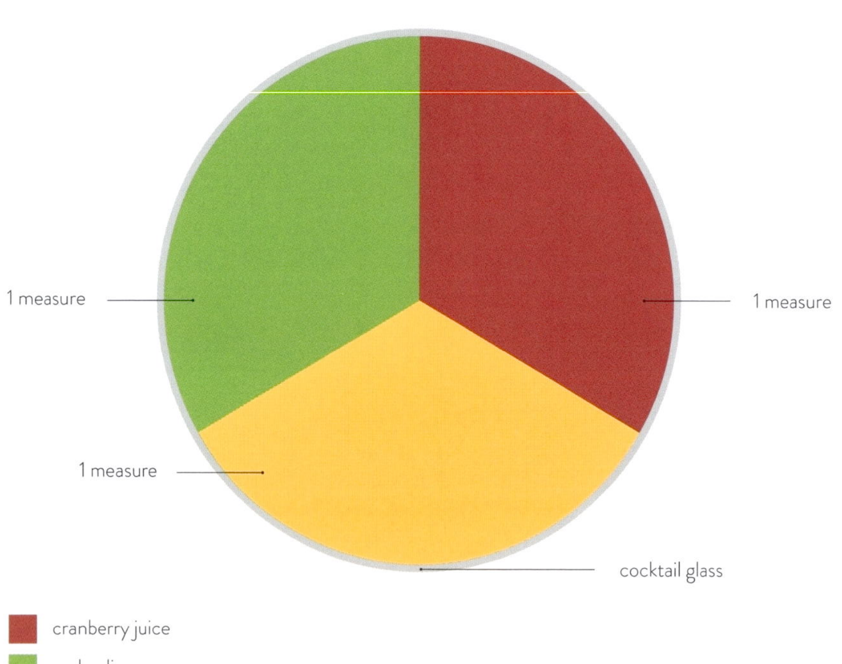

Instructions

1. Shake all the ingredients together and strain into a cocktail glass.

EL DIABLO

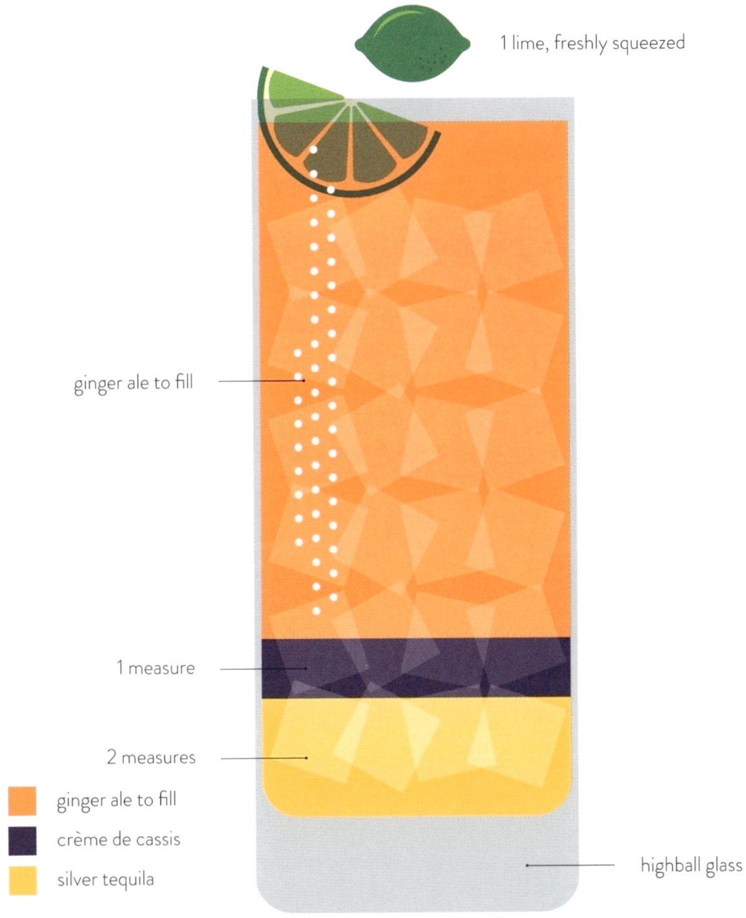

Instructions

1 Pour lime juice into a highball with crushed ice. **2** Add tequila and crème de cassis. **3** Fill with ginger ale. Stir. **4** Drop in a lime wedge and serve with a straw.

ELDORADO

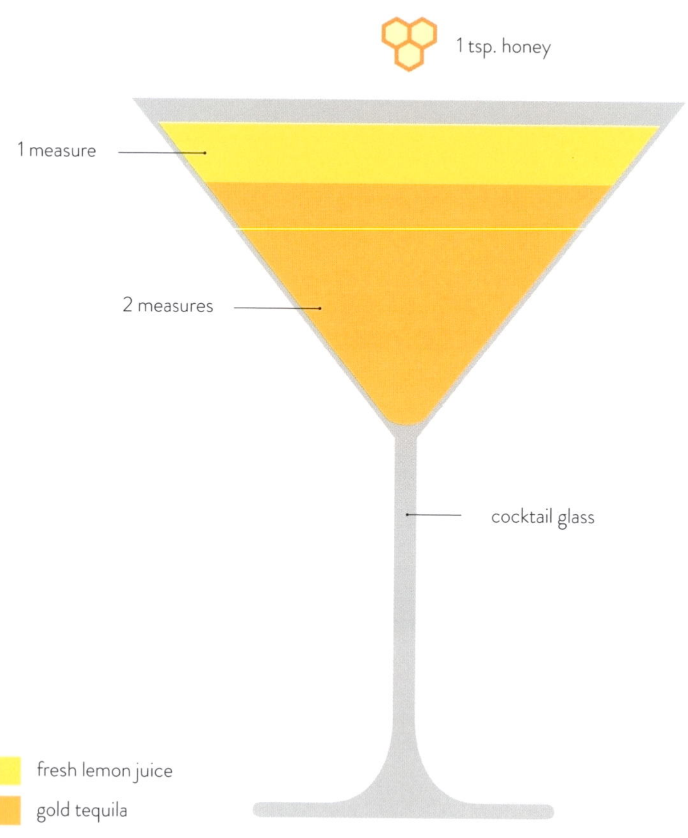

Instructions

1 Shake all the ingredients together, then strain into a cocktail glass and serve.

FROSTBITE

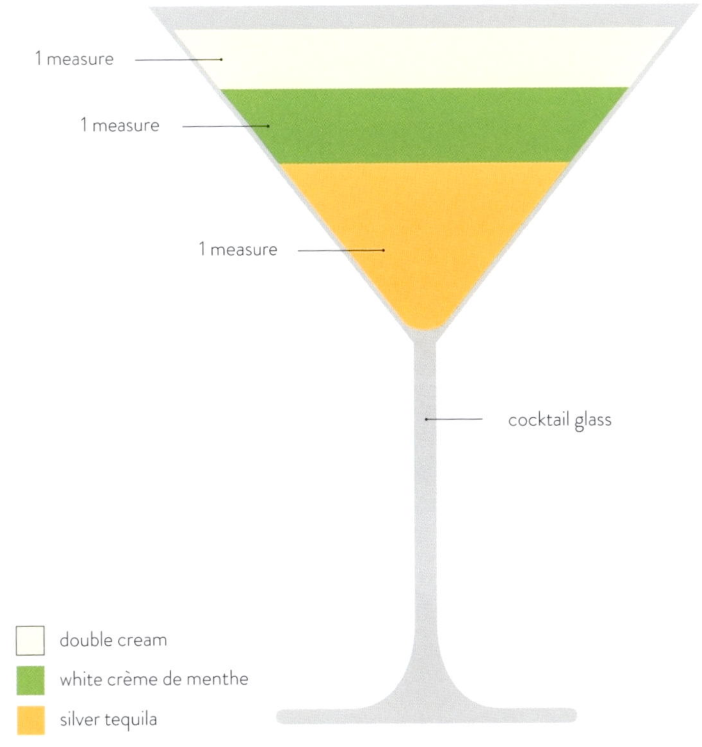

Instructions

1 Mix the ingredients together in a shaker, then strain into a cocktail glass and serve.

LA BOMBA

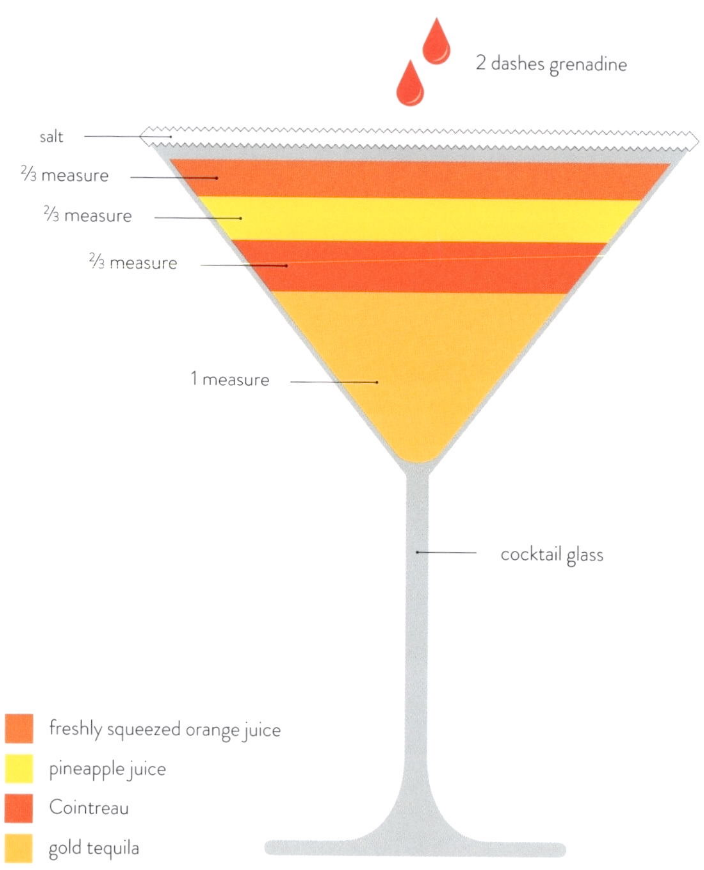

Instructions

1 Shake the tequila, Cointreau, pineapple and oranges juices, then strain into a cocktail glass with a salted rim. **2** Add the grenadine.

LASER BEAM

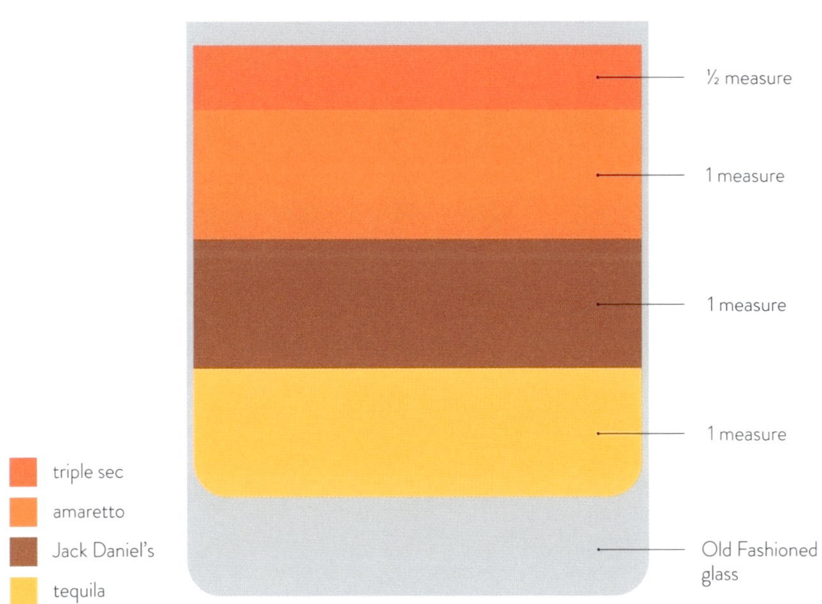

Instructions

1 Shake all the ingredients together, pour into an Old Fashioned glass, and serve.

MATADOR

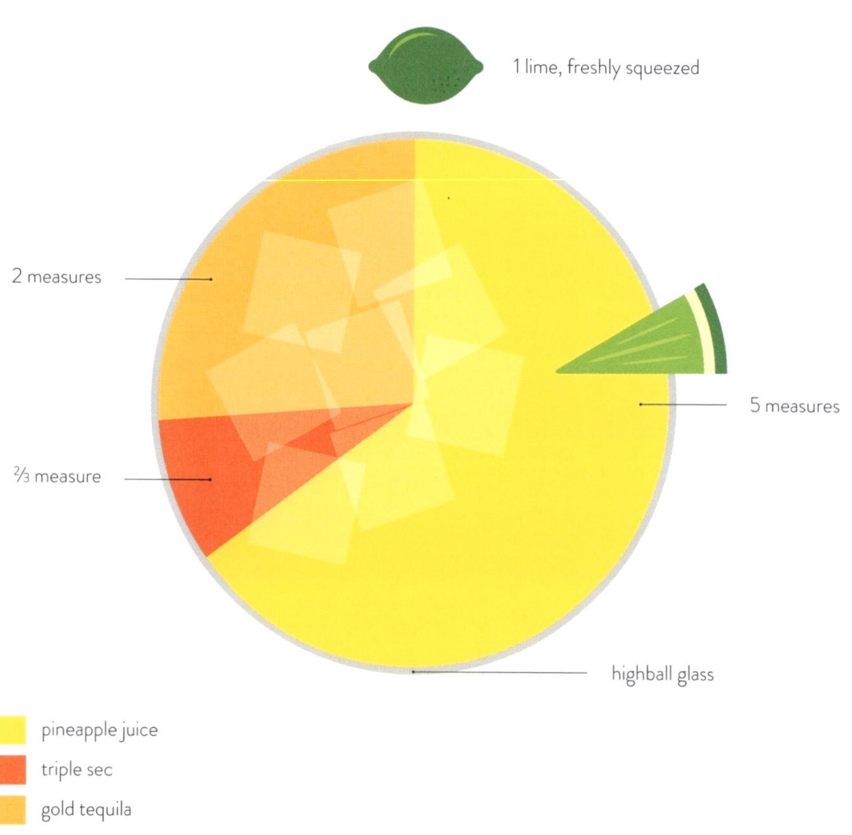

pineapple juice

triple sec

gold tequila

Instructions

1 Shake all the liquid ingredients, then strain into a highball with ice. **2** Add a lime wedge.

MEXICAN MULE

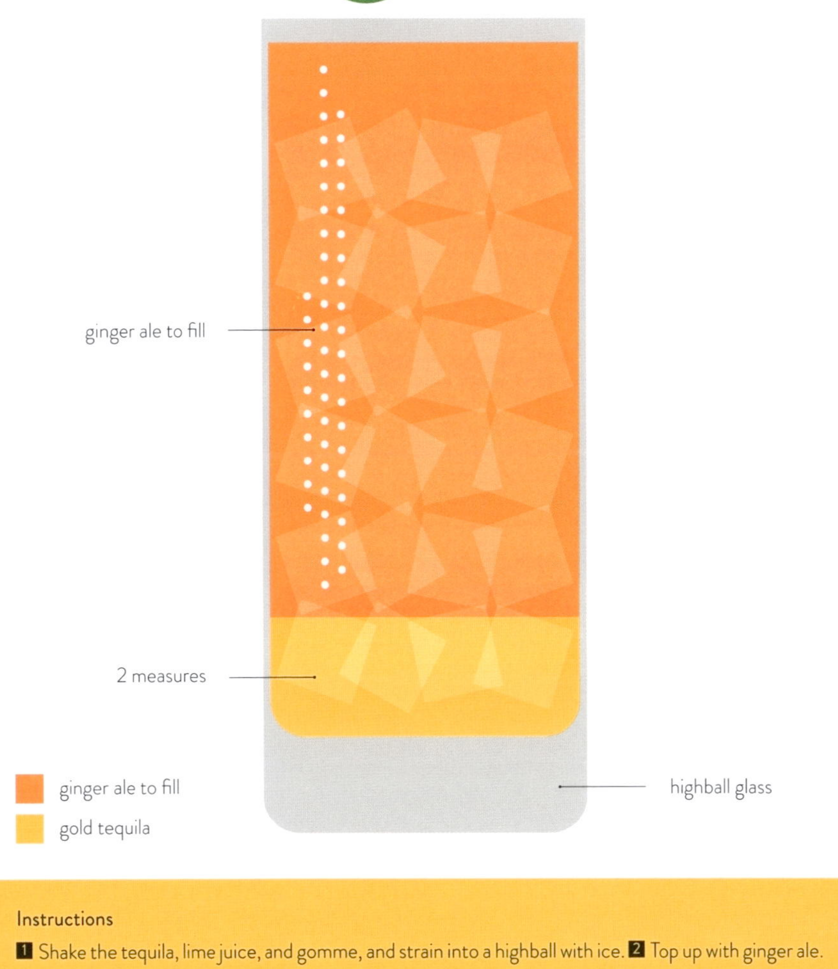

Instructions

1 Shake the tequila, lime juice, and gomme, and strain into a highball with ice. **2** Top up with ginger ale.

MEXICANA

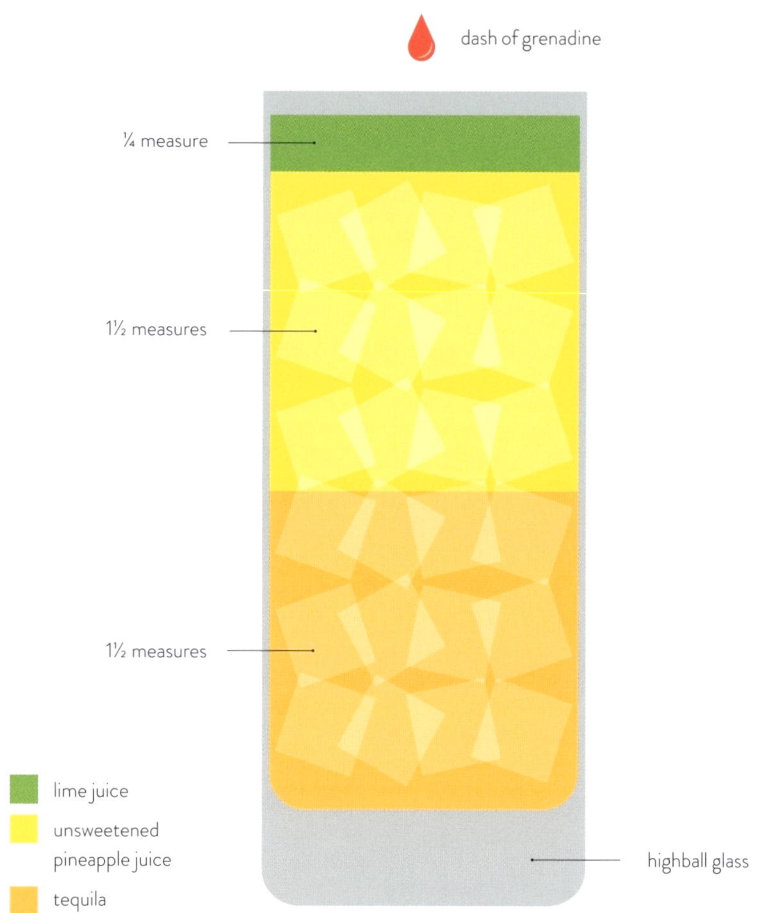

Instructions

1. Shake all the ingredients together and strain into a highball glass filled with ice.

RED DESERT

Instructions

1 Shake all the ingredients and strain into a salt-rimmed highball glass. **2** Garnish with a lime wedge.

ROSALITA

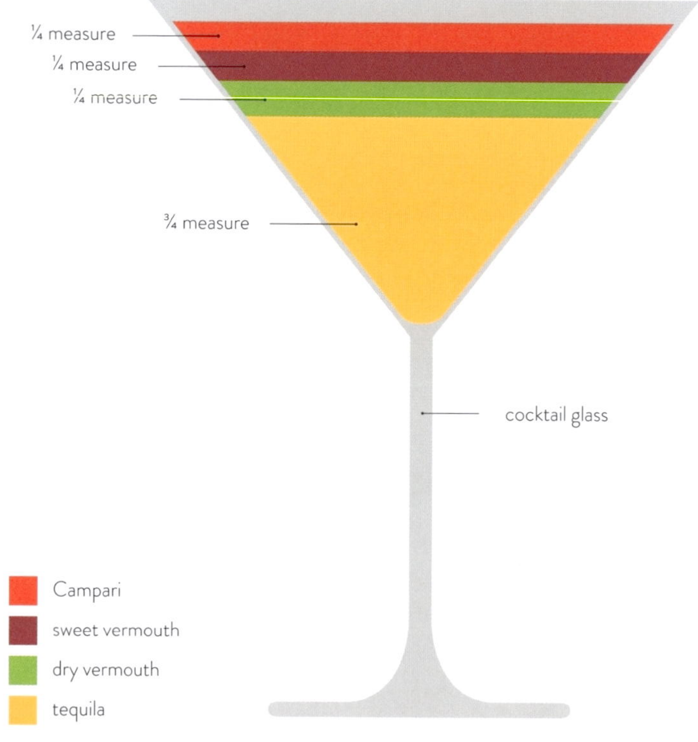

Instructions

1. Shake all the ingredients together and strain into a cocktail glass.

SHORT FUSE

Instructions

1 Shake all the liquid ingredients together and strain into an ice-filled highball glass. **2** Add a lime wedge.

SILK STOCKING

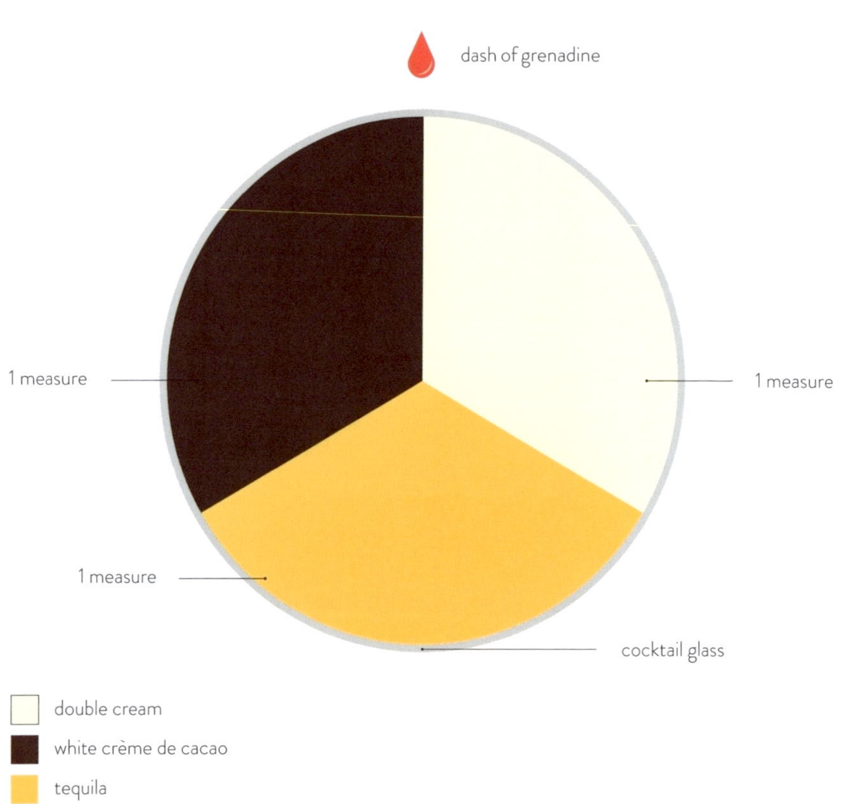

Instructions

1 Mix the ingredients together in a shaker, then strain into a cocktail glass and serve.

SOUTH OF THE BORDER

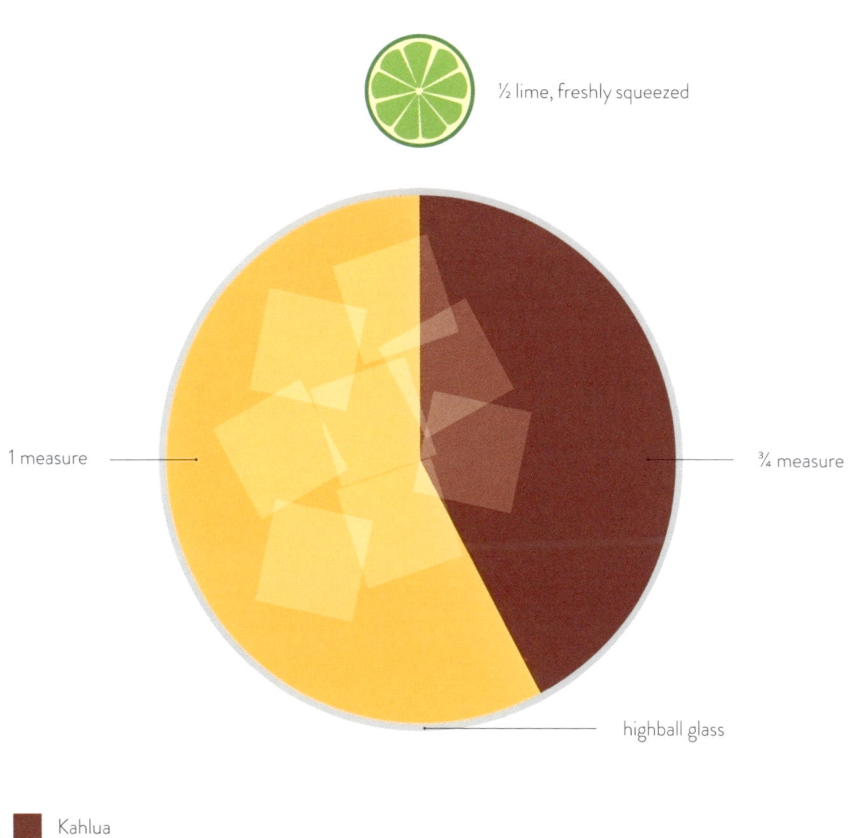

Instructions

1 Squeeze the lime over ice in a highball glass and stir before adding the spirits. **2** Stir again to mix.

TEQUILA SUNRISE

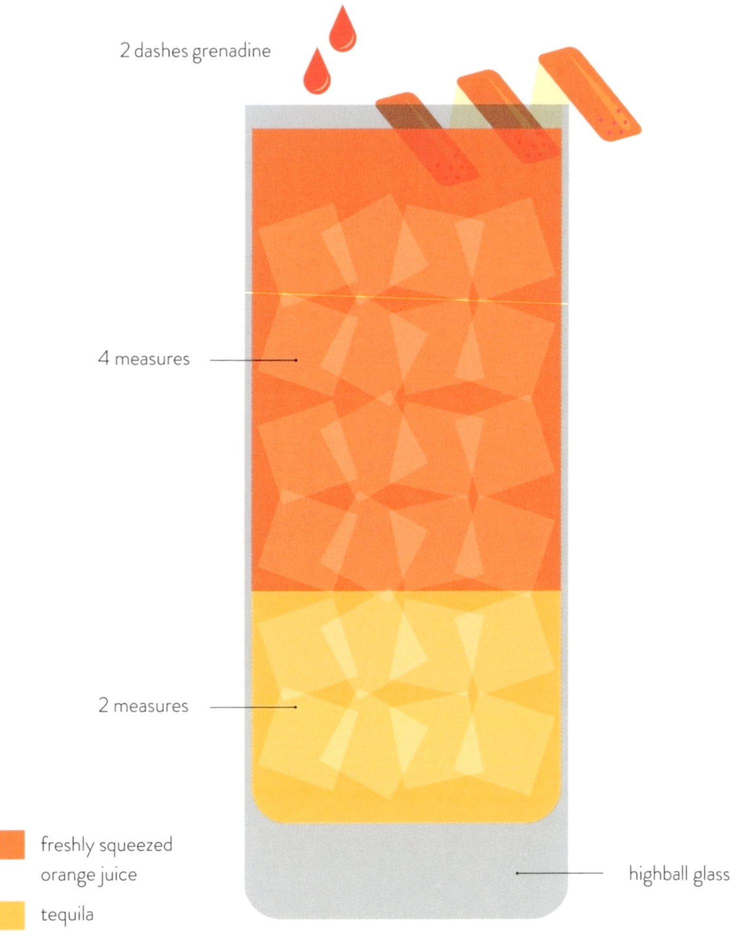

Instructions

1 Pour the tequila and orange juice into a highball glass filled with ice. 2 Stir, then slowly add the grenadine. 3 Add an orange spiral to garnish and serve with a stirrer.

TIJUANA TAXI

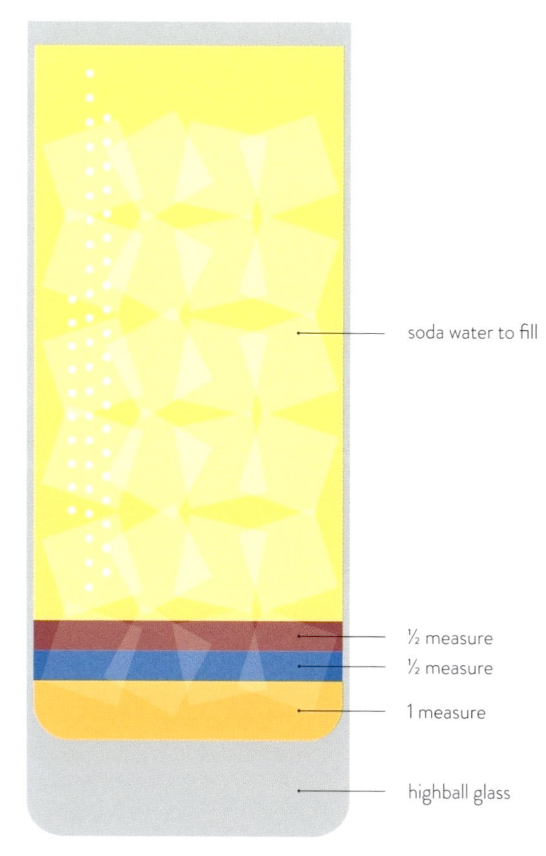

soda water to fill
tropical fruit schnapps
blue curaçao
gold tequila

Instructions

1 Pour the tequila, curaçao, and schnapps into a highball glass filled with ice. **2** Top up with soda.

TOMAHAWK

pineapple juice
cranberry juice
triple sec or Cointreau
tequila

Instructions

1 Shake all the ingredients together and strain into a highball glass filled with ice.

VAMPIRO

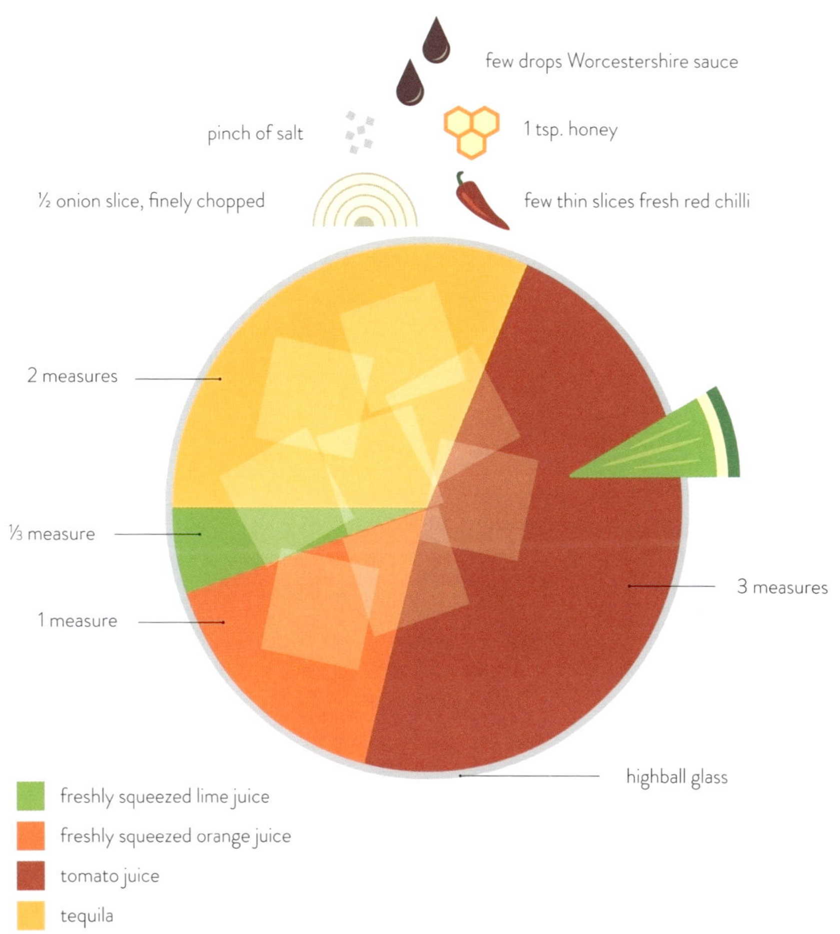

Instructions

1. Shake all the ingredients, except the lime wedge, and strain into an ice-filled highball glass.
2. Garnish with a lime wedge.

CHAMPAGNE

BASTILE

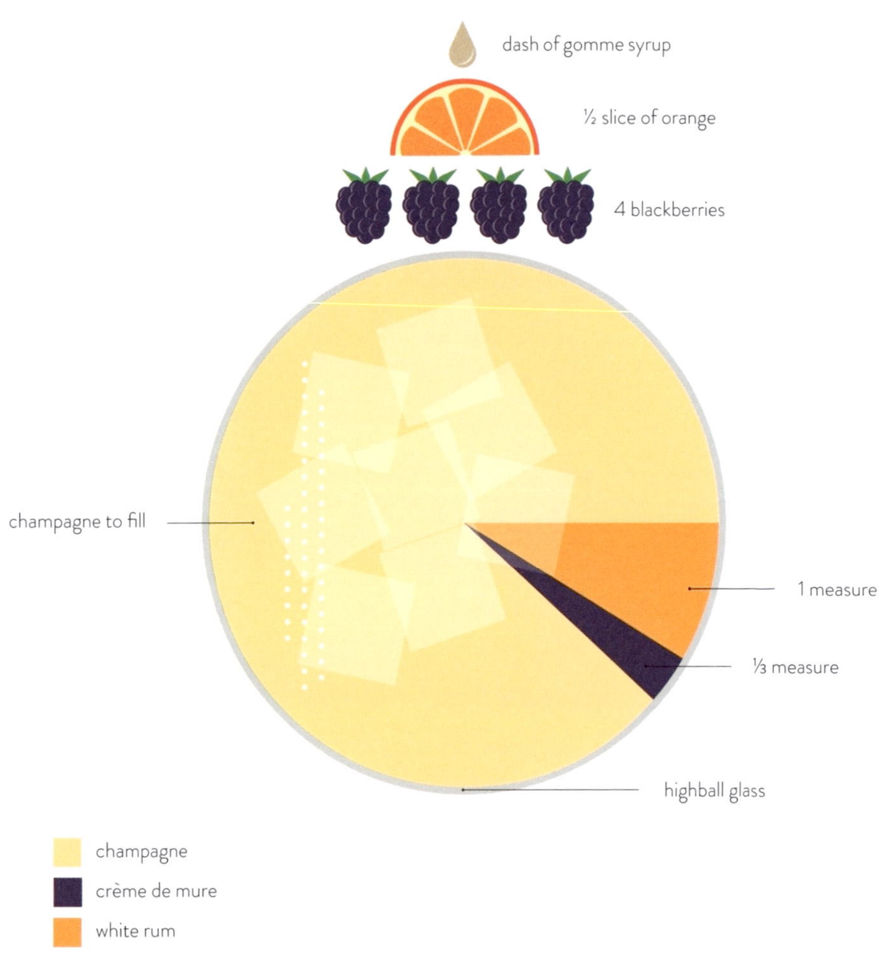

Instructions

1 Muddle the blackberries with the gomme and the crème de mure in a shaker. **2** Add the rum and squeeze a half-slice of orange over the mixture. **3** Add ice cubes, shake, and strain into a highball glass with crushed ice, then top up with champagne and stir gently.

BLACK VELVET

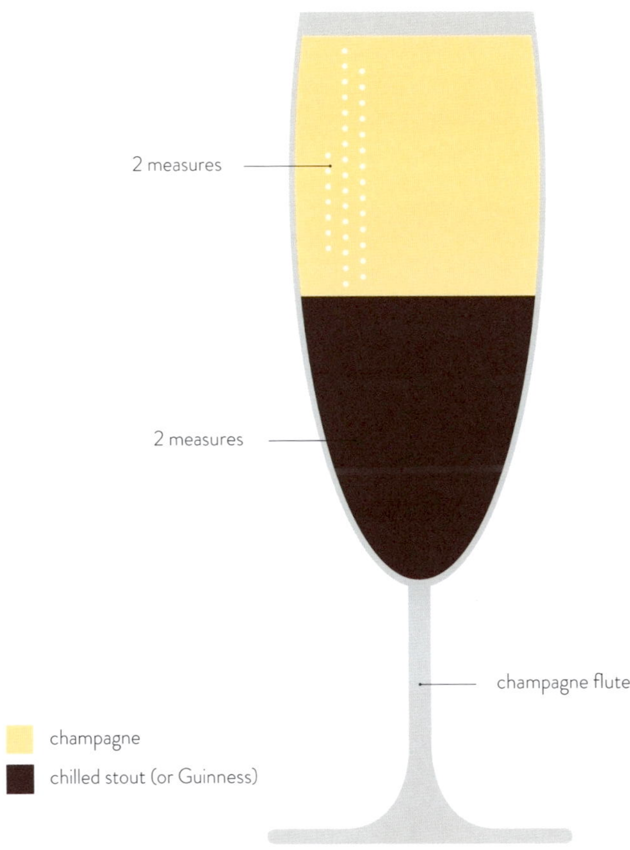

Instructions

1 Pour the stout and then the champagne into a champagne flute and serve.

CASANOVA

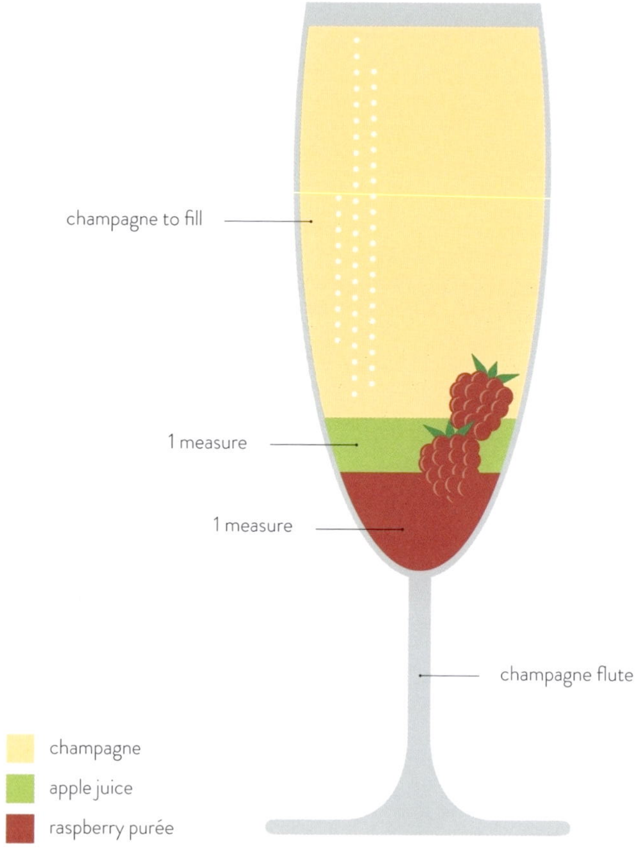

Instructions

1 Pour the raspberry purée into a champagne flute. 2 Add the apple juice and stir, then top up with champagne and stir gently. 3 Drop two small raspberries into the glass and serve.

CHAMPAGNE COBBLER

Instructions

1 Fill a large goblet with crushed ice, then pour the champagne until it is three-quarters full.

2 Stir in the Cointreau and garnish with fruit and mint.

CHAMPAGNE COCKTAIL

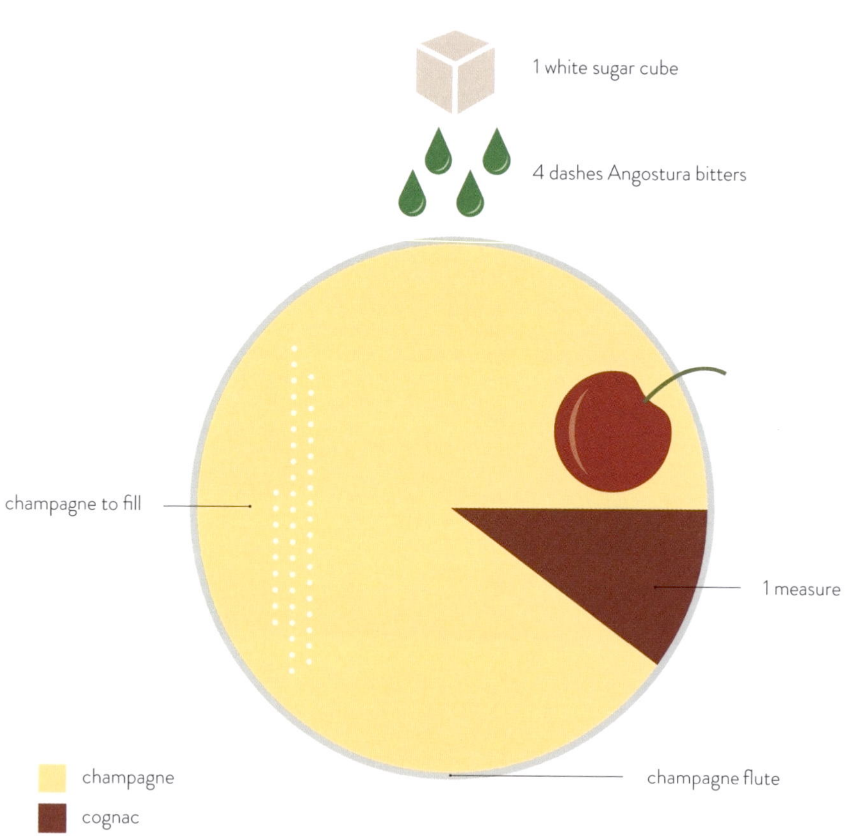

Instructions

1 Place the sugar cube in a champagne flute and soak with the Angostura bitters. **2** Pour on the cognac and top up with champagne. **3** Garnish with the maraschino cherry and serve.

CHAMPAGNE COOLER

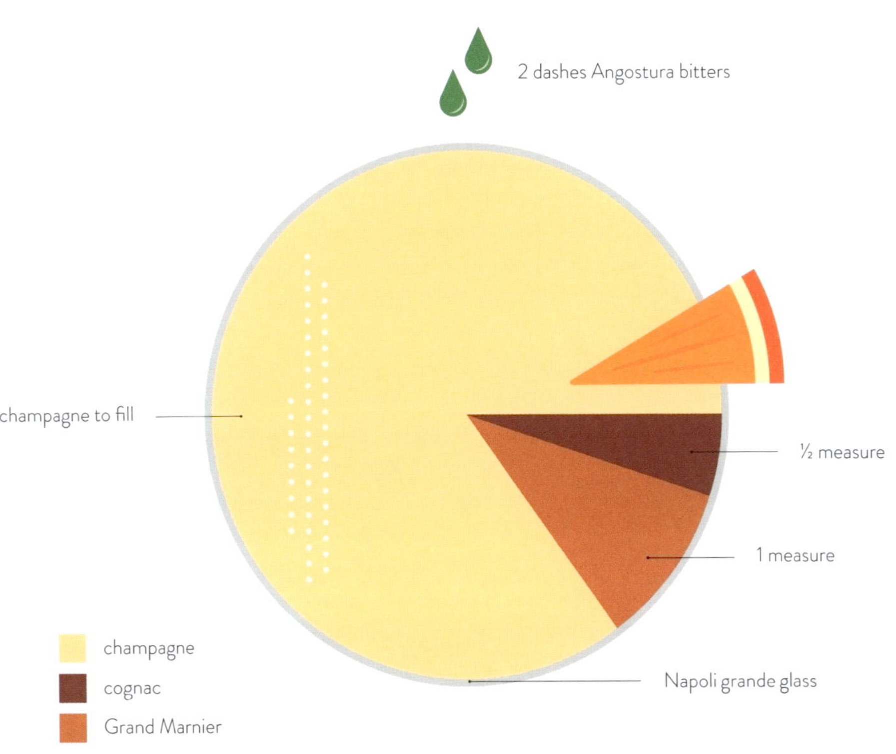

Instructions

1 Pour the Grand Marnier, cognac and bitters into a napoli grande glass. **2** Top up with champagne and garnish with an orange slice.

COOL CUCUMBER

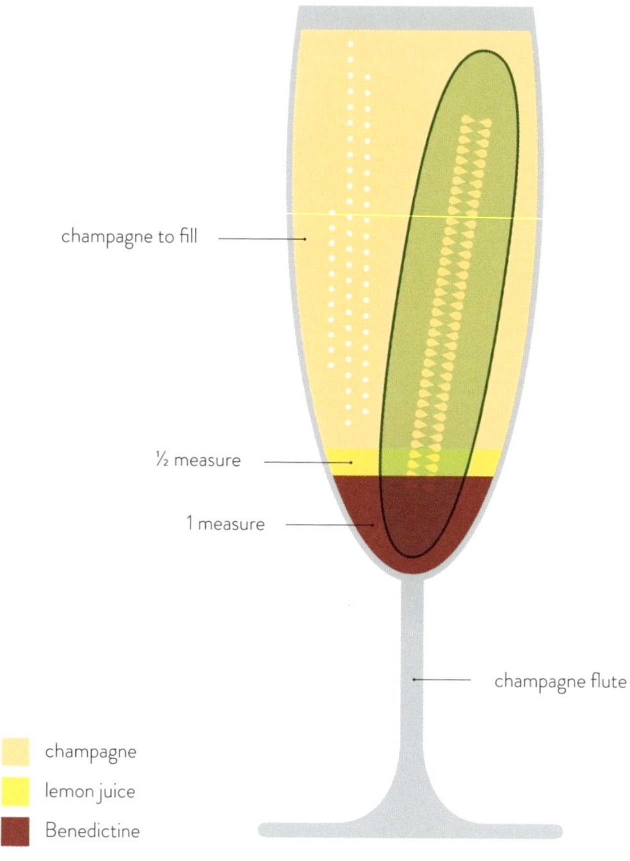

Instructions

1. Pour the Benedictine and lemon juice into a chilled champagne flute and top up with champagne.
2. Add a strip of cucumber as a garnish.

DEATH IN THE AFTERNOON

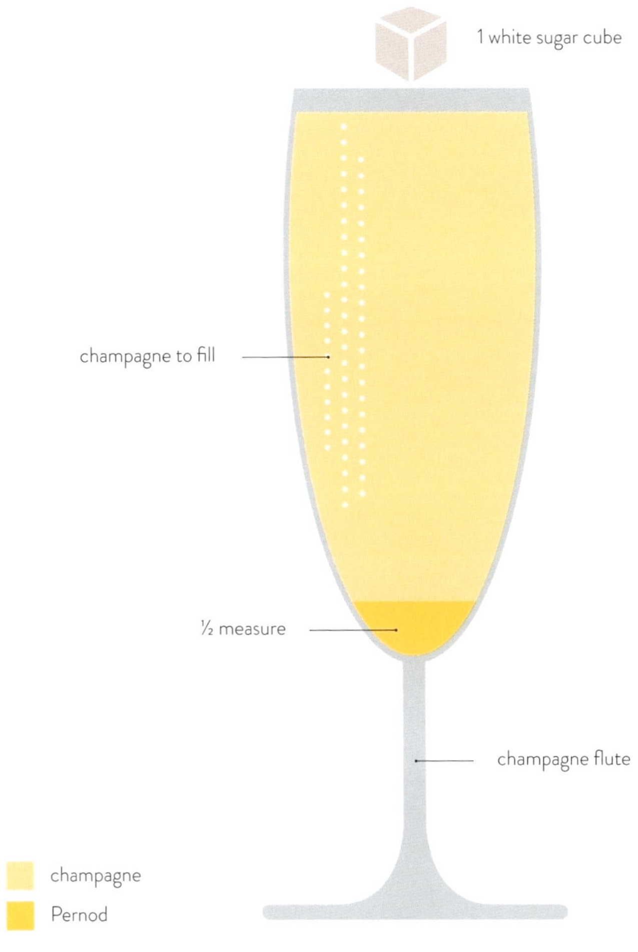

Instructions

1 Place the sugar cube in a champagne flute and add the Pernod, then top up with champagne.

FRENCH SHERBET

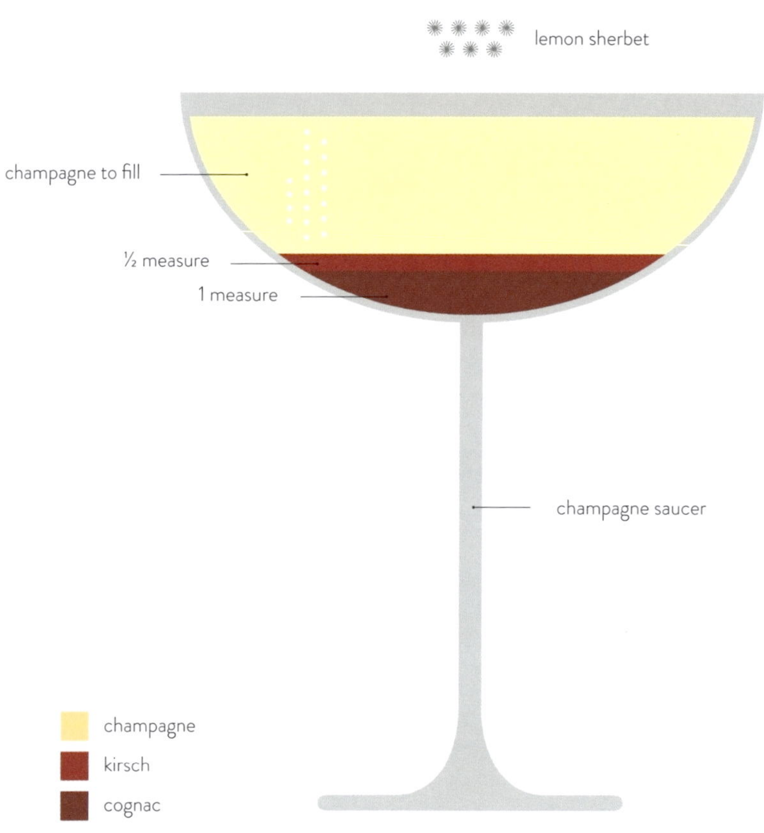

Instructions

1 Stir the sherbert, kirsch and cognac in a deep champagne saucer, and fill with champagne.

HONEYMOON PARADISE

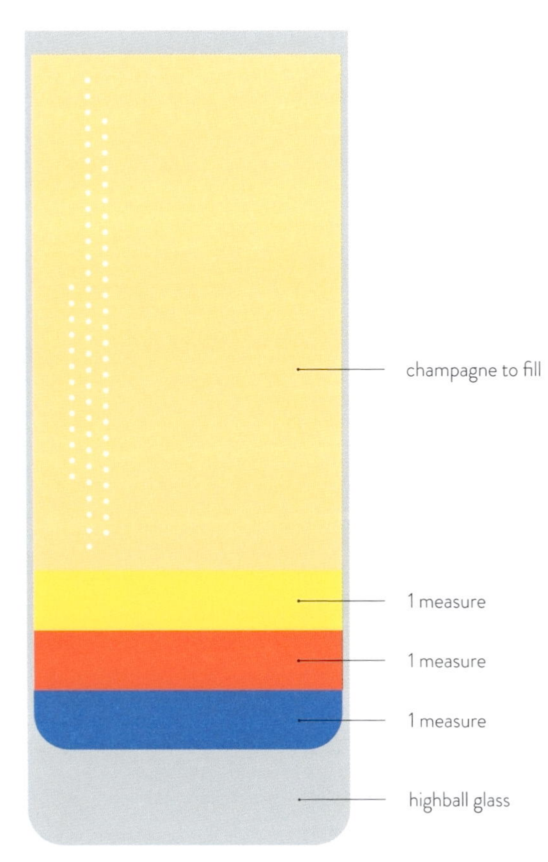

champagne

fresh lemon juice

Cointreau

blue curaçao

Instructions

1 Pour the blue curaçao and Cointreau into a highball glass, then top up with champagne and serve.

JAMES BOND

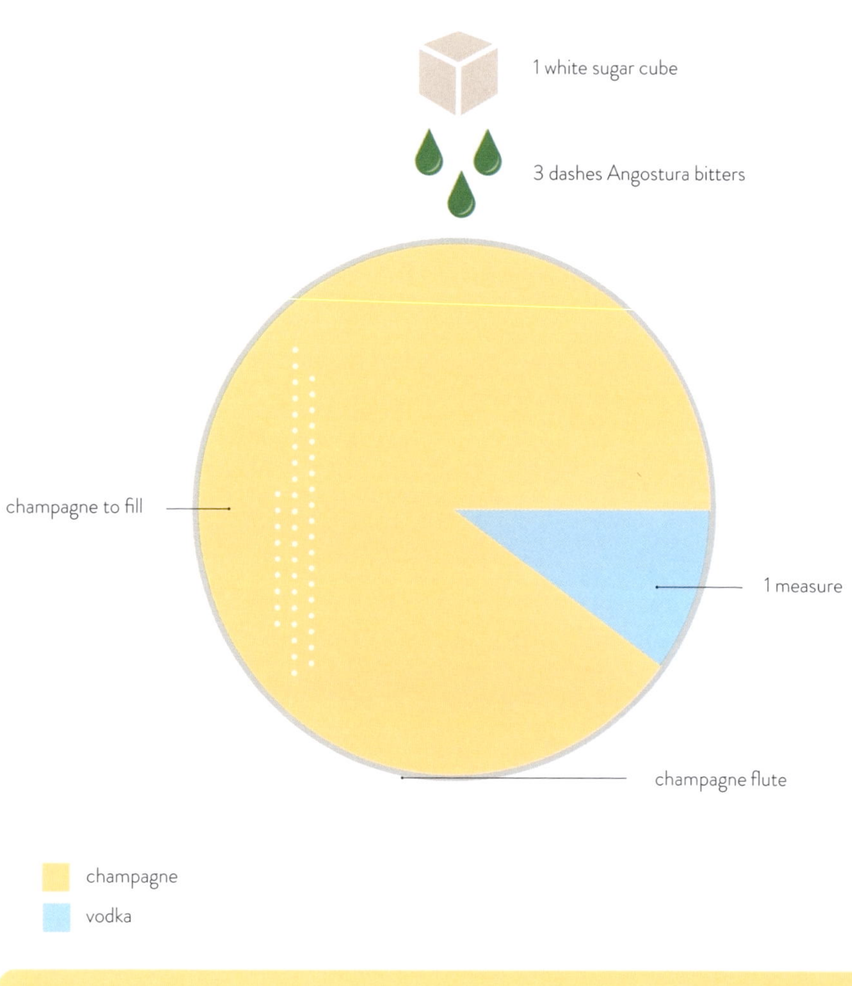

Instructions

1 In a champagne flute soak the sugar cube in the bitters, then pour on the vodka.

2 Top up with champagne and serve.

KIR ROYALE

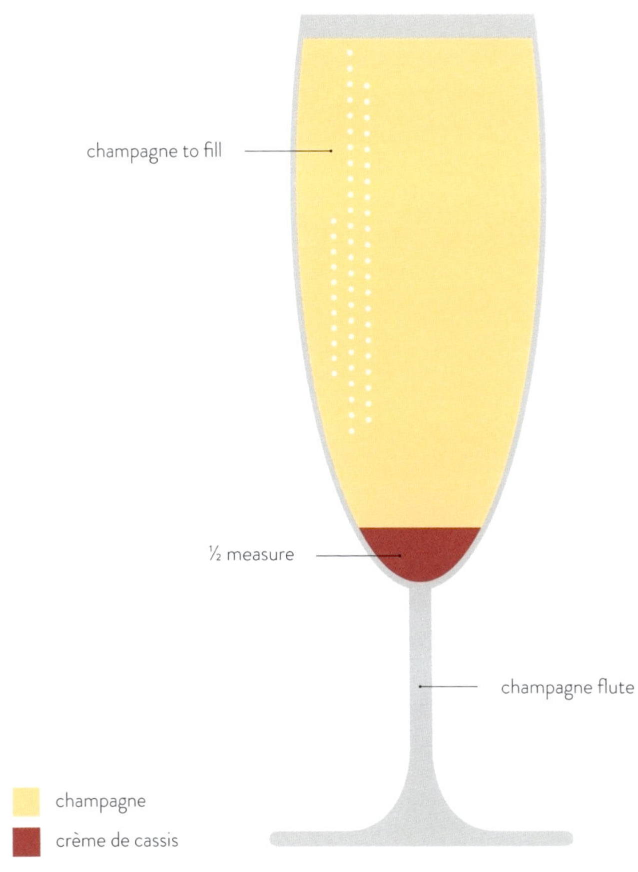

Instructions

1 Put the crème de cassis in a champagne flute, then pour on the champagne and serve.

LA DOLCE VITA

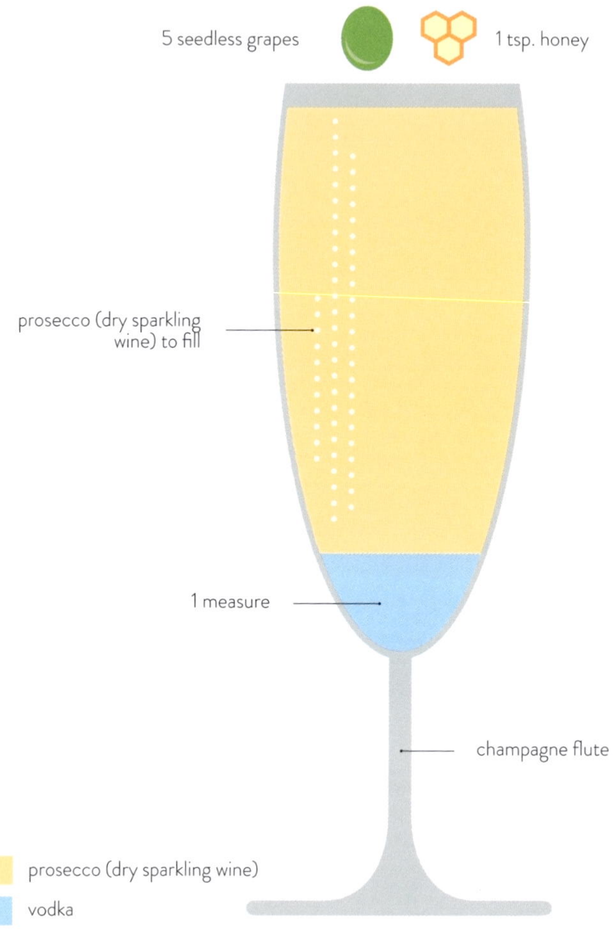

Instructions

1 Muddle the grapes in a shaker, then add the vodka and honey. **2** Shake and strain into a champagne glass, then top up with prosecco.

MIMOSA

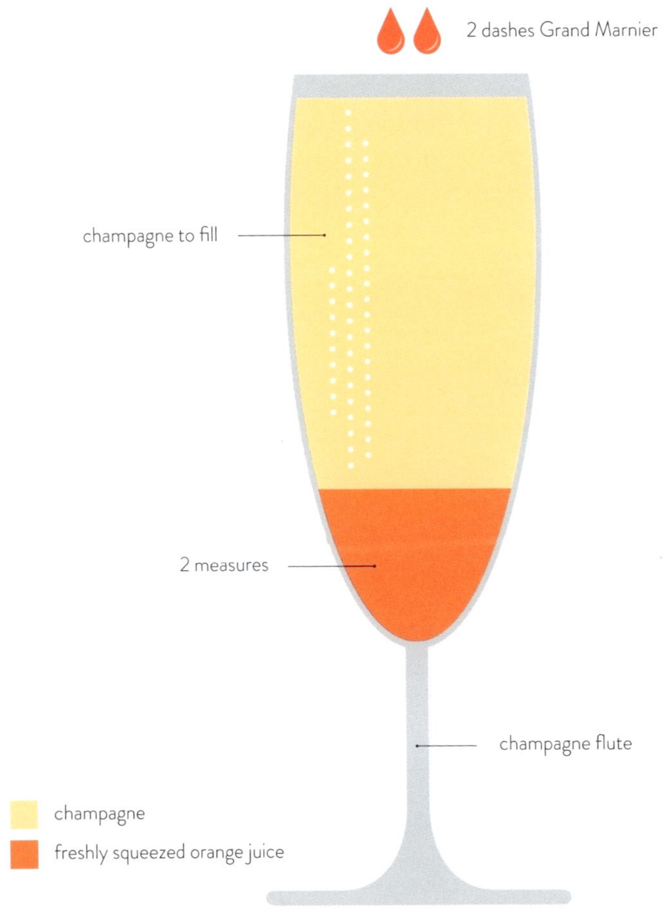

Instructions

1 Fill a champagne glass to a quarter-full with orange juice. **2** Add the Grand Marnier, then top up with champagne.

POINSETTIA

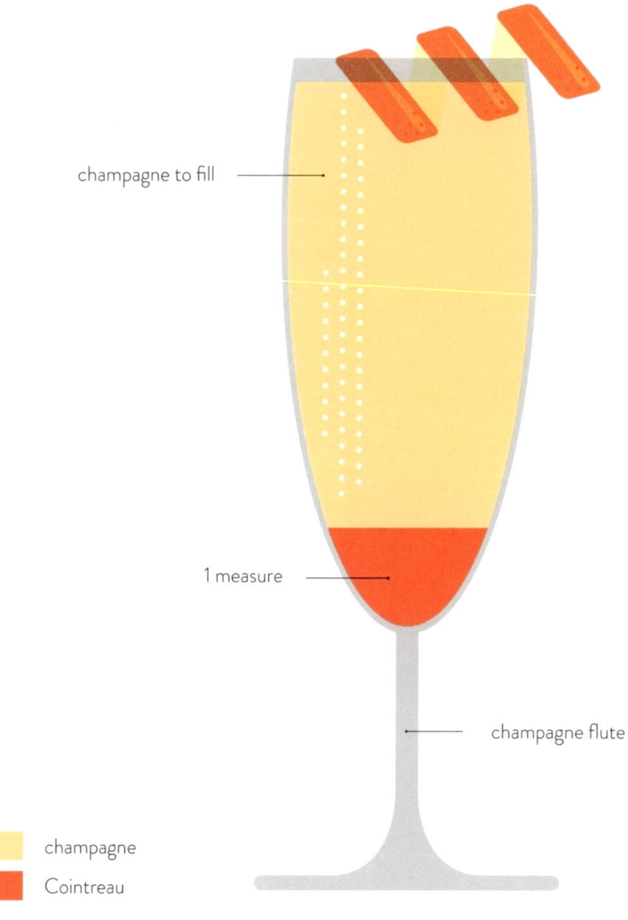

Instructions

1 Pour the Cointreau into a champagne flute and top up with champagne. **2** Add an orange twist and serve.

RASPBERRY SIP

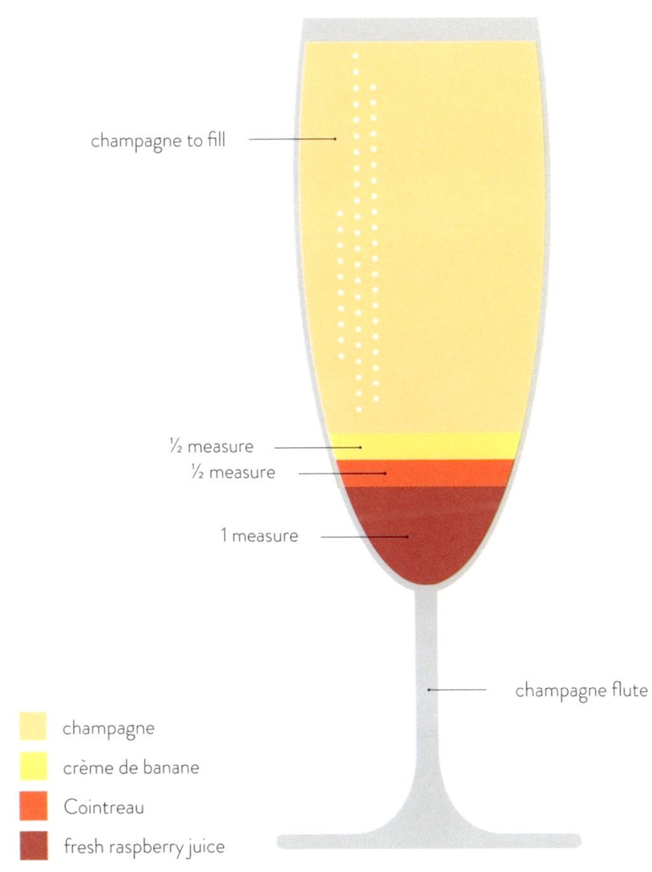

Instructions

1 Pour ingredients, except champagne, into a shaker with ice. **2** Strain into a champagne flute, and top up with champagne.

RITZ FIZZ

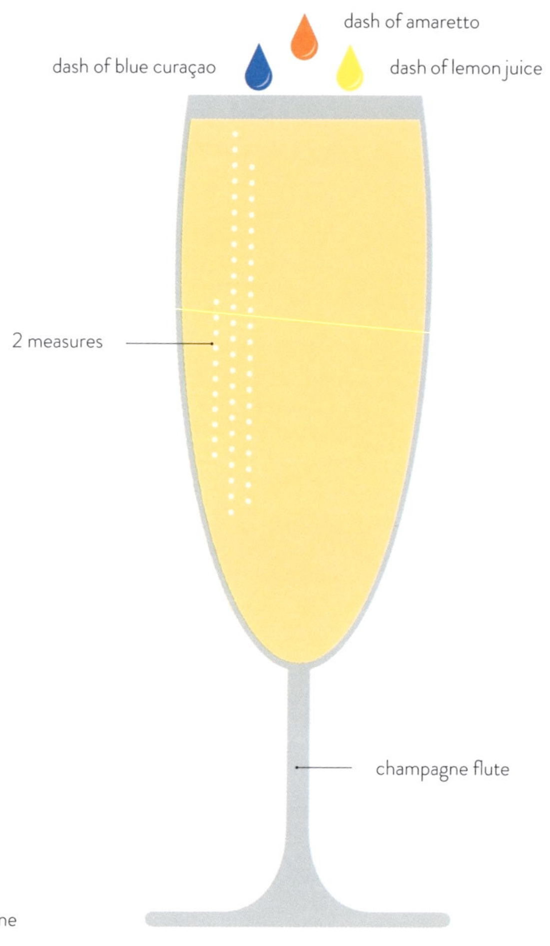

Instructions

1. Pour the amaretto, curaçao and lemon juice into a champagne flute, top up with champagne, and serve.

SOIXANTE-NEUF

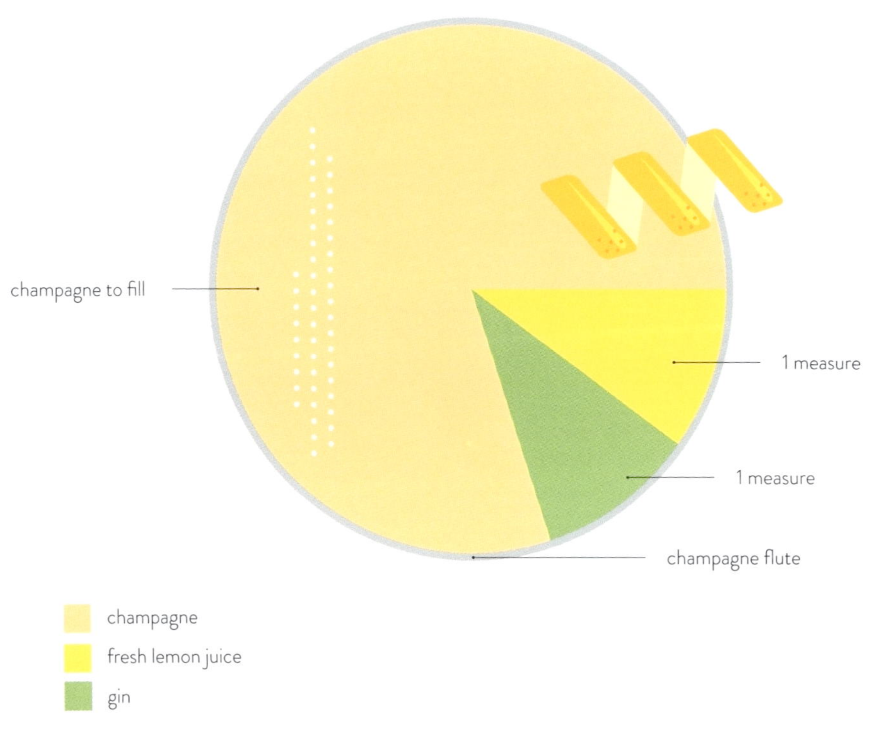

Instructions

1 Shake the gin and lemon juice together, then strain into a champagne flute. **2** Top up with champagne, garnish with a lemon twist and serve.

SWEET SURRENDER

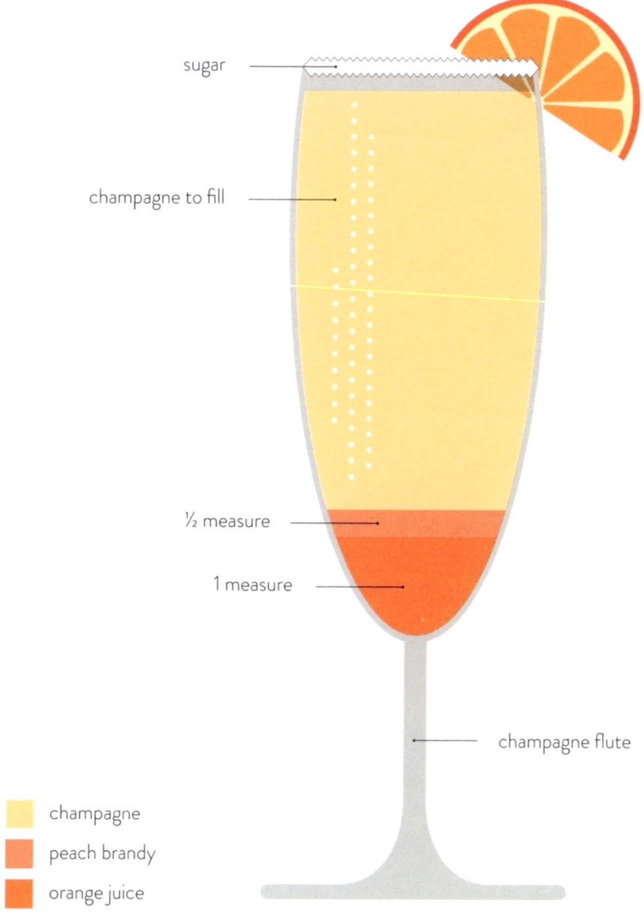

Instructions

1 Rub an orange slice around the rim of a champage flute, then coat the rim in sugar. **2** Mix the orange juice and peach brandy together in an ice-filled shaker, strain, and pour into the glass. **3** Top up with champagne.

TYPHOON

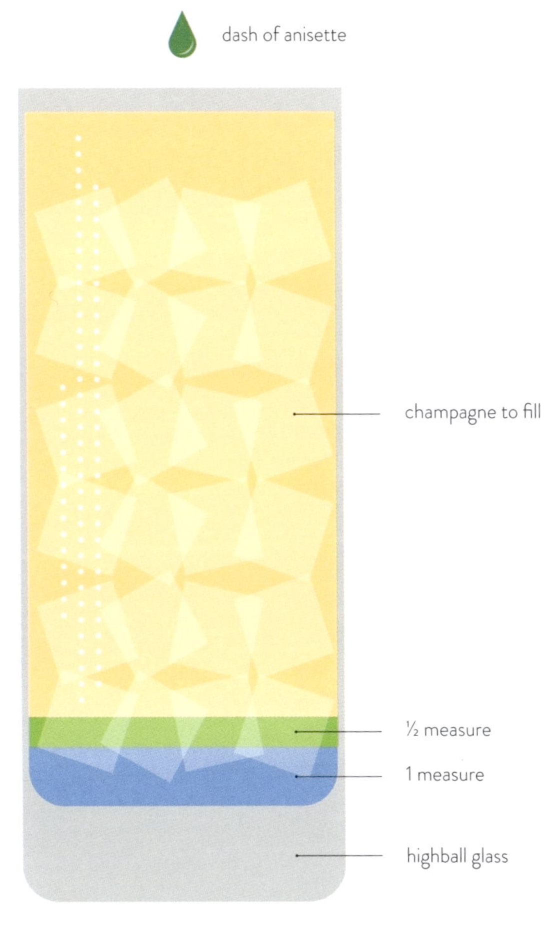

champagne
fresh lime juice
gin

Instructions

1. In a shaker mix together the gin, anisette and lime juice, then strain into an ice-filled highball glass.
2. Top up with champagne and serve.

LIQUEUR

AFTER EIGHT

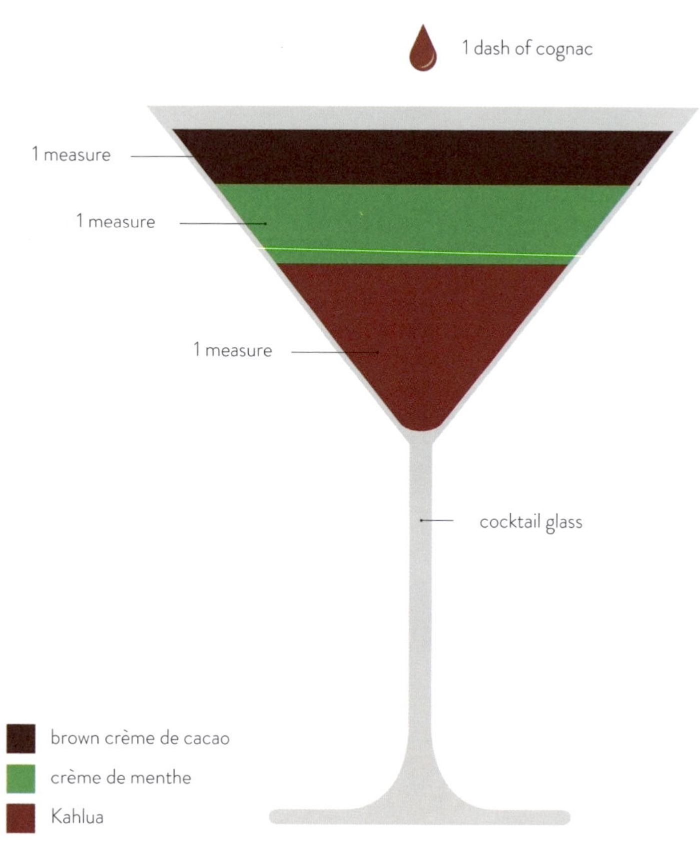

Instructions

1 Shake all the ingredients together, then strain into a cocktail glass and serve.

AMARETTO COMFORT

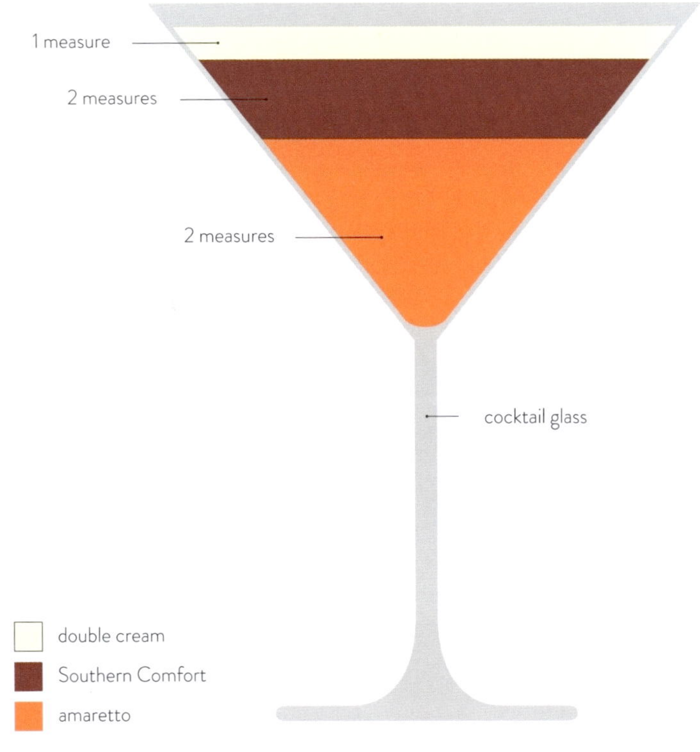

Instructions

1 Stir the amaretto and Southern Comfort together and strain into a cocktail glass. **2** Float the cream on top then serve.

ARISTOCRAT

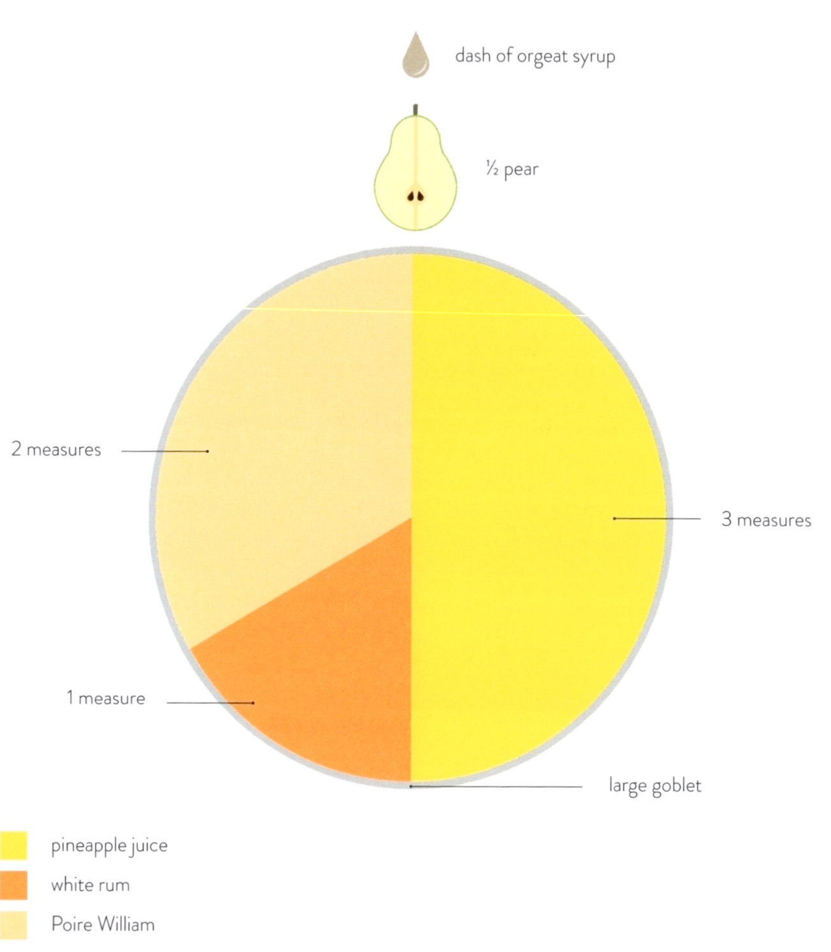

Instructions

1 Blend all the ingredients together and pour into a large goblet.

BAD GIRL

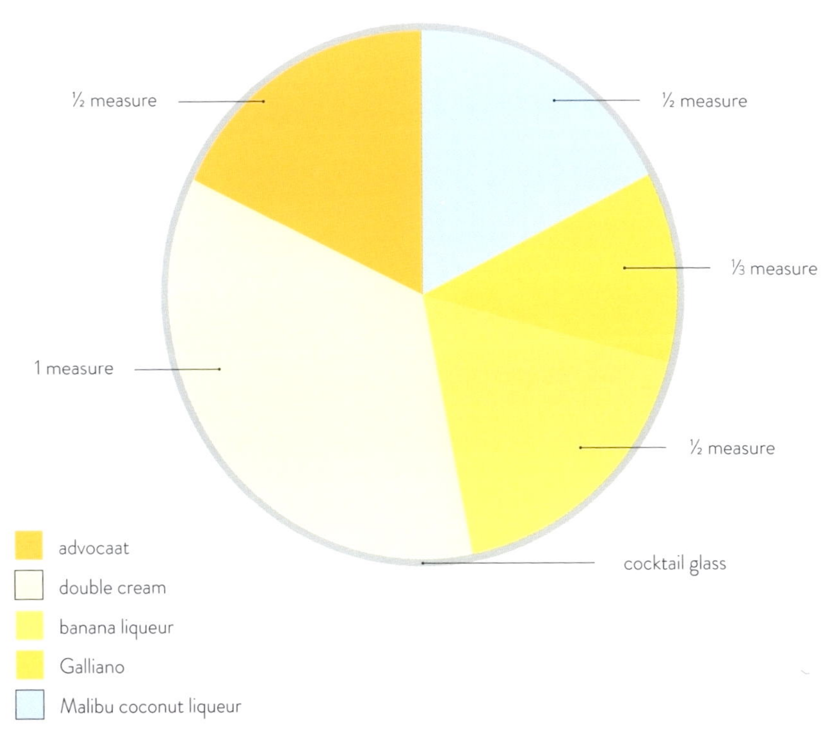

Instructions

1 Place all the ingredients in a blender with ice. **2** Blend, then pour into a cocktail glass.

BANSHEE

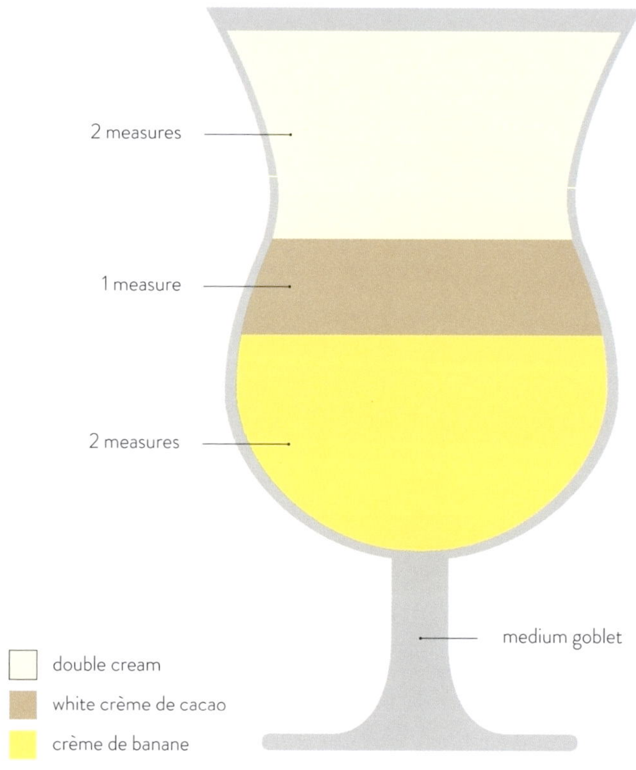

Instructions

1 Mix all the ingredients together in a shaker with ice, then strain into a medium goblet and serve.

BEE STINGER

Instructions

1 Pour the crème de menthe and crème de cassis into a brandy glass. Stir and serve.

BLACK AND TAN

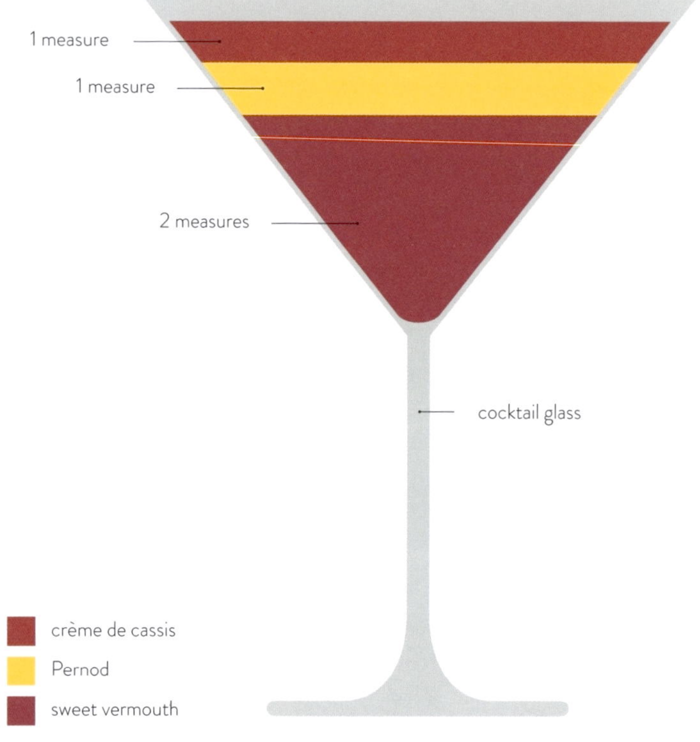

Instructions

1 Shake all the ingredients together, then strain into a cocktail glass and serve.

BLACKJACK

Instructions

1 Stir all ingredients over ice in a mixing glass. **2** Strain into a chilled cocktail glass.

BRIGHTON ROCK

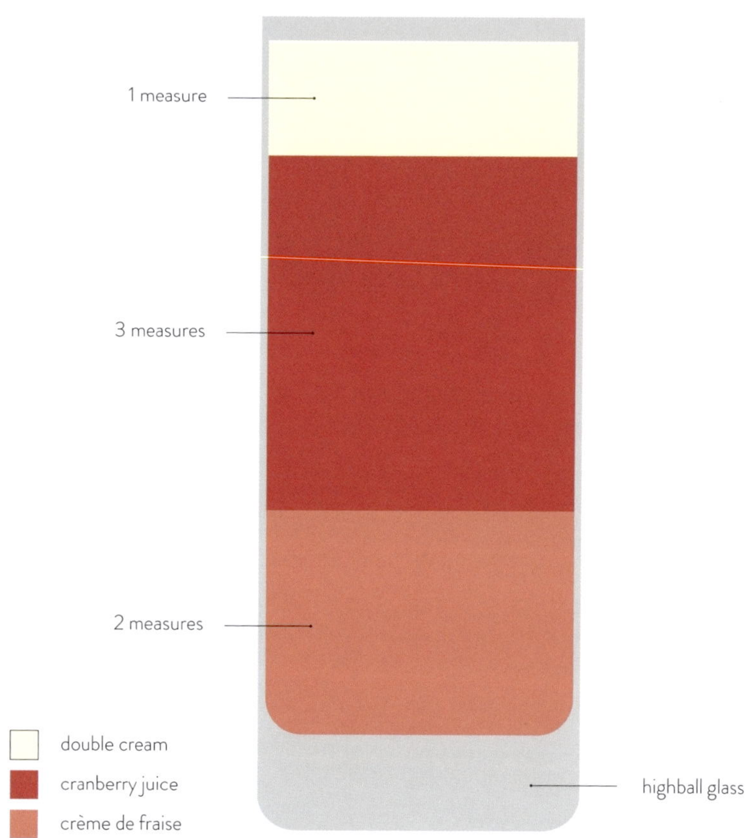

Instructions

1 Mix all the ingredients together in a shaker with ice, then strain into a highball glass.

DEATH BY CHOCOLATE

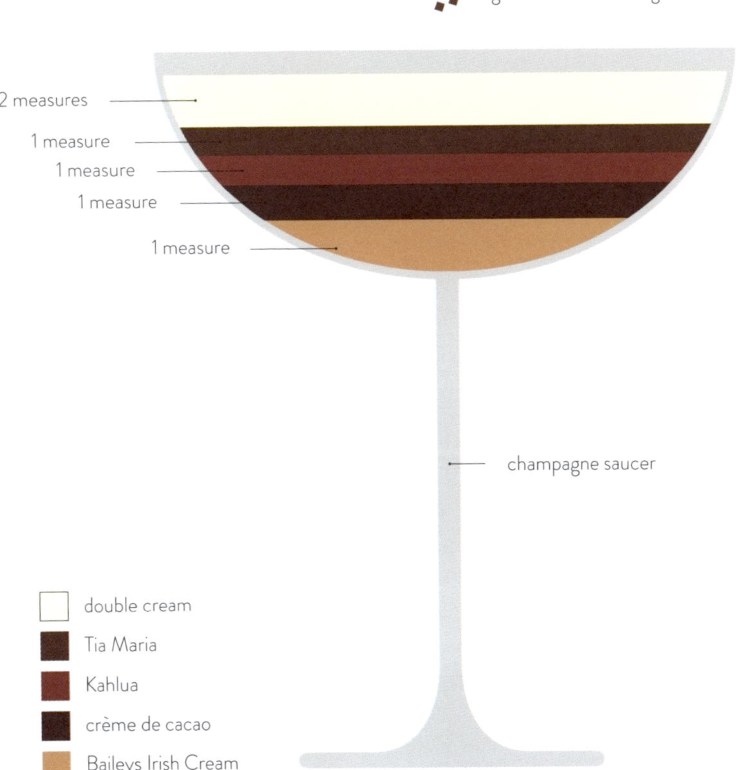

Instructions

1 Shake all the ingredients together with ice and strain into a large champagne saucer. **2** Garnish with grated chocolate.

FUZZY NAVEL

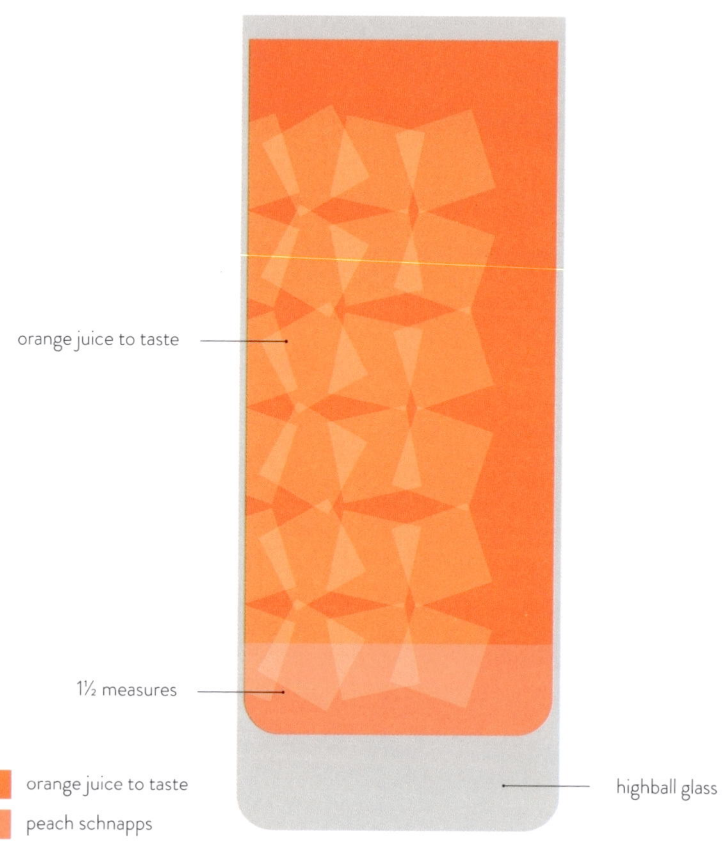

Instructions

1 Pour the peach schnapps into an ice-filled highball glass. **2** Fill with orange juice and stir to combine.

GRASSHOPPER

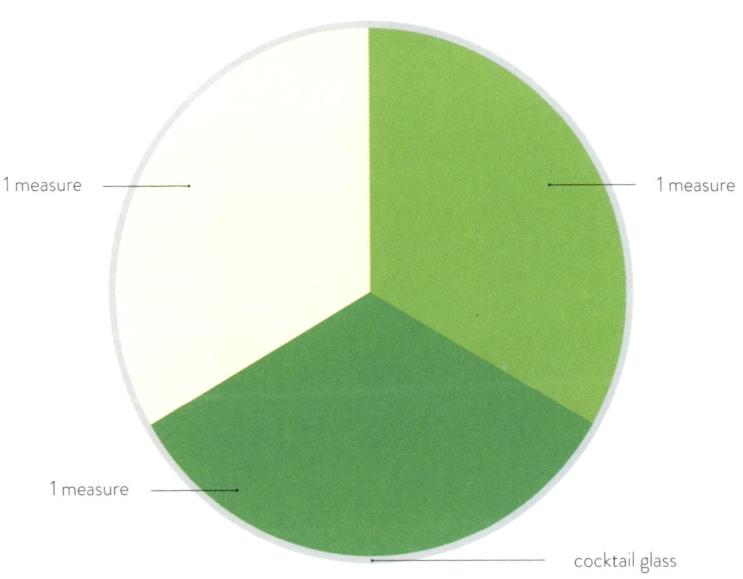

double cream

white crème de menthe

crème de menthe

Instructions

1 Mix all the ingredients together in a shaker with ice, then strain into a cocktail glass.

IRON LADY

Instructions

1 Mix all the ingredients together in a shaker filled with ice, then strain into an ice-filled highball glass.

PINK CADILLAC

Instructions

1 Mix all the ingredients together in a shaker with ice, then strain into a cocktail glass.

RED DEATH

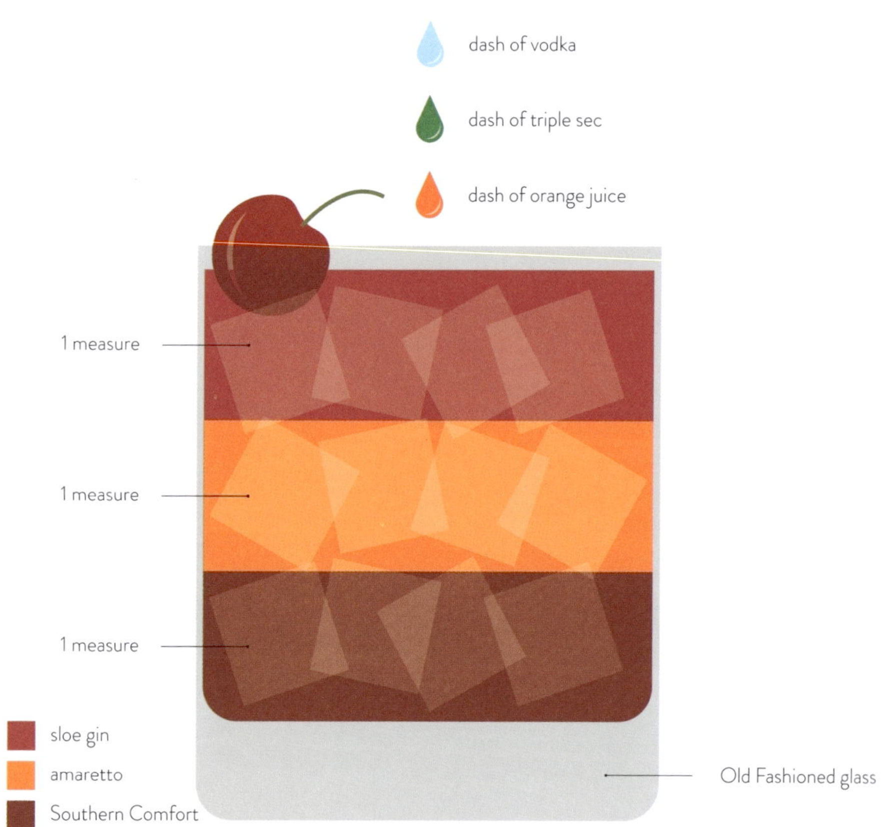

Instructions

1. Shake all the ingredients together with ice and strain into an Old Fashioned glass filled with ice.
2. Garnish with a maraschino cherry.

SCREAMING MULTIPLE ORGASM

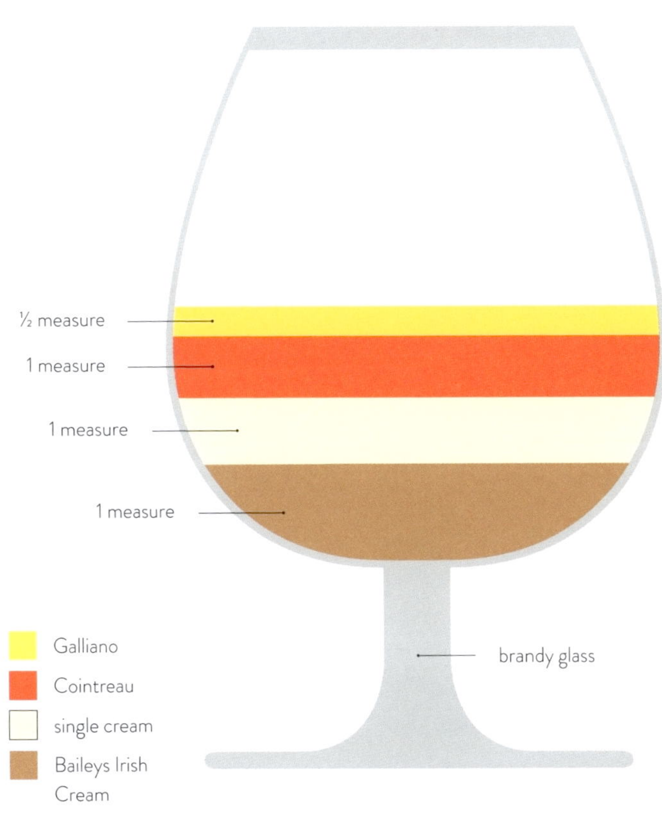

Instructions

1 In the exact order above, layer in a brandy glass and serve.

SHOOTING STAR

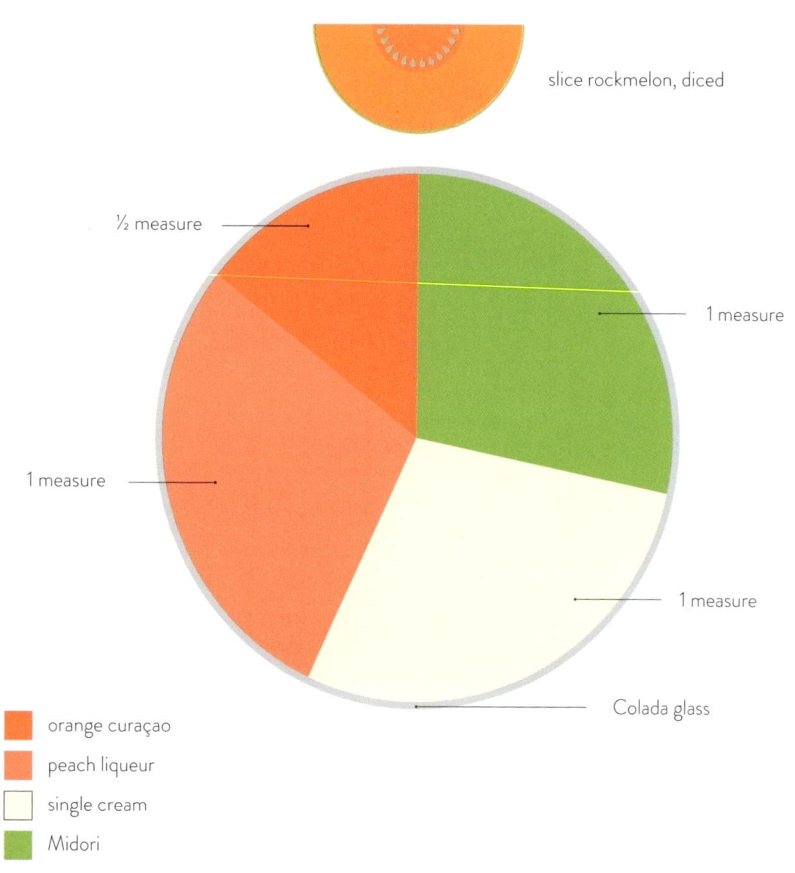

Instructions

1 Blend all the ingredients together until smooth, then pour into a colada glass.

SWAN SONG

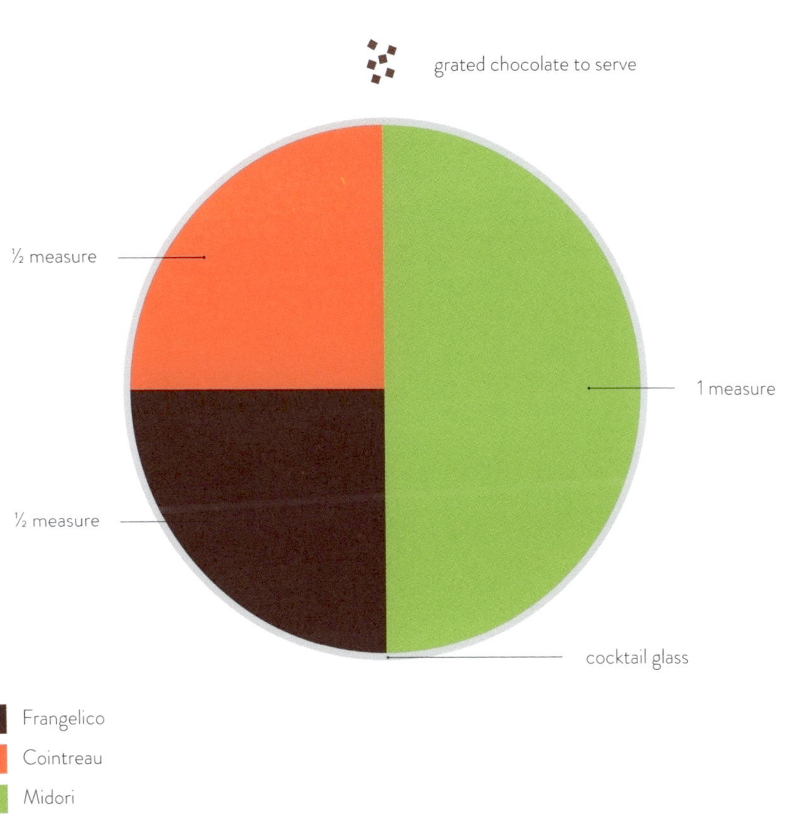

Instructions

1 Mix all the ingredients together in a shaker, then strain into a cocktail glass. **2** Sprinkle with the chocolate and serve.

SHOTS

ALABAMA SLAMMER

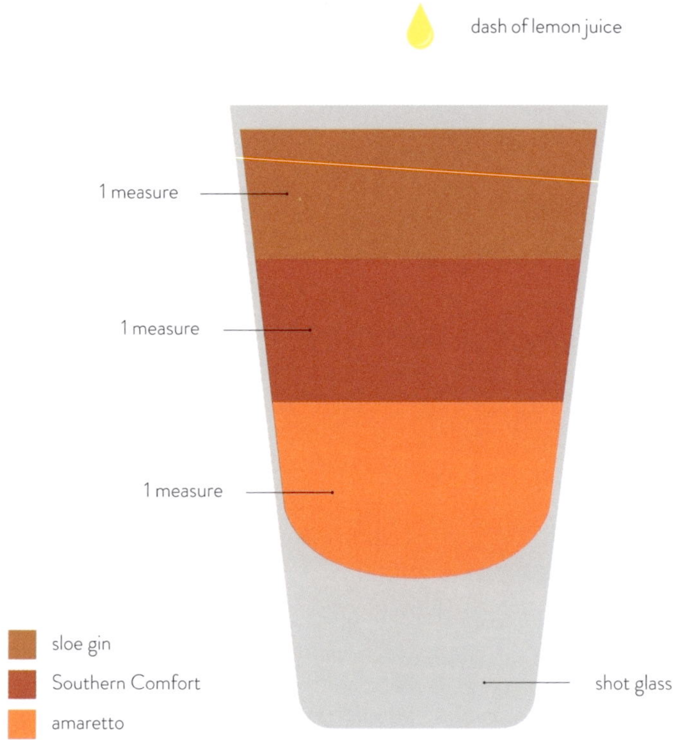

Instructions

1 Stir the amaretto, Southern Comfort and gin together, then strain into a shot glass. **2** Add the lemon juice and serve.

ANGEL'S KISS

Instructions

1 In the exact order above, layer each of the ingredients in a shot glass and serve.

ANGEL WING SHOOTER

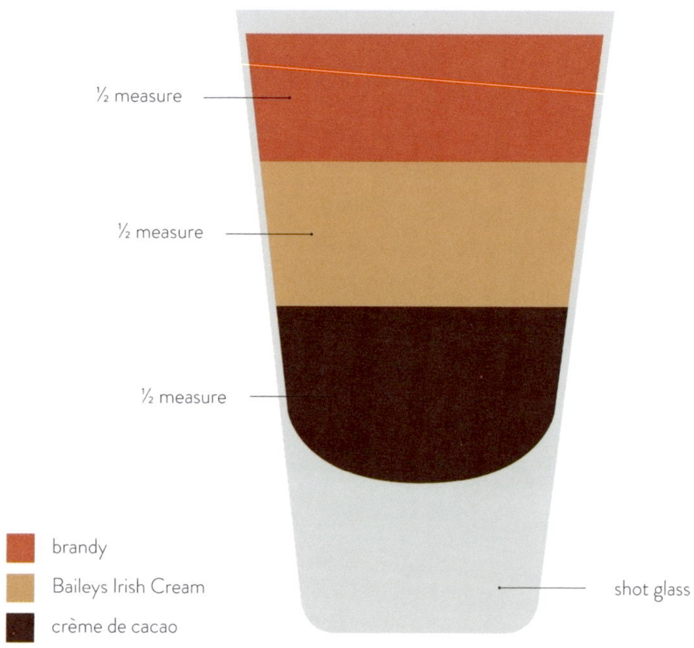

Instructions

1 In the exact order above, layer the ingredients in a liqueur glass.

B-52

Instructions

1 In the exact order above, layer the ingredients in a shot glass and serve.

BLACK JACK SHOOTER

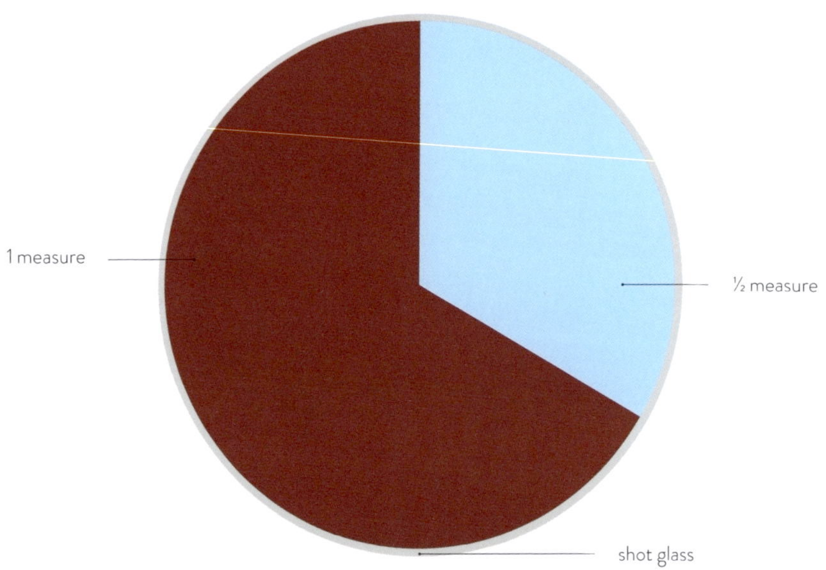

Instructions

1 Layer the ingredients in a shot glass and serve.

CHASTITY BELT SHOOTER

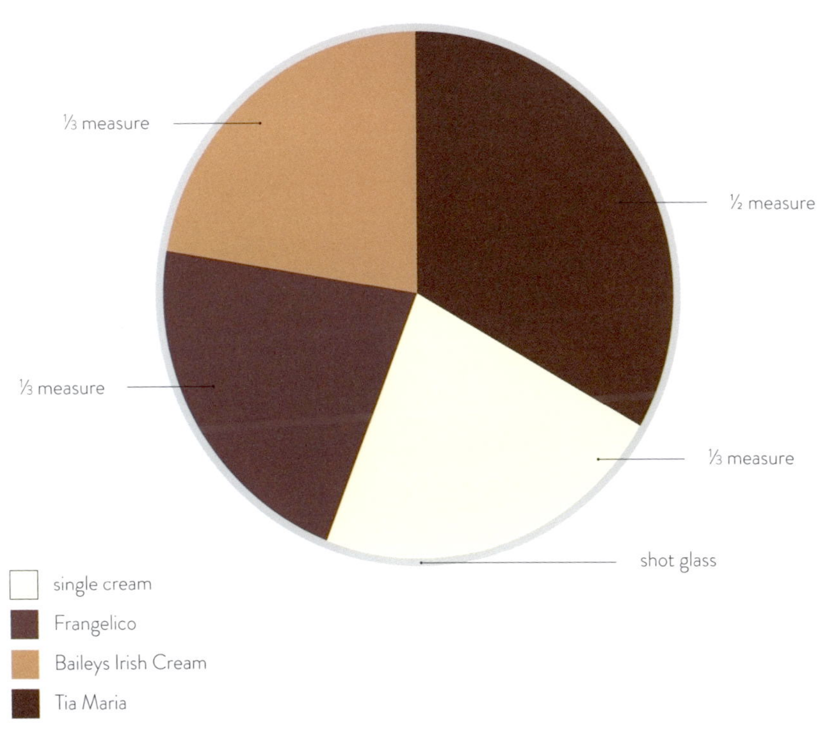

Instructions

1 In the exact order above, layer the ingredients in a shot glass and serve.

DEEP THROAT SHOOTER

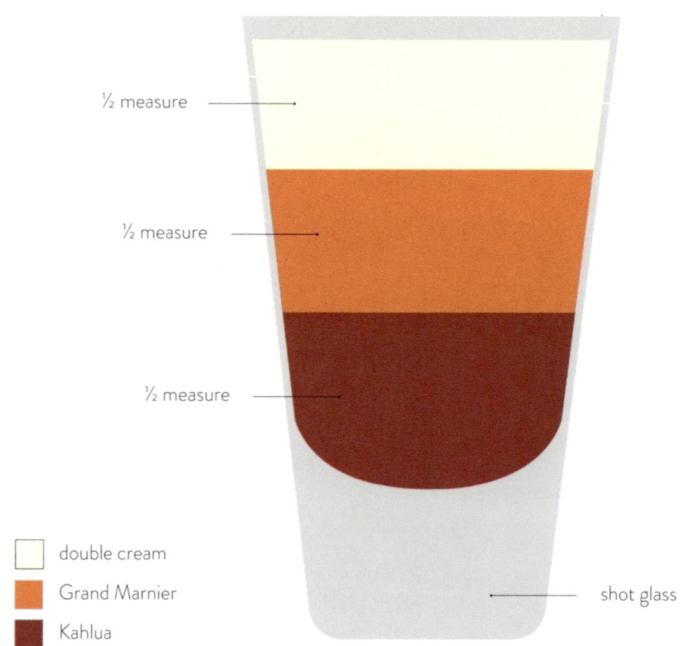

Instructions

1 In the exact order above, layer the ingredients in a shot glass and serve.

SEX ON THE BEACH

Instructions

1 Stir all the ingredients together, then strain into a shot glass. **2** Top up with the cranberry juice and serve.

SLIPPERY NIPPLE

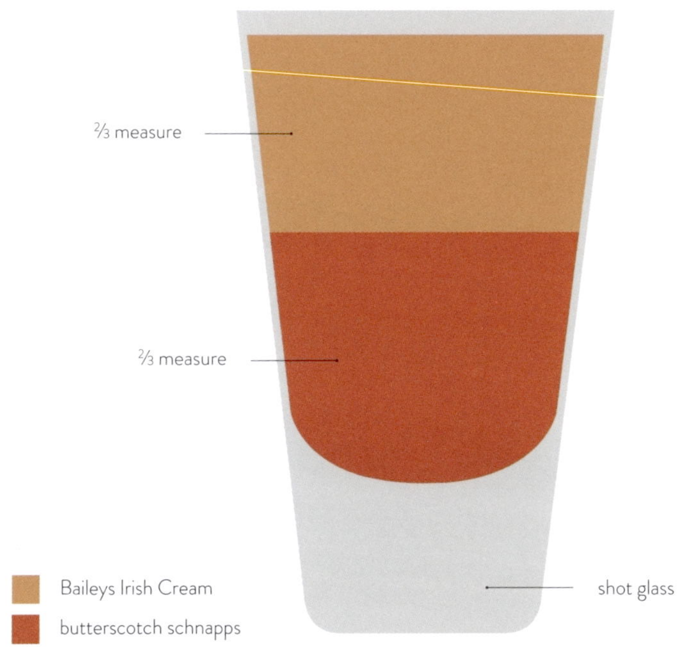

Instructions

1 Pour butterscotch schnapps into a shot glass and layer the Baileys on top.

TRAFFIC LIGHT

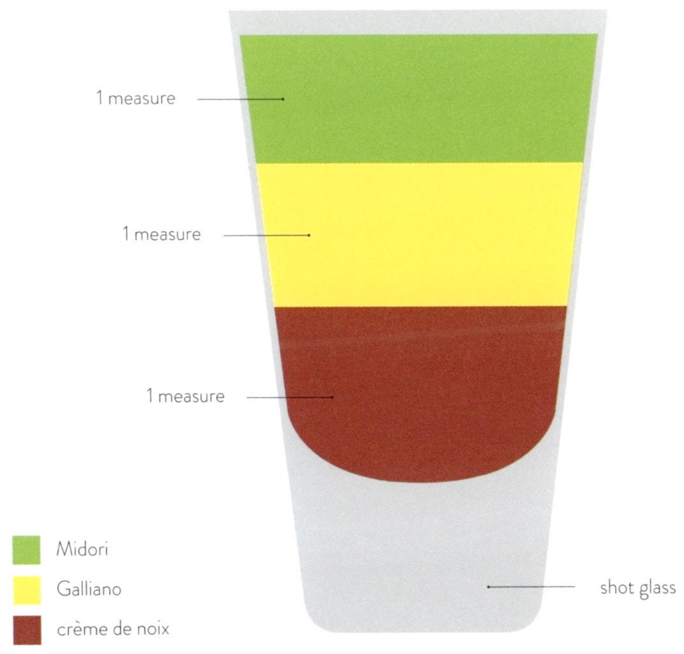

Instructions

1 Layer the ingredients in the exact order above, in a shot glass, and serve.

INDEX

Index of ingredients: for full list of cocktails see A–Z at front of book.

A

absinthe 169
Absolut Mandarin vodka 66, 68
advocaat 87, 227
amaretto
  Alabama Slammer 242
  Amaretto Comfort 223
  Bella Donna 133
  Godfather 161
  Laser Beam 185
  Red Death 236
  Ritz Fizz 216
Angostura bitters
  Alaska 80
  Ballantine's 154
  Brandy Cocktail 111
  Champagne Cocktail 204, 205
  Champagne Cooler 205
  Chicago 115
  Colonel Fizz 159
  Imperial 90
  James Bond 210
  Joe Collins 65
  Last Emperor 164
  Manhattan 41
  Old Vermouth 97
  Old Fashioned 48
  Pisco Sour 49
  Rob Roy 167
  Tom Fizz 100
  Woodstock 103
anisette 163, 219
apple juice 74, 114, 202
applejack 120
Appleton Special rum 138
apricot brandy 96, 121, 125, 145, 165, 191
armagnac 17, 19

B

Baileys Irish Cream 21
  Angel Wing Shooter 244
  B-52 245
  Chastity Belt Shooter 247
  Death by Chocolate 231
  Mudslide 69
  Screaming Multiple Orgasm 237
  Slippery Nipple 250
banana 142
banana liqueur 227
Barcardi 143
beef bouillon 60
Benedictine 21, 51, 108, 109, 160, 206
bourbon 12
  Angelic 153
  Chapel Hill 158
  Colonel Fizz 159
  dash of lemon juice
  Colonel Fizz
  Kentucky Sunset 163
  Liberty Bell 165
  Lieutenant 121
  Milk Punch 166
  Mint Julep 46
  Old Fashioned 48
  Sazerac 169
  VIP 171
brandy 17–19, 50, 104–25, 229, 243, 244
butterscotch schnapps 250

C

cachaça 37
calvados 116, 125
Campari 47, 92, 165, 190
Canadian Club whisky 157
Captain Morgan rum 138, 143
Chambord 63, 249
champagne 22, 198–219
  Barracuda 131
  Bellini 34
  French 75 88
  Jacuzzi 91
  Juniper Royale 93
  Moulin Rouge 96
  Raja 124
  The Swinger 99
Chartreuse 21, 80, 170
cherry brandy 51, 114, 117, 155
Cherry Heering 149
clam juice 179
coconut cream 128, 130, 134, 136, 142, 146, 147
coffee 132, 229

cognac 17, 18–19
Adam and Eve 106
After Eight 222
Brandy Alexander 36
Brandy Cocktail 111
Champagne Cocktail 204
Champagne Cooler 205
Eggnog 118
French Sherbet 208
Frenchie 119
Mikado 122
Raja 124
Cointreau
B-52 245
Between the Sheets 110
Blue Monday 82
Casablanca 135
Champagne Cobbler 203
Cosmopolitan 38
Fluffy Duck 87
Honeymoon Paradise 209
Jasmine 92
La Bomba 184
Mai Tai 43
Margarita 44
Mikado 122
Nicky Finn 123
Poinsettia 214
Raspberry Sip 215
Red Desert 189
Screaming Multiple Orgasm 237
Sidecar 50
Singapore Sling 51
Swan Song 239
Tomahawk 196
VIP 171
White Velvet 102
cola 137
cranberry juice 23
Brighton Rock 230
Cape Codder 61
Cool Gold 180
Cosmopolitan 38
Dizzy Gillespie 138
Juniper Royale 93
Mai Tai 43
Sea Breeze 73
Sea Horse 74
Sex on the Beach 249
Tomahawk 196
Woo Woo 77
crème de banane 67, 215, 225
crème de cacao
After Eight 222
Angel Wing Shooter 244
Angelic 153
Angel's Kiss 243
Banshee 225
Brandy Alexander 36
Death by Chocolate 231
Floridita 140
French Kiss 1 62
Iron Lady 234
Pink Cadillac 235
Silk Stocking 192
Whizz Doodle 173
crème de cassis 154, 181, 211, 226, 228, 234
crème de fraise 128, 230
crème de menthe 21, 170, 183, 222, 226, 233
crème de mure 62, 200
crème de noix 251
crème de noyaux 122
curaçao 70, 82, 134, 195, 209, 216, 238

D
Drambuie 142, 168

E
egg 118
egg white 49, 53, 84, 85, 145, 177

F
forbidden fruit 106
Frangelico 239, 247

G
Galliano
Apollo 13 129
Bad Girl 227
Barracuda 131
Gumdrop 162
Harvey Wallbanger 64
Pink Cadillac 235
Screaming Multiple Orgasm 237
Traffic Light 251
garnishes 23
gin 14–15, 78–103
Gimlet 40
Long Island Iced Tea 42
Martini 45
Soixante-Neuf 217
Tom Collins 52
Typhoon 219
Vesper 75
Whizz Doodle 173
ginger ale 23, 181, 187
ginger wine 172
Grand Marnier

Apollo 13 129
Brandy Kiss 113
Cadillac Lady 85
Champagne Cooler 205
Deep Throat Shooter 248
Frenchie 119
Last Emperor 164
Leap Year 95
Mimosa 213
grapefruit juice 23, 71, 73, 121, 130, 176, 191
Grenadine
All Night 177
American Beauty 107
Angelic 153
Apollo 13 129
Barracuda 131
Bellini 34
Bombardier 83
Brandy Daisy 112
Broadway 84
Chapala 178
El Presidente 139
Floridita 140
Hurricane 141
Jack Rose 120
Juniper Royale 93
La Bomba 184
Madonna 143
Mexicana 188
Mikado 122
Moulin Rouge 96
Naked Lady 145
Pink Cadillac 235
Silk Stocking 192
Tequila Sunrise 194
Union Jack 101
Zombie 149
Guinness 201

I

ice 10

J

Jack Daniels 185

K

Kahlua
After Eight 222
Black Jack Shooter 246
Black Magic (alt) 58
Black Russian 59
Death by Chocolate 231
Deep Throat Shooter 248
Dizzy Dame 117
Mudslide 69
South of the Border 193
White Russian 76
Kirsch 208, 229
kummel 21, 94

L

lemon juice
Aviation 2 56
Bellini 34
Between the Sheets 110
Black Magic (alt) 58
Bloody Mary 35
Brandy Daisy 112
Brandy Kiss 113
Cadillac Lady 85
Canadian Sherbet 157
Chapala 178
Chapel Hill 158
Cocoloco 136
Colonel Fizz 159
Cool Cucumber 206
Eldorado 182
French 75 88
Frisco 160
Honeymoon Paradise 209
Jasmine 92
Joe Collins 65
Leap Year 95
Metropolis 68
Moulin Rouge 96
Naked Lady 145
Nicky Finn 123
Red Snapper 98
Ritz Fizz 216
Sidecar 50
Soixante-Neuf 217
Tom Collins 52
Tom Fizz 100
Whisky Sour 53
Woodstock 103
lemonade 87
Lillet 75
lime cordial 40, 43
lime juice
All Night 177
Barracuda 131
Bombardier 83
Caipirinha 37
Casablanca 135
Cherry Picker 114
Clam Digger 179
Cosmopolitan 38
Cuba Libre 137
Daiquiri 39
Dizzy Gillespie 138
El Diablo 181
El Presidente 139
Floridita 140

Hurricane 141
Jack Rose 120
Long Island Iced Tea 42
Margarita 44
Matador 186
Mexican Mule 187
Mexicana 188
Mojito 144
Pisco Sour 49
Pussy Foot 148
Red Desert 189
Sea Horse 74
Short Fuse 191
Singapore Sling 51
South of the Border 193
Typhoon 219
Vampiro 197
Zombie 149
liqueurs 21
lychee liqueur 67

M

Malibu 138, 227
Mandarin Napoléon 68
maraschino cherry juice 191
maraschino liqueur 56, 90, 156
melon liqueur 180
Midori 70, 238, 239, 249, 251
mint 46, 144

N

noix de coco 234

O

orange bitters 80, 81, 135
orange juice 23
Afternoon Delight 128
American Beauty 107
April Shower 108
Blood and Sand 155
Bombardier 83
Chapala 178
Dizzy Gillespie 138
Fuzzy Navel 232
Harvey Wallbanger 64
Hurricane 141
Jacuzzi 91
Juniper Royale 93
La Bomba 184
Last Emperor 164
Long Island Iced Tea 42
Love for Sale 66
Madonna 143
Mai Tai 43
Mimosa 213
Old Fashioned 48
Painkiller 146
Pink Cadillac 235
Pussy Foot 148
Red Death 236
Screwdriver 72
Singapore Sling 51
Sweet Surrender 218
Tequila Sunrise 194
Vampiro 197
Zombie 149
Orgeat syrup 224
ouzo 246

P

passion fruit liqueur 66
pastis 89
peach brandy 218
peach liqueur 238
peach purée or nectar 34
peach schnapps 77, 91, 165, 232
Pernod 74, 123, 169, 207, 228
Peychaud bitters 152, 169
pineapple juice 23
Acapulco 176
Algonquin 152
Aristocrat 224
Bahia 130
Barracuda 131
Blue Hawaiian 134
Broadway 84
Dizzy Gillespie 138
El Presidente 139
French Martini 1 63
Hurricane 141
Jungle Juice 142
La Bomba 184
Love for Sale 66
Lychee Martini 67
Madonna 143
Mai Tai 43
Matador 186
Mexicana 188
Painkiller 146
Piña Colada 147
Poison Arrow 70
Pussy Foot 148
Sex on the Beach 249
Singapore Sling 51
Tomahawk 196
White Velvet 102
pisco 17, 18, 49
Poire William 224
port 107
prosecco 212

R
raspberry 202, 215
rum 13–14, 126–49
Acapulco 176
Aristocrat 224
Bastile 200
Between the Sheets 110
Bikini 57
Daiquiri 39
Eggnog 118
Long Island Iced Tea 42
Mai Tai 43
Poison Arrow 70
rye 12, 41, 152, 156, 160

S
sloe gin 101, 242, 243
sour cherry syrup 189
sour mix 133
Southern Comfort 223, 236, 242
stout 201
strawberry 128
Strega 163

T
tequila 19–20, 42, 44, 114, 136, 174–97
Tia Maria 157, 231, 245, 247
tomato juice 23, 35, 98, 179, 197
triple sec
Chapala 178
Chapel Hill 158
Chicago 115
Hurricane 141
Laser Beam 185
Long Island Iced Tea 42
Matador 186
Red Death 236
Tomahawk 196
tropical fruit schnapps 195

V
vermouth
Algonquin 152
American Beauty 107
Astoria 81
Ballantine's 154
Black and Tan 228
Blood and Sand 155
Brandy Cocktail 111
Broadway 84
Brooklyn 156
Corpse Reviver 116
Dirty Martini 86
Floridita 140
Harry's Cocktail 89
Imperial 90
Kaiser 94
Last Emperor 164
Leap Year 95
Manhattan 41
Martini 45
Negroni 47
Old Vermouth 97
Rob Roy 167
Rosalita 190
Shamrock 170
Tulip 125
VIP 171
vodka 16–17, 54–77
Bloody Mary 35
Cocoloco 136
Cosmopolitan 38
Fluffy Duck 87
Gimlet 40
James Bond 210
La Dolce Vita 212
Long Island Iced Tea 42
Red Death 236
Sex on the Beach 249

W
whisky/whiskey 12, 53, 150–73